The New Testament Always News

The New Testament Always News

by ETIENNE CHARPENTIER

Translated by Philip G. Roets

ST. NORBERT ABBEY PRESS
De Pere, Wisconsin
U.S.A.
1969

Edited by Lisa McGaw

Translated by Philip G. Roets

Originally published as *Ce Testament Toujours Nouveau* by Librarie Artheme Fayard.

Standard Book Number 8316-1037-9
Library of Congress Catalog Card Number 78-87817

Printed in the United States of America
ST. NORBERT ABBEY PRESS
De Pere, Wisconsin 54115

CONTENTS

"Don't you believe in Jesus Christ, Neuville?" he asked him bluntly.

"I don't know."

"Don't you believe that God loves us and that we love only through him? That Jesus Christ is his Son and that he saved us from the lie and from pride which is nothing but a lie?"

"Yes!"

"And that the union of all those who respond to his love is a union animated by His Spirit and that it has from him its holiness and that the apostles entrusted the message of Jesus Christ to it?"

"Is not the Church hiding under these words?"

"On the contrary, Neuville! These realities are hidden under the Church."

"They are certainly hidden!"

"No more than the love in any human face."

"That is not the same thing," said Frances. "We communicate with a face. We can force it to give up its secret."

"But it is the same thing," says Blanchet.

P.-A. Lesort, **The Wind Blows Where It Wills**

INTRODUCTION

Frances, baptized, unbelieving. Yves Neuville, not baptized. Two upright people, who love each other with a love that is true and demanding, for whom the only thing of real importance is this love with the human solidarity and the close friendship. And the spiritual drama is tied together: This human love brings Yves, and through him, Frances, to the divine love. Both feel the demands of this discovery threaten their happiness: say Yes to God and he demands a total love. Does this not destroy the other Yes which has given them everything? . . . "How could I have been so foolish," says Frances to herself, "as to write to him that he could say the same Yes (by his baptism) as the Yes of their marriage, when it is the first Yes that is tearing him to pieces?" . . . "No, I will not leave you," says Yves, "we shall be together, you are with me, I am with you, our little ones are with us, the world is with us, God wants us all, the other life is now, it is the now in our love, the now in all love, these are but parts of a single love, a single love through the earth and through the centuries, which will one day unite everything."

This is certainly an unusual way to open an introduction to the New Testament, through a history of love! But is this not the way in which we should have ended the introduction to the Old Testament? Is the story of mankind anything else but the story of God becoming man in order to wed this mankind? To give to man the being in this very love?[1] The Old Testament is young because it is the history of this meeting, of these first stutterings of the love of an engaged couple. And then, at the very crossroads of the ages, God comes in his Son to wed mankind. On the Cross. For he must first cleanse it. The New Testament, this is the history—our history—of Christ loving with a love that demands mankind to become his Bride: "Christ loved the Church: he gave himself for her by purifying her through this nuptial bath[2] which the Yes of love and of faith accompanies. For he wished to present her to himself, completely glorious, with no speck or wrinkle, or anything like that, but holy and faultless" (cf. Eph. 5:25-27).

It is "to communicate with the face of the Church" that these few pages would like to help you "force it to give up its secret" hidden in this "internal diary" which is the New Testament: The history of its meeting and its engagement with the Son of God, in which each of us, all mankind, the entire world are carried along.

The plan of this book? We shall attempt to live again with the Church the discovery of his love by following, as far as we can, the literary chronology of the birth of these texts. Seven Chapters: The Paschal Mystery of Jesus (his descent into death, then his being raised, and his being lifted into the presence of the Father) were his own "baptism," were **The Nuptial Bath** in which he cleansed his Church in advance. **Born of the Spirit,** the Church truly lives only from the moment in which Christ sends his spirit to "animate" it: The Acts of the Apostles tell us of this adventure. A life of love between husband and wife is definitely something ever new, and unceasingly renewed: It is **A First Yes Which Is Reconquered Each Day:** The letters of Paul are filled with emotion because they show us precisely this young Church finding day by day its life of union with Christ, discovering the demand of this Yes in the very heart of daily life, led, through fidelity to this love, to pour it out on men and on the world. For this Christ created his Church: In her we are **Baptized to Consecrate the World,** as Peter and the author of the Letter to the Hebrews tell us. As married people on the eve of their golden wedding anniversary begin to understand the entire fullness of the Yes in their marriage, the complete riches contained in hope in their first meeting, the Church, rich with a half century of life with Christ, can turn back upon its past and give us this wealth through its four evangelists. They give us **The Story of a Love,** while depicting in these texts the true face of **Jesus of Nazareth**. But Jesus is not in the past. The history of this first love is still only a prefiguring and anticipation of the eternal wedding of which the Apocalypse sings: **As a Young Bride Prepared for Her Husband,** the Church awaits the final coming of her Lord.

Warning

It is always amusing to start a book with the second half. This allows the reader to imagine what went before, or to invent what he could only receive from someone else, but this is not always the best way to understand the book! The New Testament is only the second half of the Scripture: before it, there is the Old Testament. Therefore, be so kind, if you have not read **The Old Testament—Always Relevant,** to begin with this.[3] It will help you, perhaps, to discover this long time of engagement between God and his people. Here are scattered the seed whose fruits we gather. It will recall to you also what you can expect from these pages, but should not. Before the books of the masters, which I am not on any score, these pages would ask the confidence of a friend about that which he loves in the Bible.[4]

[1] "'The force with which I love you,' declares Lady Prouheze, 'is no different from that by which you exist'" (*Le Soulier de Satin*).

[2]Among the Jews as well as the Greeks, the bath of the girl about to be married was part of the ritual of marriage.

[3]*The Old Testament—Always Relevant* by Charpentier, English translation published by St. Norbert Abbey Press (1969). This will be cited as OT.

[4]How are we to thank such masters as Fathers Léon-Dufour, Guillet, Tremel, Feuillet, who so kindly accepted the task of supervising each part of this book. Special acknowledgment must also go to Jacqueline, Marie Therese, Alain, Christiane, Marie-Louise, and so many others. With the friendly assistance of my colleagues in the seminary, I have been able to complete this work.

I.

THE NUPTIAL BATH: THE PASCHAL MYSTERY

In a street in Jerusalem, one night in the year A.D. 30

14 Nisan, the year 30. Evening was just falling, opening the most solemn Sabbath of the year: the Paschal Sabbath. Progressively the silence silvered by the full moon, which was already taking possession of the now deserted streets, becomes a prayer.

Today, Jerusalem has broken all records for noise. The temple courts still resound with the bleating of thousands of lambs which the busy priests are killing. The shops experienced this ceaseless jostling and shoving of a motley group buying the bitter herbs for the paschal supper, as they called to one another or insulted each other. In the morning there was also the organized mob which moved toward the governor's palace to demand of him, according to their yearly custom, the release of one prisoner. This time it was Barabbas. And as if all this was not enough, the Holy City was being offered the luxury of a triple execution on the empty lot very near the gates: two criminals and a certain Jesus of Nazareth. The howling mob still does not understand how this could have happened. They have just wrested his death sentence from wishy-washy Pilate with the cry: "Crucify him! Crucify him!" This Jesus had been their hero. Very many had followed him, had loved him, had accepted favors from him, words which helped them and miracles. They had even raised the question: Is this not the Messiah?

It had taken all the skill and cleverness of a few leaders of the people and the chief priests to turn them against him in an instant. They had seen him then crossing these crowded streets, stumbling under the terrible weight of the cross, shoved and struck by the Roman soldiers. They had seen him suffer for three long hours. They had insulted him (the sight of blood awakens the disturbances in the heart of a man) . . . but now all this was ended. They had turned now to serious matters, to the only serious matter: the sacrifice of the Pasch. The immolation of the Paschal Lamb at the temple was complete; by eating this victim in the course of the nocturnal Eucharist, of the sacred liturgy of the Pasch, they continued to communicate in God who saves, to enter into the Plan of Love of God for his people. And in each family the same deeds and the same prayers ascend during this solemn meal.[1] The rite is well known. Let us recall it: it still forms the outline for our Mass.

Entrance: The father of the family, who presides, blesses the feast and the first cup: "Blessed by you, O Lord, our God, eternal king who created the fruit of the vine."[2]

First Service: To recall the bitterness of the years of captivity in Egypt, they consciously munch some bitter herbs dipped in salty sauce.

The Principal Meal can now begin. The Paschal Lamb is brought in. The father of the family recalls "the meaning of the feast and the symbolism of the different foods: the unleavened bread, the memorial of the bread that had not had time to rise on the night of the exodus; the lamb calling to mind the first Pasch in which the blood sprinkled on the doorposts had preserved the Hebrews from the blows of the messenger of destruction (Exod. 12:23); the wine a symbol of joy and thanksgiving for all the favors of God" (Benoit). After this recalling (which the father of the family could extend as he pleased), they sang Ps. 113 and blessed the second cup of wine and then washed their hands.[3]

Blessing the Bread: Then the father blesses the bread: "Blessed be you, Lord, our God, who caused the bread to grow in the earth." He breaks it and distributes it. Then they eat the Paschal Lamb.

The Third Cup: Then the father blesses the third cup of wine after he has mixed it with a little water.[4] This blessing undoubtedly begins during this period with the solemn dialogue:

> "Let us give thanks to the Lord our God. Blessed be the name of the Lord now and forever! With your assent we shall bless him who has made us share in his goods. It is by his goodness that we live."

Eucharist: Then there is the "Eucharist" for all the marvels of God toward his people,[5] for this marvel especially: the covenant, sealed in blood at the foot of Sinai (OT, p. 24).

Conclusion: With this blessing the meal is completed. Then the singing of Pss. 114-118 which serve as the conclusion will send each into the silence of the night and the meditation on the mystery fulfilled.[6]

In the now deserted streets a man wanders, a stranger to the feast. These words of the prayer, he sang them the evening before. He ate the eucharistic bread. He drank the cup of the covenant . . . and now all this appears empty, absurd, the words of this evening as well as yesterday. So many things have happened between these two nights! Yesterday, he, Peter, was there in the upper room with his eleven companions. And Jesus officiated. There was no Paschal Lamb and yet it was truly the Pasch, this feast around the sacrificed Lamb. This meal had taken on a solemn character which none of the participants missed. They felt that it was the flowering of these extraordinary months with Jesus, with Jesus the Messiah. But then, there was the Cross. Peter has not succeeded in expelling this long day from his memory: Jesus arrested in the Garden called Gethsemane, forbidding him to draw the sword to defend him, bound by the servants, imprisoned in the home of the high priest . . . but then . . . Peter was not quite so clear . . . his memories were flooded with tears. He, Peter—"Bedrock" this surname which the Master had given him (before he was only "Simon" the fisherman), this new name which should create in him a new being—he, Peter, has sworn on oath before a servant girl that he "did not know the man"! From that whole long night only one thing stands out in his mind: the look that Jesus turned on him. Then everything went to pieces within him. He had dashed out of the palace courtyard where John, his friend, had brought him, and had burst into bitter sobbing. Everything was ended. Jesus had died as a criminal at the gates of the city, condemned by the priests, executed by the Romans. Immediately after, they had brought him to the completely new tomb of Joseph of Arimathea, and had buried him. The heavy stone of the tomb had rolled over the hope of Peter and over his love. He had betrayed his Master. He had not stopped believing that he was truly the Messiah. But he betrayed him. Everything was finished.

Interminable Sabbath

The Sabbath's dawn awakens Peter in this friend's

house where he had finally gone to sleep. The Sabbath with its rigorous obligation of rest allowed him nothing more than to think of his Master.

For Peter, Jesus remains the Master. There is no doubt that it seems as if God has abandoned Jesus, since he allowed him to die on the wood of the Cross. But perhaps, he, Peter, and the others had not rightly understood him. They were awaiting the glorious Messiah who was to bring back the kingdom of Israel by expelling the Romans. They had thought this had happened. They had glimpsed for themselves already the twelve thrones. . . . Almost as an obsession, these scandalous phrases of Jesus kept returning to the mind of Peter, words which he had refused to accept—and Jesus had treated him as Satan. "The son of man must be put to death." He was sent by God and he had been put to death! Is this not the realization of this mysterious figure described by the prophet Isaiah, the "Suffering Servant"? "If he offers his life as a guilt-offering, he will see a posterity. . . . He will see the light and will be filled. . . . I will give to him the many" (Isa. 53:10-12).[7] But how will all this take place? When will it take place? Undoubtedly on the "last day." Peter had thought this last day had arrived with Jesus. He has left everything, his family and his work because he believed this. Now there was nothing else to do but to return to all this, to flee this city which killed his hope, to take up his nets again while awaiting this day on which God will himself come to give to this Jesus "whole hordes for his tribute."

Flee. An interminable Sabbath with its rigorous obligation of rest which forces him to go through all his memories again.[8]

They have stolen his body

Mary Magdalene comes to warn them about this. "They have taken the body from the tomb, and we do not know where they have put it!" She was waiting anxiously for this end of the Sabbath and the night that followed it so that she could, at the first light of dawn, run to the tomb and weep there. But the stone was rolled away, the body was gone!

Peter jumps up immediately. He also runs to the tomb, he sees the stone shelf on which they had placed the body, the linen bands and cloths which they had used for the burial. They have stolen the body.[9]

As the Sabbath wore on, a certain balance had been struck in his sorrow. Jesus was dead. Now he had to wait for the day, the "last day," on which God would come to establish his Kingdom.

The death was a rupture, it had put an end to the relations between Jesus and his disciples. Now there remained only this last bond with him: the tomb. Behind the cold stone, the body lay.

And now in a final coup, this last bond is snatched away. The body has disappeared. Now there remains nothing to take hold of. This last human bond, poor as it was—a corpse—is broken. Total upset. . . . Flee this city and its memories.

"Peter went back to his house . . . ."[10]

Surrounded by two thousand years of Christian living, the discovery of the empty tomb would appear to us immediately as a proof that Jesus is raised. This would also appear to the first Christian generation who edit the Gospels. But it was not so on Easter Sunday. If we were to come to the cemetery, the morning after the burial of a dear one, and find the tomb open and empty, we would not think immediately of a possible resurrection but of a violation of the burial. This discovery is not a proof but a question for Peter. A question which disturbs him. The body of Jesus has disappeared. There is nothing more to which to attach himself.

It is beyond this breaking point that the resurrection will be given as a gift of God surpassing human expectation. Peter begins this approach to the true faith which Jesus had announced to him (Luke 22:32). This **conversion,** the three steps of which each of us has to go through unceasingly:

1. Everything starts with a **question**. I feel secure in the mental universe which I have made for myself, I have a global vision of the world which permits me to live (e.g., the Marxist synthesis). Then something which does not square with these categories shakes everything up or brings everything into question: a miracle (and the spectators in the Gospel cried out: "Who then is this man?" or indeed in the Acts: "In whose name do you cure?"), an extraordinary event (this discovery of the empty tomb, the transformation of the apostles at Pentecost, the new attitude of John XXIII, or a personal event), or even the authentically involved attitude of a militant Christian, or better of a team of militant Christians who posit to the Communist comrade the question "Why?"

Before a message can be proclaimed, the man must be open, in expectation of something. Perhaps we too frequently forget this necessary role of the "signs" before the announcement of the Gospel.[11] In this stage we are in the domain of the "history" of facts knowable to all.

2. To the question posed by the event, an explanation will be furnished, the meaning of this event will be revealed. On Pentecost Peter cried out, "No, these men are not drunk . . . they are filled with the **Holy Spirit**." Before the Sanhedrin questioning about the cure of the lame

beggar, he testifies: "It is through the **name of Jesus** that we have cured him," and the Christian comrade will explain his attitude, "It is because of Jesus Christ."

Here is something entirely new which surpasses our history and which gives meaning to it: the total significance of the event. Here I am forced to take a position.

3. The response which I will give will come now from the very depths of my being because it involves me totally: If I say Yes to the interpretation which has been given me; this is **faith**. If I refuse to say Yes, this is **unbelief.**

This response is no longer strictly in the order of material history. It involves me on the level of my personal existence to rethink the entire universe according to another synthesis.

"Jesus is raised, he has appeared to Peter" (Luke 24:34)

Jesus is living! This is the response of God to the question set before the apostles by the death of Jesus and the disappearance of his body. Faced with this response, they will have to involve themselves and us. The Gospel writers did not describe this appearance of Christ to Peter, but all recount this scene in which Jesus presents himself living to his disciples to establish them as witnesses to his resurrection.

The details differ but the very differences are reassuring for our faith: these texts are not the invention of forgers who agree on one text. All of them show us in the apostles, first, a reaction of doubt so clearly that Jesus reproaches them for their unbelief and hardness of heart.[12] Jesus is obliged to show them his hands and his feet. It is truly the Jesus they had known before his Passion. He is exactly the same and yet he is also totally different, since he makes himself present with them as he wishes, for short periods of time.

But if God has raised Jesus, this same Jesus in whom they believed before his death, then nothing is at an end. On the contrary, everything is beginning. At the foot of the Cross, the priests had mockingly jeered: "He trusted in God, let him deliver him now if he loves him" (Matt. 27:43; Wisd. 2:18-20). And apparently God was dead. Was this his refusal to answer? Or rather, was this his refusal to answer the question as it had been asked by the priest and the apostles?

The real response of God is the resurrection of Jesus. A response that is given first to Jesus himself: it is the sign that the Father accepts his sacrifice of the Cross. A response given especially to the disciples (and to us), but entirely different from what they expected. They wanted a human messiah, a human response; deliverance from the Cross. God gives them "his" response, a totally unlooked-for response: Jesus is truly the one he claimed to be, the Messiah charged with fulfilling the plan of God, but not a messiah in a merely human measure. A Messiah, not glorious but filled with pain (Isa. 52:13-53:12), not only Son of man but Son of God!

"God has lifted him up to his right side, he has made him Lord"

Thus Peter ends his first discourse to the people on Pentecost. Jesus is **Lord**. We are so accustomed to this word that it has lost all its strength for us. Yet it is through this word that the apostles summed up everything they understood of the mystery of God. God has made him Lord, which means that he has not only restored him to life but has "lifted him up to his right side." And the **Ascension** is the visible expression of this being lifted up. As Son of God, Jesus does not have to be introduced into the bosom of the Trinity, since he has never left it. But Jesus, **Man-God,** Jesus in his humanity is introduced into heaven to receive the full power over our world which he has redeemed. And with him our humanity is already in hope received into heaven. The **Ascension** is the sign that Jesus inaugurated another kind of presence among us, that he ceases to be present here with his body of flesh. It is especially the sign of his taking possession of the world and the entire universe; **The feast of Christ, the King**. It is the realization for him and the anticipation for us of this Lordship over the world which Paul stresses so much in his first Letter to the Corinthians: "And when everything is subjected to him, then the Son himself will be subject in his turn to the One who subjected all things to him, so that God may be all in all" (1 Cor. 15:28; cf. 1 Cor. 3:22).

This entrance of Jesus into the glory of God ("Glory," another name for God, God-insofar-as-he-is-glorious) is his Lordship over the world. But this Lordship will actually exist in the world only in the measure in which his Church will establish it. For this reason Jesus lifted up sends his Spirit to the Church.

"For there was no spirit as yet because Jesus had not yet been glorified" (John 7:39)

Fifty days after Easter, the feast of Pentecost, the apostles "were all filled with the Holy Spirit" (Acts 2:4). We shall see how this coming of the Spirit, a presence of Jesus continued in his Church, gives life to it. But this coming is first the completion of the paschal mystery of Christ. The Spirit could be given to us only from the bosom of the Trinity, but he could be given us only through the humanity of Christ, through which all goods come to us. This pouring out of the Spirit on the world on Pentecost is then the sign that Jesus has completed and fulfilled his paschal mystery, that, in a sense, the humanity of Jesus is "completed," that it has reached its fullness; his sacrifice on the Cross, the peak of his whole life of interior offering, has been accepted by the Father. The resurrection is fully meaningful. God has given him Lordship over the world, as the Ascension shows. Now he can send upon this world his Spirit, which, from a sinful world filled with despair, will become the spiritual world in which God can be all in all.

Note on the Historicity of the Events of the Paschal Mystery

In trying to relive the paschal mystery through the psychology of the apostles, I have been careful to take from the Gospel accounts only that which appears solidly established to the exegetes. I could have given the impression that these accounts are "on-the-spot reports" on which we can support ourselves without any problems at all. And yet these events do pose problems for the historian, whether believer or unbeliever. Thus we must take them up again from a more technical point of view in order to experience solidity.

The difficulty is that these events are less "historic facts" than "mysteries," or, to use Gabriel Marcel's distinction, they are less problems which I understand or discern, in relation to the surroundings, than they are mysteries, which involve me, into which I am inserted without being able, like the insect enclosed in the crystal ball, to grasp all the fullness globally. The events of the life of Jesus before Easter—his Passion, his death on the Cross, his burial—are all historical (statistical) facts which can be observed, which are "demonstrable" through historic science. The events of his life after Easter are mysteries, i.e., their essential aspect escapes me. Their effects, the traces of their passage in our world, are historically knowable and reassure my reason, but they are especially to lead me to accept in **faith** this mysterious passing of God which they reveal to me and which the inspired authors try to the best of their ability to make me feel.[13]

The Resurrection. Neither the apostles nor the women were present for this. They saw Jesus living after the resurrection. Jean Guitton poses the question in this manner: If Pilate or Herod had been present in the Upper Room at the time of the appearances of the risen Christ, would they have seen him? Probably not. For the resurrection of Jesus is not, as for Lazarus for example, a mere return to physical life. It is the entrance of Jesus into true life, a life more real than ours, a "physical" life, but of a physique different from ours, a life which does not end (and I myself will have to be at the end of time to be able to know historically that it does not end). This is not a fact which is offered to my faith, to my free decision, which involves my entire existence.

This does not mean that this act of faith is irrational. In fact, we can sense this mystery in the effects that it produces: the experience of the apostles that this Jesus whom they had seen dead is now living; their transformation: some men deceived by his death, despairing, refusing to believe even on Easter morning, fearful, are suddenly changed to the extent that twenty-five years later they have borne through persecutions, imprisonments, death-penalties, this faith up to the end of the known world: Rome (and perhaps Spain). The effect of the resurrection remains visible before our eyes: the multitude of Christians, spread out through the world for twenty centuries. **For us today, the sign of the resurrection is the Church.**

The Ascension. You will say, there are no difficulties connected with the Ascension. This is a fact well attested and even dated. Indeed! If this is true, is it not curious to note that never in the New Testament do the apostles or Paul appeal to it? **Well-dated**

fact?: "40 days after the Passover?" Yet we know that it is only in the fourth century that the Church fixed the liturgical feast on this date. (Before, the Christians celebrated this mystery on Easter Sunday or the Sunday after or even on Pentecost.) Moreover, Luke, who, in the Acts, places the Ascension on the fortieth day (a stereotyped number in the Bible) presents it to us in his Gospel as fulfilled on the evening of the Pasch! Furthermore, this "ascending" of Jesus toward "heaven" shocks many of our contemporaries, who feel that this is the language of the mythologies. Copernicus taught us that the universe is not built in stages or layers; and in his Sputnik, Gagarin assured us that he did not meet God in the "heaven." It is quite evident that "heaven" is not above our heads. But the apostles, like ourselves, with our extremely young science, have no other way to express certain ideas than in spatial language. We speak of our feelings "being picked up," or someone whose health improves "has picked up," "Let us lift up our hearts," says the priest to us at the Mass and none of us is deceived by these expressions. But what did happen on the day of Ascension? The mystery in which **Jesus is lifted to the right side of God.** And this, like the resurrection, is a fact offered to my faith. Does this mean that the description which Luke gives us is nothing but imagination? There is no reason to refuse to Jesus the possibility of having carried out visually before his apostles, by an "ascension" toward the sky, his "exaltation" into the presence of the Father. But we could also think, without losing any of the mystery, that this description in biblical language (Ascension, cloud, angels) is a literary form which appeared to Luke as the most appropriate to bring us to experience the mystery, to express for us the inexpressible.[14]

Pentecost. Like the Resurrection, we have an event historically well dated, at the time of the Jewish feast, fifty days after the Pasch. But does this mean that all the details of Luke's description are to be taken as a Huntley-Brinkley newscast? Are they "his story" in our modern sense of the word? These details are not proper to the Christian Pentecost: the noise of the wind, fire, are in the Bible the sign that God is manifesting his presence or his action. The "tongues of fire" are evidently more surprising. But they are less surprising for one who has read the "targums" (paraphrased translations) of Philo (Jewish philosopher living in Alexandria in the time of Christ). In commenting on the account of the gift of the law of God to Moses on Mount Sinai, the rabbi explained that this "voice" (or this "noise," the same word) was visible like "tongues of fire" (recall the flashes of lightning in **The Ten Commandments** by which Cecil DeMille attempted to materialize this tradition), tongues of fire to the number of seventy according to the number of nations on the earth in Genesis, a magnificent way to express that this law has a universal import for all people. In his account, does Luke wish to tell us that there were really tongues of fire? Or is this a way to tell us that the Spirit will now be the new law poured into the heart of all believers? This voice of God leaping formerly from the cloud, a sign of the presence of God, is now presented in the bosom of the Church, because the Spirit has been given to it. The entire mystery of Pentecost is contained in the one phrase: "They were all filled with the Holy Spirit" (Acts 2:4).

Our modern, Western minds are in danger of being sidetracked by these statements. We distinguish very exactly (or we think we do) between an event and the interpretation we should give it. This is a very practical way. But why should it be the only way? Ignoring perspective, painters of former times put side by side, on one and the same plane, that which, in fact, is situated on varied planes of depth. But regarding the laws of perspective, the modern artist will suggest this depth . . . if we know how to read it. So also for the reading of our biblical texts (and ancient profane texts) the problem comes back to a knowledge of the laws of perspective, namely, to discern before an account what rises from the plane of the event which really took place and that which rises from the plane of its deep meaning which is perceived only through the faith of witness. Does this seem complicated? Do not be fooled! We are going ahead. Gradually your eye will get used to it.

[1]Jesus celebrated the banquet with his disciples on the vigil in the evening. (Anne Jaubert maintains that the Last Supper took place on Tuesday evening, but this theory runs into too many difficulties to be held. Cf. OT, p. 188). This last meal of Jesus was not a paschal meal in the strict sense, since he could not have immolated the lamb in the temple. He himself was the true Lamb who was to be immolated on the morrow. Thus in his last "paschal" meal around the only true Lamb, did he wish to respect the customary rites which we gather from between the lines of the Gospels.

[2]Undoubtedly the blessing of the first cup in Luke (Luke 22:17-18).

[3]To sign the abasement of his Passion, Jesus washes the feet of his disciples.

[4]For the Jew does not drink straight wine. There is perhaps no other symbolism to be sought in the drop of water the priest mingles in the cup of wine.

[5]"Eucharist." For the Catholic this word has become synonymous only with "Real Presence." We "adore the Eucharist!" But this is not the proper meaning of the word. Because we have forgotten the primary meaning of the word, i.e., "praise," "thanksgiving," it is not true that we have lost in part the meaning of the Mass. To make the Eucharist means, first and foremost, to thank God for all his benefits. The Mass is the "Sacrifice of praise" par excellence, because Jesus, in pronouncing the Eucharist over the wine (the second cup in Luke 22:20), has given a new meaning to Jewish praise by saying, "Do this in memory of me": i.e., "Give thanks to God for the benefits he has accomplished through me." We do not treat of "adoring the Eucharist" (what can this actually mean?) but of making "Eucharist adoration," i.e., of entering into the true prayer of thanksgiving which can be pleasing to the Father: that which his Son offered him in his paschal mystery and which the Mass renders present.

[6]For Jewish theology, the meaning of this rite is very rich. It is a *memorial* of the past; not only a recall, but a way of rendering it present by recalling it. In performing this rite, the participant becomes really contemporary with the deeds of the past which have value also for him. There is also *expectation of the future:* the liberation which God performed in former times for his people, we know that he will one day complete. The night of the Pasch becomes also the night on which they expect the Messiah, on which they leave the door open so that he can come and sit at their table. Finally, *this rite expressed the present:* recalling (by rendering them present) the past benefits of God, awaiting those of the end of time, he expresses the fidelity of God toward his people, today. The meaning of this Jewish paschal rite will blossom forth and be realized in truth in our sacraments.

[7]Concerning the Suffering Servant: a figure which will so much aid the first Christians to understand the mystery of Jesus, OT, pp. 114-116.

[8]It is quite clear that all of this is a bit in the form of a novel: the Gospels do not tell us anything of the psychology of Peter. This is in a way quite easy and also dangerous, trying to give the life situation of the paschal mystery. It is dangerous if it gives the impression that the Gospels are a biography, an exact diary of events. We shall come back to this.

[9]We are following for the moment the account of John (20:1-2).

[10]"To his house," i.e., to Capernaum in Galilee. This is at least a possible reconstruction of the facts. The history of the apparitions of Jesus risen is quite complex. Jesus presents himself living to his disciples both in Jerusalem and in Galilee. A certain number of exegetes think it was first in Galilee and then in Jerusalem.

[11]How many working people, for example, have heard the resurrection and the divinity of Jesus proclaimed at a religious ceremony in which they participated through human sympathy (marriage, funeral, etc.), apparently without result, because they were not open, looking for an answer because they had not met in their work (or did not know how to look for them) authentic Christian workers whose lives posed a question to them.

[12]This also is important to assure our faith in the resurrection.

We are far from the theories worked out at the beginning of our century, showing us the apostles, after the death of Jesus, awaiting his resurrection with such impatience that they end up by taking their expectation for the reality. The Gospels are very outspoken in this: the disciples were not psychologically prepared for this resurrection, since, when they came face to face with the risen Christ, they had so much difficulty in believing.

[13]I put myself here on the plane of the "historicity" of the events, of the trace that they leave in our history. It is quite evident that the events from before the Pasch also reveal to us particularly the mystery of the passage of God and hence the mystery of our own existence. And they become perfectly clear—and hence involve us—through the perfect and definitive revelation of the paschal event.

[14]Father Benoit in the *Dictionary of Biblical Theology* (English translation published by Herder/Desclee, 1967), expressed the meaning of the Ascension very well. (This *Dictionary* is a "must".)

II.

BORN OF THE SPIRIT: ACTS OF THE APOSTLES

"Pentecost changed everything in the world, because that morning the Church was born."

J. Guillet

Dance of the Dead—In this oratorio, Honegger, on a text of Claudel, raises before our astonished eyes the extraordinary chapter 37 of Ezekiel. The year 587 B.C. has come and gone. The people are in exile, destroyed as a nation. Before the eyes of the prophet there appear dry bones scattered over an immense valley. God brings Ezekiel to glimpse how he will restore life to his people: "Prophesy over these bones: say 'Dry Bones, hear the Word of Yahweh.'" With an enormous clattering noise, the bones gather together, flesh appears on them—nerves, muscles, skin, all take shape. But in these reconstructed bodies there is no life. "Call the Breath on them," commands God. "Come from the four winds, Breath, breathe upon these dead that they may live . . . ." And the Breath came into them and they came to life again—stood up on their own feet.

Between the resurrection and Pentecost, the Church is present in these 120 disciples gathered in the Upper Room around the Twelve and Mary.[1] This is the Body of the Church, born of the **Word of God** incarnate who is Jesus Christ, born of his preaching and from his side opened on the Cross. But there was no life. Then, Jesus became Lord by his Ascension, and sent the Spirit (Breath).

A. The Church: The Body of Jesus Living by His Spirit

"All were filled with the Holy Spirit . . . ." The Church now lives. This body is now "animated" by the Spirit, the continued presence of Jesus. Jesus will be able through this presence to pursue his work, to construct his own body out of mankind, since there are two agents whom he has commissioned for this: his Spirit and the group of apostles. And these two agents will, till the end of time, collaborate, the one proclaiming externally the Word of God, the "Event Jesus Christ," while the other interiorizes it in the heart of believers. The apostles and their successors transmit Jesus Christ through the sacraments, the Spirit brings men interiorly to cling to the efficacy of these sacred signs.[2]

As the breath inflates the pneumatic lifeboat to give it its full dimension and efficacy before launching it on the water, so the Spirit will bring this Church to its full extension—will lead it to discover that it is the Body of Christ made for all men of all times before launching it to the limit of history. Or rather, it is by launching it in this world that the Spirit will make it conscious of what it is. In Acts, Luke shows us the Church faithful to a double movement: the Spirit is constantly pushing the apostles outside—outside the Upper Room, outside the Near East—outside the provincialistic narrow ideas, always further and at the same time, unceasingly, he leads them back to Jesus Christ to make them realize that what they are living is what he wanted and prepared. **From this fidelity to life and to the Spirit our Gospels will be born** (Acts 2:42-47).

In order to perceive this double movement in reading Acts, let us first try to outline it.

1. To Know Jesus Christ Build His Body

> "The Christian knows Jesus Christ insofar as he bears witness to him in the world."
>
> J. Guillet

A paradox: To know Jesus, the apostles are tempted to "contemplate" him, to lock themselves in the Upper Room to find him behind them, in their memories. To know Jesus, the prophets look down upon the Church which the apostles are building. "We spread the gospel [i.e., Jesus Christ who is the Good News proclaimed to men, Rom. 16:25] writes St. Peter, the Gospel of which the messengers long to catch a glimpse (1 Pet. 1:12), and Paul declares: "So that the sovereignties and powers should learn only now through the Church, how comprehensive God's Wisdom really is; exactly according to the plan which he had had from all eternity in Christ Jesus our Lord" (Eph. 3:10).

Illusion of the Apostles: They think that Jesus has completed his earthly life, that his entire life is behind them and that they can grasp it completely by turning back to it. **The declaration of the Spirit:** Jesus is behind you; he is in front of you; he is in your hands. Jesus is not finished. He will be only when he has reached his "stature as a perfect man" (Eph. 4:13). He will be definitively incarnate at the moment in which he "comes" definitively, at the end of the world to gather us all in him and in which he will finally be able to present himself to the Father so that God may be all in all (1 Cor. 15:28).[3]

A disturbing revelation which transforms us from historians of the past into creators of the present! As to the enthusiastic hands of the artist is delivered the material to be fashioned so as to reveal the idea that he knows is living there, so the body of Jesus Christ is given into the hands of his Church (you and me) so that taking in hand our humanity and the world we may cause the rise of the countenance of Jesus Christ! "Pentecost changed everything in the world because, that morning, the Church was born. The Church was born because Peter and his companions, instead of joining their Master in their memories, felt themselves suddenly under the impulse of the Holy Spirit entirely given over to the tasks of the present moment. . . . The life of Jesus from this hour is no longer a series of touching or uplifting episodes. It is God flowering forth in his plan—reconciling mankind to himself in his Son."[4]

Jesus is before us, in the hands of his Church. But it is also true that he is behind us. What he will be at the end of time, Jesus has already been in "sacrament" in image, but in real and efficacious image, i.e., which contains in advance and produces what it re-presents. Thus, to know Jesus Christ whom it builds, the Church must at the same time turn back to the human countenance of Jesus of Nazareth as he lived.

2. To Build His Body Know Jesus Christ

Know Jesus Christ? Nothing could be easier—or so we think! It is enough to open his Gospel, to look upon Jesus living, to listen to his words. Nothing easier for us! But at the moment in which we are, Pentecost, there are no Gospels!

There are no Gospels! First of all we must rid ourselves of a false idea which we all, unconsciously, carry in ourselves. Instinctively we imagine the apostles during the earthly life of Jesus in the form of modern reporters. They accompany him, camera in one hand, notebook and tape-recorder in the other, carefully jotting down the acts and words which they will then have only to put down in writing.

Nothing could be further from the truth! Of a certainty the camera and tape-recorder did not exist, but even more so, the very idea of which they are the symbol, i.e., reporting, was not yet invented. And even if it had existed, would they have considered it? Certainly when the apostles left everything to follow Jesus, they accompanied him as someone of importance, but Jesus did not yet have the importance in their eyes that he will later have. They follow a man—a prophet, and soon **the** Prophet, the Messiah: but no more. They do not follow him as men who will later have to give an account of what they have seen and heard. On Easter morning, the apostles are like people who, coming out of a tunnel, suddenly burst out into the blinding light of the sun: they see nothing, not because it is dark but because it is too light. The apostles are overcome because they discover Jesus. They have accompanied him for two years without knowing with whom they were walking. They have walked through this night of the Passion in which the "half light, half dark" which they had known has become darkness, and they burst forth suddenly into the light of Easter. The full flowering of Easter! Of the life of Jesus, they now know only one thing: "Jesus died, God raised him, lifted him up. We are saved!" The details of the life of Jesus, his words, all this is pushed out of their clear consciousness. The fact of Easter stands out completely and its consequence: "We are saved."

But then our Gospels? The Gospel—there is a statement important from many points of view—the Gospel: the Church gradually in the course of twenty, thirty, forty years forms the Gospel. The Gospel is born as the fruit of the "reseeing" of life of the first Christian generation.

A "reseeing" of life: to judge this fact in which we are involved, this situation, this mentality, reflection will recall to us one or other of the texts of our Gospels. To reflect upon its life, upon all these actions which the Spirit brings alive for it, to know whether they are in accord with what Jesus wanted, the Christian community will bring back to its immediate consciousness what Jesus said and did. In the midst of the circumstances and needs of its daily life, without preconceived idea or plan, words and episodes of the earthly life of Jesus will be recalled, twenty, thirty, forty years in the course of which, **little by little,** the Gospel is formed.

"History of the formation" of the Gospels.[5] **Full of feeling and yet disturbing!** Disquieting also at first glance for the historian! Full of life and feeling because the Gospels cease to be static "books," "manuals of the perfect Christian," or codes of morality. They become what they really are, a Person living in the midst of a community, constantly asking him questions and constantly responding to him, the history of the dialogue of a community with its Lord whose life and teachings are the light (more: a presence) in each of the events of daily life, they become what they should be for us also: the expression of a fidelity and a companionship with Jesus.[6] Disquieting for the historian also (believer or unbeliever). Sociology has brought back to us the importance of the "life situations,"[7] carriers of tradition, of this soil in which the seed that has been sown there sprouts. But what is the share of "creativity" of these "life situations"? We know the danger in the reseeing of life, "interpreting" a text from its functional value for our own life. Did the "reseeing" of life of the original community escape this danger of "creating" Gospel texts and a face of Jesus in view of the functional value for their own lives?[8]

For the moment, let us not complicate the problems too much. Let us begin by visiting this original community.

Guided by Luke we shall attend closely to the double movement which the Spirit brings alive in the disciples: He constantly pushed them forward, making them understand that to know Jesus Christ is to build the Church and constantly he leads them back to the life of Jesus, not only that which he lived with them for two years and for some thirty years on earth, but also this "life" which the Word of God lived for 1,500 years in the midst of his people. Word of God proclaimed by prophets, priests, and wise men; Word of God put into writing in the "Scriptures" (in what we now call the Old Testament).

The Acts recount for us this history from A.D. 30 to 50 and beyond. It is enough for you to read it. To help us to do this with new eyes, why not attempt to interview this or that person who lived at the time? The idea may seem far-fetched, but Luke will be here as a technical adviser.

B. The Year 35—with Simon Peter, Peter, and John

I find them near the Beautiful Gate of the temple at 3:00 in the afternoon, the time for evening prayer. The lame man whom they had cured some months ago "in the name of Jesus Christ the Nazarene" assured me of this: they go up every day to the temple for the three daily prayers. How willingly they get ready and give themselves to my questions. Peter answers most of the time.

"You are among the principal leaders of this group of disciples of Jesus. Can you tell me how this group began?"

My answer is going to surprise you: For me, **the true beginning** took place after the departure of Jesus, the day of our Jewish feast of Pentecost. That day I began to understand truly who Jesus is. I had followed him for two years, two marvelous years, but also two hard years—I had followed him because John the Baptist had pointed him out as a prophet. Some were asking whether he might not be the Messiah. Gradually my conviction took shape, and at Caesarea, near the sources of the Jordan, when he asked who we thought he was, I answered without hesitation: "You are the Messiah!" From that very moment he began to make proposals which really bothered me. "The Son of Man [this was the name he used of himself] is to suffer and be put to death . . ." And there would be his condemnation, his death on the Cross. And I denied him . . . . But we have seen him alive: God has raised him up, and one day on this hill [he points out the Mount of Olives which turns to gold in the rays of the setting sun] we came to realize that his earthly life was ended.

"But you mentioned Pentecost!"

Yes, I did! That is the day Jesus sent upon us his Holy Spirit as he had promised. Then everything seemed simple. He had promised that his Spirit would recall his words and lead us to understand everything. The two years passed with Jesus we are just beginning to understand, I think. From now on there is only one thing that is of importance to us: to be witnesses of what Jesus said and did.

[We are walking back and forth under the portico of Solomon, where the group of the disciples gather spontaneously. How surprised I am at the favor which Peter and John seem to enjoy with the people.]

Yes, this is extraordinary! But we are really nothing. It is the Word of God that does everything and the name of Jesus is so powerful.

[They tell us of the miracles that Peter worked as he went along. But it is clear he does not like to talk about it. I do not insist.]

"What is your relation to official Judaism? Granting that the Sanhedrin holds you for suspects and even imprisoned you, I was a little surprised to note your diligence in frequenting the temple."

But why? We are Jews and we remain so. Certainly, our chief priests suspect us. Several times they have summoned us to appear before them and have even scourged us: that was the day we came to understand the Passion of Jesus better and the joy there can be in suffering with him and for him. But we are Jews. Jesus is the Messiah whom God sent to our people to establish his Kingdom. It is true, not everything was carried out the way the Pharisees and we ourselves expected it: a Messiah King who would expel the Romans and re-establish the supremacy of our people over the entire world. No, his Kingdom is not of this world. And we have only one hope, he whom our entire people recognize as the Messiah, he in whose name alone we can be saved.

"But was Jesus Messiah and Savior only for the Jews?"

Yes and no! You were present, I think, at the last feast of Pentecost? You recall the crowds climbing in pilgrimage toward Jerusalem, Jews by race, but also men coming from every nation under the heavens who have become Jews by their convictions. Read our Scriptures again: the prophets, especially Isaiah, announce that at the end of time, in the "Day of the Lord," all people will come up here to the mountain of God to adore him. Even Egypt and Assyria, our hereditary enemies, God will welcome as his people. The whole world will embrace the Jewish faith to adore the true God. Now! That day I have seen. On the feast of Pentecost, five years ago, I realized that all these people, to whom the Spirit made me speak, were the first fruits of the whole world. One day, the whole world will have become Jewish and will recognize Jesus as the Messiah.[9]

[While he was speaking, we left the temple esplanade and walked in the uphill streets. We stopped before one door]: "This is the house of Mary, mother of John-Mark. Here we usually hold our prayer meetings."

"Good, I shall ask you more on this topic . . . ."

[Peter knocks on the door and Rhoda, a servant girl comes to listen. She recognizes Peter's voice and she is filled with joy. She hurries to let us in.]

1. Liturgical milieu

. . . . our prayer meetings? An immense topic, because, in a sense, it is our essential activity. You know that for us, Jews, "to serve" God through worship is the purpose of our life. This also sums up our entire daily life offered to God.[10] To be more clear we distinguish the prayers and cultic acts: "breaking bread" and baptism.

For prayer (I am not speaking of the prayers in the temple—you have noted that we are diligent in these), we do not make innovations on what we were doing before Jesus. It is simply that everything has a new meaning. To be specific, take as an example the outline of one of our last vigils. We had just been released by the Sanhedrin and when we arrived here with our brothers, we spontaneously set ourselves to praying: an invocation of God, the singing of the psalm, "Why this uproar among the nations . . . ?" This is the story of our community who is singing it, or better the story of Jesus continued in our community. This is what I have tried to explain. Then we prayed in silence and then I concluded this prayer by asking the Lord to extend his hand over us and permit us always to preach boldly.[11]

"This is a prayer vigil born of a particular circumstance. Do you not have prayer proper to your community?"

Of course! First, the Psalms of David. Does this surprise you? They are not proper to us, but the way in which we pray them is very personal for us: We know that the Lord in whom we pray is Jesus and this gives the psalms their whole meaning. We address ourselves also to God, the Father of Jesus, but we do this in union with Jesus, in his name, because we know that everything that the psalms sing and hope for is realized in Jesus, his Son. We also have psalms that originated in our community, for example, "Blessed be the Lord, the God of Israel," in which we thank God for his benefits and especially for having sent Jesus, the rising sun which enlightens our darkness and guides us in the path of peace.[12] Or again: "My soul proclaims the greatness of the Lord," in which Israel, "the virgin, Israel" as the people always loved to be called, humiliated because she is barren, rejoices because she has begotten her Savior.[13] We have the acclamations: "Holy, Holy, Holy is the Lord God of Hosts!" or indeed, "Praise, glory, wisdom, thanksgiving, honor, power and strength to our God, forever and ever. Amen!" And this pressing appeal which runs through our worship: "**Maran atta**; Come Lord Jesus."[14] Above all, we love to repeat the prayer which Jesus himself taught us: "Our Father . . . ."

"Does the reading of the Scriptures hold as great a place in your life as before? What are they now?"

The Scriptures remain the Scriptures for us, i.e., the Word of God, and we read them diligently. But now we feel that we finally understand them. The Spirit of Jesus enlightens us, and we know that they all speak of Jesus. Thus, while meditating on them, we like to discover the life of the Master there. His Passion and death, for example, ceased to be a stumbling block for us the day that we understood that Jesus is the "servant" of whom the prophet Isaiah speaks, who gives his life as a guilt-offering, who was the "suffering Just Man" of the psalms, who bears in himself all our sufferings, or again in the "Just Man" of whom the book of Wisdom speaks.[15]

"This Jesus whom you discover thus announced in the Scriptures, he whom you pray to, is also he with whom you lived for two years. Does this not change a little the memories you have of him?"

This is quite evident. The **light of the resurrection** throws light on the entire life of Jesus. His Passion and death, for example could appear at the moment as a tragic but ordinary fact. The Romans had already crucified many a Jew in the same way. But in recounting his death now, we are attentive to everything that manifested that Jesus was aware that he was the "Servant," offering himself voluntarily to death in sacrifice. Another example: the title "Son of God." For us, it was a title that belongs to the Messiah: David the King was Son of God. I proclaimed Jesus "Messiah, Son of God." Now I understand there was infinitely more in these words that I spoke than what I thought at the time. You have noted that we speak freely of the "Lord Jesus"; in fact, it is only on the day of the resurrection that God has made him "Lord" over the whole world.

"You spoke just now about the 'breaking of the bread.' This is an expression very common in our period to express that they broke bread together, that they shared the same meal. I thought I understood that it had an entirely different meaning for you."

In one sense, it means a meal in common for us also,

but you are right that it has taken on a technical meaning for us: It no longer means just any meal but the meal which we do "in memory of Jesus," by reproducing this last meal which he took with us before he died. It is extraordinary what a deeper understanding we have of Jesus because of re-presenting this meal. I take into my hands the bread and at the end of the meal the cup of wine and, while passing them to my brothers, I repeat the words of the Master: "This is my body given for you, my blood which shall be poured out for you . . . ." So many memories come to mind. [I notice here that Peter is making a real effort to contain his feelings.] First he is there as he was at the Last Supper. We began our meal almost alone, almost orphans, but now, he is there! And it is he who explains to us his death, for at this Last Supper, it was his death that he offered. I did not understand what was happening when I saw him hanged upon the Cross. I know now that this was not an ordinary death, but a sacrifice. That evening he is the Paschal Lamb who saves us. And during this time I betrayed him. I see again his look at me when he came out.

[Peter is overcome with emotion and John delicately takes over.] I followed him to the Cross. Mary, his mother, was there. He entrusted her to me. I saw the water come out of his side. I carried him to the tomb. But when we recall his entire Passion we are not sad. For it is not the story of a dead man that is being called to mind: Jesus is living, he is with us at this meal. When I think of him upon the Cross, I see him as the king; his crown of thorns is a royal crown; his Cross is the throne that he has ascended to judge the whole world and to draw all men to himself.[16] This liturgical celebration of the death and resurrection of Jesus permits us to recall his Passion, but also many other events of his life—for example, the joyful meals eaten with the Resurrected on the shore of Lake Tiberias, and also the anticipations that he gave us of these, (now we understand that he was acting in anticipation): the multiplication of the loaves in which the Master presented himself to us as he who offers the true meal, the meal which we shall all, one day, eat together, with God in heaven and of which the "breaking of the bread" is already a foretaste.[17]

"Entrance into your community is through baptism. Why have you chosen this rite? Were you influenced by John the Baptist or the Essenes?

It is true that the Essenes had numerous washings, but you will note that they are repeated over and over and so do not have the same character as our baptism. Our baptism would come nearer to that of John: His was a rite of penitence signifying the desire to be rid of one's failures. In fact, during his lifetime, Jesus sent us to baptize, and at the moment I scarcely saw any difference from that of John, our first master. But after the death and resurrection of Jesus, we understood how completely different it is. We recalled, of course, that Jesus wanted to receive this baptism of penitence; but one of his statements, strange at first glance, came to mind also, a statement which gives this baptism a completely different meaning. One day when we were going to Jerusalem where he was to die, he said to us: "I have a Baptism with which I am to be baptized and how anxious I am that it be fulfilled" (Luke 12:50). Hence his true baptism was his death, and the baptism that he wished to receive from John was only a prefiguring of his descent into death. You know how this baptism took place: they descended into the water until they were completely covered by it. We know now that this was an image of the descent of Jesus into death, but also of his departure from the waters of death by his resurrection. This is the meaning of this rite: to be baptized is to enter with Jesus into death in order to come out with him, raised for a new life.[18]

"Is there anything magical about this?"

Not at all! The descent into the waters unites to Jesus only if we believe. He who is baptized must express his faith.

"How do you express it? Are there obligatory formulae?"

Obligatory? No! We say: "I believe that Jesus Christ is the Son of God,"[19] or "Jesus is Lord"[20] This contains our entire faith, and he who pronounces it can do so only because the Spirit has inspired it.[21]

"This is a global expression of your faith. Have you more detailed formulae?"[22]

Yes, for example:

I believe in the Christ
who died
who is raised
who is at the right of God
who is to judge the living and the dead.[23]

For this occasion also, the leaders of the sacred music have composed some canticles. This one is well known:

Wake up from your sleep,
rise from the dead,
and Christ will shine on you.[24]

Or this other:

He was made visible in the flesh,
Justified by the Spirit,
Seen by the angels,
Proclaimed to the pagans,
Believed in, by the world,
Lifted up in glory.[25]

"We have spoken very much about prayer and worship. I suppose this is not your only activity?"

2. Catechetical milieu

No, of course. For us, the apostles, a great portion of our time is dedicated to teaching. Did not Jesus choose us as "witnesses" for this? And we are amazed at seeing how diligent the believers are.

"Do you have a set plan for this teaching?"

Yes and no. We always start with the Scriptures. For it is in Scripture that God has presented in advance his wonderful plan for saving us, and Jesus came to fulfill these prophecies. The life of Jesus brings us to an understanding of Scripture, but the Scripture in its turn explains Jesus to us. Let us take an example. One of the titles the Master liked was "Son of man." This is a current expression for "a man." This is the sense in which we first took it. But you know that the prophet Daniel gave a very special and precise meaning to it: in a vision he saw a "Son of man" coming on the clouds of heaven before God and receiving from him dominion and power. Daniel explains to us that this mysterious being is the symbol of the whole people of God. Jesus, at the time of his trial, solemnly declares to the Sanhedrin that he is the Son of man—and for this reason he is condemned to death as a blasphemer. Hence Jesus, entirely man as we are, gathered together in himself the entire people of God. He explained this to us with crystal clearness: "Whatever you do to the least of these my brothers, you do to me." But the life of Jesus brings us to understand Daniel. The question was being asked: Who would this "Son of man" be (a man—a mere image representing a collectivity) and how will it be brought to reality? Now we know.[26]

We thus compose the life of Jesus. We start with his

baptism by John, then his teaching in Galilee, his going up to Jerusalem, and his death.[27]

But most of the time our teaching consisted in **answers.** To be disciples of Christ brought up many a question. Some came from the Pharisees: Why do you not wash your hands in the ritual way before meals? Why do you not fast? . . . The majority came to us from the brothers. One has been invited to eat in the home of a tax collector and another keeps company with people who are looked down on: what should they do? Another would like to dedicate himself to the service of the Word, but he is hesitant about leaving his parents. Is the non-Jew also our neighbor? Must we pay the temple tax? Is divorce allowed? . . .

"How do you answer? Do you have rules for conduct which you try to apply?"

Our only rule of conduct is the **person of Jesus.** Before each question we ask ourselves: What did Jesus do in such a case? What would he do here? This is wonderful because everything takes on a light. And you know this makes us remember very many words and deeds of Jesus which we had almost forgotten. My neighbor? One day, Jesus told this story: "A man was going down from Jerusalem to Jericho . . ." (Luke 10:29). Can we keep company with sinners? He was called: "The friend of sinners" (Luke 7:34); the day on which he was invited to the house of Simon, the Pharisee, there came the woman who is called simply, "A woman with a bad name": these people, he said, will be before us in paradise because they are "poor," and when they allow themselves to be loved by Jesus as a poor man who awaits everything from him, they are pardoned and they love him in return (Luke 7:36-50; Matt. 21:31). It is also recalled how demanding the Master was when he treated of leaving everything to follow him: "We must not look back . . ." (Luke 9:57-62). Ritual washings? He said, "What goes into the mouth does not make a man unclean; it is what comes out of the mouth that makes him unclean" (Matt. 15:10-20). By starting in this way with our day-by-day living, we are led to rediscover the life of Jesus and to understand it better.

"Jesus performed very many miracles. Do you utilize these in your teaching?"

Assuredly! Already during the life of Jesus we did this: when he sent us on mission, we had to show what kind of master was sending us. I really would like to recount the miracles of Jesus because this is concrete and allows us to teach very many things.

"Does this prove that Jesus was really what he claimed to be?"

Yes, this is the first point. This proves that God sets his seal of approval on him and that we should, therefore, put our confidence in him.[28] But there is another aspect, more important perhaps—sickness (and death, which is often its immediate consequence) is the sign of sin.[29] By curing, Jesus shows that he is the Master of death and of sin because he himself dies and has borne upon himself our sins, because he is raised and therefore he is the conqueror of death. This we understand now. During his lifetime, we saw only the first aspect. Let me give you an example. One day, at the beginning of his ministry, Jesus came home with me. My mother-in-law was in bed with a high fever. I spoke to him about this. He went over to her, took her by the hand so that she sat up, and the fever was gone—and she got up and served us. When I recount this, it is to prove the power of Jesus; no one can perform such wonders unless God is with him. But frequently also I will use this to show that Jesus was able to "raise her" because God "raised" him from the dead, that he cured her and so many others, "in order that the words of Isaiah would be fulfilled: and yet ours were the sufferings he bore—ours the sorrows she carried."[30]

At times we recount a miracle only for the lesson we can draw from it and this will differ according to the group we are addressing.[31] Take an example: the miracle of the storm, which Jesus calmed with one command. That day, we were frightened by his power, because the sea for us is the symbol of all the wicked powers of which it is the hiding place. God alone is the master of the sea. A question jumped right out of our hearts: Who then is this man? But I have used this miracle at the time of a retreat with the disciples. It is almost as if it were made for that: as we were getting into the boat, two disciples asked Jesus about following him, and he recalled to them how demanding this would be: "The foxes have dens but the Son of man has no place to lay his head." Then he got into the boat and we followed him: getting into this boat is then setting out in the footsteps of Jesus, as a disciple. This boat is the Church which Jesus founded and into which we came after him. And we were afraid of storms! Jesus reproached us for not having enough faith. He invites us, the disciples, to progress always in this faith because the people around us look at us, and look at the boat. And while looking on this Church—our team of disciples embarked with Jesus—they must cry out: "Who then is this man?"[32]

3. Missionary milieu

"I will not question you about your missionary activity because I have had occasion to hear you speak to the Jews.[33] It seems to me that three elements constantly recur in your talks: Jesus is the Messiah whom you put to death.

But God raised him and exalted him: to be saved, converted. Jesus has poured out upon us his Spirit, a sign that the new times have arrived. Jesus will come definitively in glory at the end of the world, to judge all men. Is this true?"

That is our basic message.[34] Add, however, that while proclaiming it, we appeal constantly to the Scriptures. This is important because, for us, it is not so much that we "prove" that Jesus is the Messiah as that we locate him in the plan of God by showing that he has fulfilled it completely. This is the best proof. Is this not the proof that Jesus used in his controversies with the Pharisees? Very many of these controversies come to mind on this occasion.

4. Community of goods

"I would like to ask one last question about your life. I am told that you put all your wealth in common."

It would be better to say we have our poverty in common. But it is true that no one among us claims what belongs to him as his own. The essential point is this: the communion of hearts. And this is true. Then without any push one way or the other, some have given over everything they possess. But this is not the essential element for us, and others may do differently; for us this has been a need of the heart, to manifest sincerely that we have only one heart and one soul because we have given ourselves entirely to Jesus, who alone possesses the words of eternal life.

RESUMÉ

As we take our leave of Peter and John, let us try to strike a balance on what this meeting has taught us about the primitive community as Luke presents it to us in the first five chapters of Acts.

This **community**, animated by **the Spirit** who is its life, structured **by the apostles**, is conscious of being **the true people of God,** announced by the Scripture, willed and prepared by Jesus.

Thus Luke sums up the essence of the life of the believers: "They showed themselves diligent in the instruction of the apostles, faithful to the fraternal communion, to the breaking of the bread, and to prayers" (cf. Acts 2:42-47; 4:32-35; 5:12-16).

The reading of the Scripture (i.e., for us, the Old Testament) is of capital importance: they read it **in the light of the resurrection of Jesus:** It helped them to understand Jesus and his life, which is the fulfillment of the plan of God.

Because of the multiple questions which daily life brings up, this community is led to recall, and reread the life of Christ, under the guidance of the **Holy Spirit**. Or better, it recalls and rereads the episodes of this life, his acts and words, according to the extent of their needs. (Note the number of times words like "we recall" or "we now understand" come up in this interview.) Thus morsels of the Gospels were gradually born, always in the light of the resurrection.

They arise especially in these three "life situations" which the specialists recognize:

1. **The liturgical milieu.** Breaking of the bread, baptism, prayer. In this milieu the account of the institution of the Eucharist will be born.[35] The accounts of the Passion, texts which explain them, like the multiplication of the bread. The confession of faith and the hymns, baptismal or not, will be used by the Gospel writers, by Paul, by Peter, and by John in Revelation.

2. **The catechetical milieu.** Here especially we shall see the systematic rereading of Scripture to locate Jesus in the plan of God. Here again, very many of the episodes of the life of Jesus and his words come back to memory and take form in response to the questions which arise from the life of the believers. The accounts of parables and miracles gradually take on their definitive form. The miracles are recounted with two "motifs": apologetic (they accredit Jesus), and theological (Jesus has taken our weaknesses on him). The general framework of the life of Jesus also begins to be fixed.

3. **The missionary milieu.** We note first how narrow this aspect still was: Peter and the apostles seem to have remained, in the beginning, in the "centralized universalism" of the great prophets; the salvation brought by Jesus is for all men, but on the condition that all men go through this center which is Jerusalem, which all Jews do. For the moment their efforts were limited to the Jews. In this situation are recalled especially the controversies of Jesus with the Pharisees, and also the miracles and especially Scripture.

We have situations ourselves in the year 35, quite arbitrarily.[36] I had to visit with this paschal community, before it produced an event which would be a determinant for its evolution.

C. The Year 36: Stephen Is Stoned

Jesus had said to his apostles: "You shall be my witnesses in Jerusalem, in all Judea and Samaria and to the ends of the earth" (Acts 1:8). All the apostles, as we have seen, are good witnesses in Jerusalem. Everything is going forward so well that they give the impression of being contented with themselves and thinking "we have arrived."

The Holy Spirit who pushed them out of the Upper Room now pushes them out of Jerusalem.

The first nucleus of the Church is recruited especially from among the Palestinian Jews, for whom the center of the world is Jerusalem. But with the increase of the number of disciples, there appeared a new group who felt ill at ease in these traditions so completely restricted, the group of the Hellenists. These are the Jews brought up in the Greek culture, who speak Greek (and therefore read the Bible in the Septuagint translation), have lived outside Palestine, and before their adherence to Jesus Christ, had their special synagogues. A conflict within the Church could not help but arise. The apostles decide to remain at the head of the portion of the Aramaic-speaking Church (the "Hebrews") and to give this new group leaders who will remain subject to them but will enjoy great autonomy. The Assembly (of the Hellenists undoubtedly) therefore elect seven of their numbers whom the apostles "ordain" by the imposition of hands.[37] Luke insists on numerous occasions: The Holy Spirit directs this operation and fills the seven. Stephen is the leader of the group.

Stephen is a figure who stirs up our sympathy. There is nothing of the "plaster of Paris" saint about him, as our statues represent. The Holy Spirit, who is the fire cast upon the earth, had to be happy to animate him. Stephen sensed the danger: the Church is in danger of not knowing how to free itself from Judaism. Through his discussions (Luke recalls that it is the Spirit who impels him to speak), through discourses (Luke reconstructs one for us in chapter 7 and gives us the basic themes, especially the rejection from the temple), he makes himself unbearable to the authorities and acts in an irreversible way. He dies because of this.[38] But how important? Because of him, the vessel of the Church goes out beyond its own little back bay, or better, official Judaism rejects it out of Jerusalem, forcing it thus to go abroad. "That day a bitter persecution started against the Church in Jerusalem, and everyone except the apostles fled to the country districts of Judea and Samaria" (Acts 8:1).

While Stephen is being killed, a young Pharisee takes charge of the clothes of those who stone him. This internal fire which burned Stephen had already been put in the heart of this Pharisee by the Holy Spirit. For the moment he is persecuting Christians, but before long on the road to Damascus, Saul will become Paul.[39]

The Spirit has now launched the Church into the deep. The apostles will have to follow.

D. Dr. Luke Opens Up His Files for Us

Perhaps it is time to see how the book of the Acts was composed. From the beginning of this chapter we have been using it as if it were the result of regular reporting. Is this an exact approach? And if not, is it even honest?

Let us transcend time and go back to interview the author, Luke.

It is around the year 65 (a little before or after), and we are outside of Palestine (Antioch? Ephesus? Greece? Alexandria? Rome?). Luke receives us. He is a man in his fifties, who breathes kindness and goodness. He is educated and expresses himself in elegant Greek, his native tongue.

"Are you in process of composing a history of Jesus, as some have told me?"

Yes! I decided after carefully searching out the eyewitnesses to write an ordered account of the events which took place among us. A life of Jesus, if you will, but which goes beyond the time, strictly speaking, that Jesus passed on earth. A history of Jesus is a history of the time of Jesus, but certainly also of the time of the Church which continues him.

"Did you know Jesus personally?"

No! I am of a pagan family and lived in Antioch. There, ten years after the death of the Lord, I heard his disciples speak of him, and we began to call them "Christians." But I have listened so carefully to those who were eyewitnesses from the beginning, and servants of the Word, . . . and so I have the impression of knowing him better now than if I had known him only during his earthly life.

"How is that?"

You know that after my conversion I partially abandoned my profession (I am a medical doctor) to follow Paul. On the roads of Asia Minor and Greece, which we traveled together in these new communities which the Word of God stirred up everywhere, in the enthusiasm of these believers, their faith, their love, their patience in suffering—and above all, in my master, Paul—I learned the power of Jesus, his friendship for men.

"Can you tell me of your work?"

I am beginning the second part, the time of the Church. As I told you I made a minute inquiry, I gathered very many documents. [While he is talking, he shows me his files.] Now I have to put this in order.

"What is the nature of these documents?"

It varies a lot. Here is my "travel log" that I made with Paul from Troas to Philippi at the time of his first trip toward Greece; then from Troas again toward Jerusalem, when he was arrested; finally from Caesarea to Rome, where he waited two years to be judged.[40]

Now here is a completely different kind: **Archives of the Church in Antioch.** These recount the foundation of this church by the Hellenists, who were expelled from Jerusalem after the murder of Stephen. Our church in Antioch holds very much to this account of the ordination of the Seven in Jerusalem. In fact, our leaders were an innovation in preaching directly to the Gentiles at a time when the Twelve thought they had to dedicate themselves to the Jews. Hence, it is important to establish that this is not a dissident community but a daughter of the mother-church in Jerusalem.[41] In the same file, I put also my **"blue-note" of the Council,** the great assembly in Jerusalem which marked a turning point in the history of the Church. I have put it also as a follow-up on **an account recorded of a particular assembly** which James, the brother of the Lord, organized there at one time; in the area where he is the leader (Jerusalem and Syria), the agreement between the Christians of Jewish origin and the Christians of Gentile origin ran into difficulty. The question at issue was the following of the legal prescriptions of the Jewish law, especially as they concerned meals and eating. At that time James took a series of steps which prevailed only for his territory.[42]

"As a disciple of Paul, you must have many memories of him!"

I surely do. For example, the account of his call on the road to Damascus. For him and for the Church this was a major event. So Paul gave us several accounts of it: one before the Jews in the temple of Jerusalem, another before King Agrippa and his sister Berenice.[43] I myself attempted a more complete account, starting especially from the memories of Ananias of Damascus who baptized Paul.[44]

From Paul and Barnabas I also have a **Summary of the Mission,** the entire first mission in pagan land, which the Holy Spirit entrusted to them. On this mission they founded the first communities in Cyprus and then in Asia Minor.[45]

"But did you gather nothing about Peter and the twelve?"

On the contrary, I inquired carefully about everything that concerned the **Head of the Church**. Here is one account of his dealings with Herod just before Herod's death, his imprisonment and his miraculous deliverance.[46] And another about the conversion of the Roman centurion Cornelius.[47] During my stay in Caesarea with my friend Philip, one of the Seven, I collected his memories of his activity.[48] And then above all I made diligent inquiry into the first years of the Church in Jerusalem, from the ascension of the Lord and Pentecost: I think I have a very clear idea of the extraordinary situation at that time.

"Excuse me, but I am a little bit swamped by this mass of documentation and I would like to ask you two questions. The material: How did you go about organizing all this? Second and more important: Could you, in a few words, sum up the major traits of this history?"

How do I go about it? You have seen my documentation. It is very diverse: accounts that I myself composed; very rarely, little portions which I have only to recopy; most often notes which I have taken from conversations, inquiries. Now I have to bring them together by making certain necessary connectives and by carefully working especially on the discourses. Why do you smile? You have read the great historians, Herodotus, Thucydides. It is in the finesse of the discourses that the good historian is recognized. But this is only the material aspect.[49] The most difficult, and this answers your second question, is to organize them in such a way for my dear Theophilus, to whom I address the work, that he notes the meaning that animates them, the plan of God which is at work. I have reflected very much on this, and this is how the history appears to me.[50]

The work of the Messiah, Jesus, as it is announced by the Scriptures, goes from his preaching to the Jews in Jerusalem up to the preaching to the ends of the earth—this is carried out by the Church animated by the Spirit and led by the apostles.

Does this seem a little complicated to you? If you wish, there are two points I would like to stress: the history that I am writing in this second work is the history of "The extension which the Spirit gives to the Church by means of the apostolic testimony"[51] But a **second idea**, this extension, which is made after the departure of Christ, is not added to his work; it **is** his work, it is an integrating part of his mission. Recall the word of the risen Jesus in the course of one appearance: "It is written: (1) that the Christ must suffer; (2) that he must be raised from the dead on the third day; (3) that in his Name repentance for the forgiveness of sins will be proclaimed to all nations, beginning with Jerusalem" (cf. Luke 24:46-48). And of this work, Jesus himself does only the first two parts, the third, which is **his** work on the same title, he does through us, his Church.[52]

"In his history I see two great parts: from Pentecost to the Council of Jerusalem and afterward."

From the Beginnings to the Council (Acts 1:1-15:35)

Look at the extraordinary extension, both geographic

and theological (the two are bound together and one leads to the other).

We start with Jerusalem, where we see the Church living for a long time and, through her life, coming always to know Jesus better. Then we go to Samaria, to Antioch, to Damascus, to Cyprus, then always further into Asia Minor.

This geographic extension has had an important consequence to force us to depart from Judaism. This also took place in stages. In Jerusalem, the Twelve preach to the Jews and expect the Gentiles to begin by becoming Jews. Then the Hellenists proclaim Christ to the Samaritans (heterodox Jews). Philip baptizes a proselyte.[53] Peter himself, with much holding back and driven by the Spirit, baptizes a "God-fearing" Roman.[54] Until this incident they are still Jews (less and less Jews) who are converted. The essential event seems to me to be the great mission of Barnabas and Paul to Asia Minor. Note how it is the Spirit himself who wanted this and took the direction in hand. The basic contribution of this trip was to show that "The Spirit has opened the door of faith to the Gentiles" (14:27).

Do you get the full implications of what this means? Jesus had said: "Do not go to the Gentiles. . . . Go rather to the lost sheep of the house of Israel." And now the Church, prompted by the Spirit, turns to Gentiles! This clearly gave rise to a question for the consciences of the apostles: "In doing this, are they faithful to the thought of Jesus? Hence the "Council of Jerusalem"! There, Peter was really recognized: after the long discussion, in a very exact statement, he puts the finishing touches to the debate: "God has given to the Gentiles just as to us, Jews, his Holy Spirit. . . . Remember, we believe that we are saved in the same way as they are: through the grace of the Lord

Jesus." I wish you could have "heard" the silence that followed these words. Everyone felt that a page had just turned: **The Church** was recognized as the Church for the world.

The gospel preached from Jerusalem to Rome

(Acts 15:36-28:31)

Everything was said, everything was done, at least in hope. For everything remained to be done: to carry the Good News to the end of the world. And God chose my master, Paul, for this. In two great round trips from Antioch to Athens, then Corinth, where he remained two years, then from Antioch to Ephesus (where he stayed a long time) and Corinth, Paul organized Christian communities in the entire region of Asia and Greece. He remained in Rome, the capital of the world. Here he arrived in chains. But the chains were of little consequence, since he could preach there. This is the way I end my work, with the vision of Paul proclaiming the Word in Rome. In fact, since he whom God had made his chosen instrument to carry the message to all nationals could preach Jesus Christ for two years in Rome, in the heart of the capital of the Gentile world, boldly and without hindrance, I am now certain that nothing could hold back the Word of God from being carried to the end of the world and to the end of time.

E. Resumé of the Birth of the Gospels

We have been led to abandon the simplified idea about the Gospels composed as a "newscast" by the apostles on the life of Jesus. The Church exists before the Gospels and the church throughout these 30, 40 or 50 years following the death of Jesus "formed" these Gospels.

1. Life and words of Jesus: pre-paschal community.

For two or three years, Jesus acts and preaches. The apostles follow him and Jesus organizes them into a community. We have listened to Peter telling us what he recalled at the moment of the death of Jesus.

2. **The paschal community: (stage of the "Formgeschichte")**. On Easter morning, the apostles, astounded and overjoyed, proclaim only one thing: "Jesus dies. God raised him. We are saved" (the kerygma).

Gradually to answer numerous questions which their life and the testimony they gave posed for them, very many of the deeds and works of Jesus come back in memory to the disciples. This happens in three "life situations" which we have noted. Since these memories are responses, they are already interpretations.

Certain accounts are thus formed and fixed in the memories: accounts of the passion, miracles, parables, and words of Jesus.

Then these little isolated accounts tend to be regrouped: one miracle account calls for another, the parables are gathered together, it is practical for the preacher to have together the different responses that Jesus made to the Pharisees. Other factors also influence this regrouping, for example, the geography. In Capernaum they will recall all the episodes that took place there, or it might be a person; the memories around John the Baptist.

Meanwhile, the framework of the life of Jesus is fixed: they get into the habit of presenting his life according to an outline: baptism by John, ministry in Galilee, ascent to Jerusalem (after the turning point in his life which was the confession of Peter in Caesarea), ministry in Jerusalem, and Passion.

Compare this to the making of a movie. At the end

of a few decades, we have a few sequences: some "plans" (our isolated stories) are regrouped in small series. But we do not yet have a "file"; there is only the last operation, the "mounting."

3. **The four editors of the Gospels.** Around the years 50-60, an author attempts, perhaps, a first ordered account (the "Aramaic Matthew," which we no longer possess). About 65, Mark in his turn writes the first of our four Gospels. Then around 65-70, Luke edits his. At the same time (or a little later) our Gospel according to Matthew sees the light of day. Finally, very much later (90?) John puts his reflections into writing. A very complex history (the "synoptic problem")—we shall decipher it later.

In this chapter,[55] we spent a great deal of time in the second stage: "The Gospel before the Gospels." A great deal of time, because in one sense it is the most important, and the most neglected, stage for the understanding of our Gospels. We shall study the third stage as the finale of this book. Before our four texts could be born, very many other texts had to see the light of day. (These will perhaps be an influence on our Gospels.) It is these works we must now study.

[1]The desire to be "twelve" shows in the apostles the consciousness of being the true "people of God," new because founded by Jesus Christ, but still in continuity with the old people constituted by the twelve tribes of Israel. This is important: the fidelity which God had formerly pledged to Abraham, the father of the people, now flowers forth in this Church.

"With Mary": Last explicit mention of Mary in the New Testament. Not in the center of the Cenacle, as the artists depict her (Peter is in the center) but with the others, one among the believers. In the hierarchic structure of the Church, Mary is nothing. Her greatness is elsewhere: she is the "figure of the Church"; she is in advance, she alone, the image of what this Church will be at the end of time, saved by Jesus Christ, "Spouse of Christ," belonging definitively to him (read again OT, pp. 224-225).

[2]Too often, especially in the course of religious controversies, these two aspects have been opposed: the Church, according to the Protestants, would be a mere "event," constantly raised up directly from on high by the Holy Spirit who creates it at each instant of its history without bond of continuity between these different moments. The Church, according to the Catholics, would be only an "institution," a visible society founded on the apostles, enduring without interruption because of this apostolic continuity. This false opposition is fortunately beginning to disappear. The Protestants are rediscovering a certain institution and John XXIII has recalled to Catholics that the Church is constantly raised up by the Holy Spirit. Jesus Christ established these two agents to continue his work, but the Spirit is God and he added to a structure which he can overthrow even though he has established it. We Catholics too often forget this sovereign freedom of the Spirit.

[3]"Your Kingship comes" . . . . All this we are asking.

[4]J. Guillet, *Jésus-Christ hier et aujourd'hui (Jesus Christ Yesterday and Today)*, (Desclée de B., 1963). An excellent book which goes right to the heart of the Gospel without technicalities. Chapter XV, "Jesus Christ, Life of the Nascent Church," is a little discouraging to me: why try to say less perfectly what he says perfectly?

[5]When they wish to "put on the dog," instead of "history of the formation" of the Gospels, they speak of the *"Formgeschichte"* of the Gospels.

[6]The Gospel has nothing to say to him who does not attempt to live by it. Militant life and action lead us back to it, teach us to understand it. How many pages, sealed shut until now, suddenly speak to us, one evening in reviewing our life, because they have become what they actually are: a response.

[7]Here again, to be in the inner circle, the French speak of the *Sitz im Leben* while the Germans talk of the *milieux de vie!*

[8]A famous alternative between what is called "The Christ of Faith" and "The Jesus of history." A false problem born of an important discovery. For too long a time it was believed that the Gospels were a "history of Jesus" in our modern sense of the word. The evidence that the Church existed before the Gospels

and "formed" them could not but give rise to a question. R. Bultmann, about 1920, and a few others were the originators of the "School of *Formgeschichte*." He wrote in the preface to his book *Jesus:* "Of the life and personality of Jesus we can know nothing." With the resurrection of Jesus as the starting point, the original community created a certain figure of Jesus, the "Christ of Faith" whose life it will recount in the Gospels, but which will hide from us the "Jesus of history." Thus Easter would be a wall beyond which we could no longer go back. The stakes are really high and one of the purposes of this chapter is to help you get beyond this false problem to which we shall return.

[9]Note how Peter and an important fraction of the community still have a narrow notion of the Church: to be a Christian one must first be or become a Jew.

[10]Not a cult cut off from daily life but a cult which is an offering, a consecration of this daily life, and which is also its source (cf. Chapter IV). The importance of Sunday Mass, the peak and starting point of a militant life.

[11]Acts 4:23-30. You recognize the outline of the first part of the Mass and of our celebrations of the Word.

[12]This is the same song that Luke will one day put on the lips of Zechariah (Luke 1:69-79) by adding two verses about John the Baptist.

[13]Luke cannot find more beautiful words to express the dispositions of Mary's heart at the Visitation. She is the true "Daughter of Zion" (Luke 1:46-55). Concerning the "Daughter of Zion," cf. OT, pp 77-78.

[14]Cf. Rev. 4:8; 7:12; 22:20.

[15]These "Servant Songs" and the "Psalms of the Persecuted Just Man" (cf. OT, pp. 114-116, 202-204) form the basic backdrop for the Passion accounts.

[16]Artists would do well to recall this when they portray the crucified. We hear, for example, that the Church has asked that the Christ of G. Richier be removed from the chapel of Assy. However beautiful it may be from the artist's point of view, this is not the Christ of the Gospel, but a Christ like this figures for about thirty-six hours of our history: from Friday evening to Sunday morning. The best representation (from the theological point of view) remains the Christ of the Middle Ages where the crown of thorns becomes the royal crown, the linen that girded

Jesus, a royal mantle, or again the Byzantine Christ whose countenance has the majesty of the Pantokrator. Our crucifix, if we wish to be Christians, must (would that it did) make us grasp that the One hanging on the Cross is the Risen One of the Easter.

[17]John does not recount the institution of the Eucharist. His whole understanding of it he gives us on the occasion of the multiplication of the bread (John 6).

[18]Cf. Rom. 6 (we read this during the paschal vigil) and Gal. 3:27. The difficulty of this kind of interview: How to avoid anachronism? Were Peter and John, in 35, clearly conscious of this meaning of baptism?

[19]Acts 8:36-37; cf. the Jerusalem Bible on Acts 8:37.

[20]"If your lips confess that 'Jesus is Lord' and if your heart believes that God raised him from the dead, you will be saved" (Rom. 10:9).

[21]"No one can say: Jesus is Lord, except through the Holy Spirit" (1 Cor. 12:3). Does this statement seem exaggerated? A sign that we have forgotten the Holy Spirit and His action?

[22]Equivalents and predecessors of our creed. It is evident that I am boldly anticipating here: the texts of this paragraph arise before the years 50-60, but almost certainly not before 35.

[23]Father Boismard reconstructs this original creed by comparing 1 Pet. 3:18-22; Rom. 8:34; and Heb. 9-10.

[24]Cited by Paul in Eph. 5:14.

[25]As reconstructed by Father Boismard from 1 Tim. 3:16 and 1 Pet. 3:18-22. You will find other examples in 1 Pet. 1:3-5; 2:22-35; 5:5-9 as well as throughout Revelation. Read again the magnificent hymn in Phil. 2:5-11.

[26]Dan. 7 (cf. OT, p. 176). One of our difficulties of the New Testament and especially of the Gospel is that, under one aspect, it is presented as a "table of contents." If you start with its table of contents, you will have an over-all view, but it will be relatively puzzling. On the other hand, when you read it again, after reading the book, each of the words of this table will be evocative: "Son of man," "Servant," "Son of David," "Son of God," "Messiah," and also "Covenant," "Vineyard," "Shepherd"—a few words among many which have a complete history. To want to understand the New Testament without knowing the Old a

little, is to claim to know a book by reading its table of contents. The *Dictionary of Biblical Theology* will give you the history of each of these words and the meaning.

[27]Read the discourse of Peter in Acts (10:36-43); it gives us a kind of plan for the Gospel of Mark.

[28]We shall speak of the "apologetic use" of the miracle.

[29]This shocks our Western minds, and yet it is deeply anchored there: when some misfortune strikes a person, is there not a tendency too often to look for some sin in his life? "God has punished him!" This is what the ancients were doing, ignorant of medicine, and attentive, especially, to the primary cause: the world and our existence are in the control of a just God, and sickness (the vestibule of death) is an evil: if God permits it, it can be only a punishment. Clear vision for a general plan: the sin of man has blocked the original harmony with God and has given death its tragic character; death and sickness, which is its image, is truly a sign of sin. But it is false thinking when they wish to apply this to a particular person, and a particular sickness (read John 9:2 and OT, pp. 140ff., 207ff.).

[30]Compare the three accounts: Mark 1:29-31 is the "apologetic" type; Matt. 8:14-15, 17 the "theological" type (designedly he has chosen the word "raised" which means also "resuscitate"); Luke 4:38-39 follows the same sense by showing us how Jesus "threatens" the fever, i.e., "exorcises" the sickness. Since she is sick, the mother-in-law is "possessed."

[31]Always we see the importance of the "life situation."

[32]Compare the "apologetic" account of Mark 4:36-41 and the "catechetic" account of Matt. 8:18-27.

[33]Note especially the five discourses of Peter: (2:14-41; 3:12-26; 4:9-12; 5:29-32; 10:34-43) and the discourse of Paul (13:16-41).

[34]What the specialists in their jargon call the "kerygma" (Greek word signifying "proclamation"; *keryx*=the herald). The kerygma is the essence of the Good News proclaimed to nonbelievers. A priest, for example, speaking to non-Christians (or to non-practicing baptized) who have come to church for an exceptional circumstance, will seek out the essence of Christianity to preach. A militant, giving an account of his faith in a few words to a nonbelieving friend, also gives a kerygma. The "catechesis" is a more developed presentation of the message to people already converted.

[35]The accounts of the institution of the Eucharist are inserted quite clumsily into the text of Mark and Matthew and are only a reproduction of the words of "consecration" as they figured in the Mass of the period.

[36]I was unable always to avoid the danger of anachronism. I have noted the most flagrant cases.

[37]Why "Seven"? Among the reasons given, the most probable is that the number 7 is the pagan number. "Twelve" is the number of Israel and the Twelve structure the New Israel; "Seven" is the number of the nations, and the leaders of the Hellenists are thus especially consecrated for their service. Nowhere is it said that the Seven were deacons. "They had to be for the Hellenist group almost what the Twelve were for the group of the Hebrews. Perhaps they even directed their liturgical gatherings and had the power to consecrate" (Benoit).

[38]Martyrdom of Stephen, a simple, popular stoning—the Roman governor would know nothing about it. Note how well this death, according to the account in Acts, resembles the death of Jesus. Luke wants to suggest to us that the death of each of the Christians is in fact, and should be in the way it is lived, the reproduction of the death of Christ. Jesus Christ is in agony until the end of the world in each man.

[39]We shall speak later of Paul and his "Conversion" on the road to Damascus.

[40]Acts 19:10-17; 20:5-21:18; chs. 27-28. Perhaps we must add 11:27. This would therefore be the testimony that Luke formed a part of this church in Antioch.

[41]Acts 6:1-8:4 and 11:19-30.

[42]Acts 15:3-12 and 15:13-53. The dissociation of these two events which the story seems to unite is important for a good understanding of the role of Peter.

[43]Acts 22:4-16 and 36:10-18. Paul will speak of it again in 1 Cor. 15:8; 2 Cor. 11:32-33; Gal. 1:13-19.

[44]Acts 9:1-3.

[45]Acts 13:14.

[46]Acts 12:1-23.

[47]Acts 9:32-11:18.

[48]Acts 21:8-9; 8:5-40.

[49]For all this I am indebted to the studies of Father Benoit both for the distinction of the sources and for Luke's way of

composing. To clarify this we can propose an analogy: I have a dissertation to write. I read different periodicals and books. I draw up a summary of a conversation with professor. At the time of actual composing or writing, I get scissors and some mucilage and gather all my material together with a few transitional works. (An analogy, not strongly advised.)

[50]It is quite evident that here again we have hypothesis. I chose this one which seemed to be indicated by the works of Ph. Menoud, J. Dupont, P. Benoit, and others.

[51]Luke, obviously, could not cite Ph. Menoud as I did here!

[52]We find here what we said above: when a militant Christian works to establish the Church where God has placed him, it is not his little work that he is doing, but it is the very work of Jesus Christ that he is accomplishing.

[53]The "proselyte" is a Gentile who accepts the Jewish faith entirely; the "God-fearing" is also a convert, but he refuses certain practices such as circumcision and certain legal prohibitions (in the matter of cooking especially).

[54]Acts 10:44-11:15.

[55]Father Xavier Léon-Dufour will recognize here all that belongs to him. His work, *The Gospels and the Jesus of History* (Herder/Desclee, 1968) is presently *the* book on the question. His minuteness and (relative) technicality will perhaps frighten you. If these pages could introduce you to reading him, they would be one way of expressing my thanks to him.

We have cited and compared very many Gospel texts. A *synopsis*—a book which presents the Gospels in parallel columns so that they can be read "with a single glance"—would be of the greatest service. The one published by R. Bompois, from Mame, has a practical format. But if you get the opportunity, take the one from the Jerusalem Bible by Benoit and Boismard. With this synopsis, the volume of notes that accompany it, and Léon-Dufour's book, we have in our hands the means for a serious and savory reading of the Gospels.

III.

A FIRST YES WHICH IS RECONQUERED EACH DAY: LETTERS OF ST. PAUL

"I arranged for you to marry Christ so that I might give you away as a chaste virgin to this one husband."
2 Cor. 11:12

"The Church lives like our love, with a first Yes that is reconquered each day."
Yves à Francoise, in P.-A. Lesort,
The Wind Blows Where It Wills

Christianity is not a "religion." It is a meeting of love, and acceptance of a creative love. Paul calls the pagans "religious"—"Men of Athens, I have seen for myself how extremely scrupulous you are in all religious matters." Of Christians he says that they are "believers," that they have faith, confidence in God. "Religion" is an approach of man to God; and search starts from below. And the religions with a thousand faces illustrate this effort of man to organize the way to reach the divine: they multiply mediations (sorcerers, rituals, incantations) to attain their object. Christianity is not a religion that will come to an end. It is the approach of God who, in Jesus Christ, the only Mediator, seeks man. It is true, this search of God meets the "religious" aspirations of men, but even more, it stirs them up. God comes toward man, he speaks to him and man responds: by his faith, he accepts this coming of of God and he accepts himself as a new being, born of this meeting. In this exchange of love, man "creates himself."

This marvelous adventure of the creative Yes, two men especially have the grace to glimpse: John and Paul. **John** personally lived it in the intimacy of two years. Thus he will chant the first Yes and will see all Christian life radiate from it. **Paul**, confronted by Christ on the road to Damascus, discovered Jesus more at work in himself and in his Christians: he will be more attentive to this reconquering to be unceasingly redone from the original Yes.[1] "I have given you to a single husband . . . ." For thirty years, Paul will be the "the best man" (the friend of the husband): like the best man who in the marriage ceremony presented the young girl to her husband-to-be, so Paul presents to Jesus innumerable communities. But he will remain near them to help them repeat their Yes, and his letters remain the most beautiful effort of Christianity to grasp the meaning of daily life with Christ. But before he takes up a pen to write, fifteen years elapse. At the moment, Paul is a Pharisee persecuting the Christians.

I. The Best Man: The Friend of the Husband: Paul Meets Christ

A. On the Damascus Road

1. Panic among the Damascus Christians

One morning in the year 36, the news spread in the lower quarters like a powder blast: "Paul of Tarsus is at our gates. The leaders in Jerusalem have given him power: he is here to arrest the Christians who fled the Holy City after the persecution of Stephen. He is to take them back in chains."

Who is this Paul, the cause of so much upset? Listen as he presents himself: "I am a Jew, born in Tarsus in

Cilicia, citizen of a town that is quite well known. Circumcised on the eighth day, Israelite by race, of the tribe of Benjamin, a Hebrew son of Hebrew parents. I was a student in Jerusalem and at the feet of Gamaliel, I was instructed in the Torah of our fathers in all its exactness. All the Jews have known me for a long time and they can, if they will, bear witness that I have lived since I reached my teens following the strictest sect of our religion, a Pharisee. As for the justice of the law I am irreproachable. I am also a Roman citizen. Others, even Roman tribunes, have bought this right of citizenship at a very dear price. I have it by birth."[2]

This man who thus expresses himself, proud of his past and what he is, before King Agrippa, before the Jews of Jerusalem who want to stone him, before the Roman tribune who trembles because he scourged a Roman citizen, is at the time thirty years old, of robust constitution (read 2 Cor. 11:21-29), perhaps married: a strong personality profoundly marked by the human conditioning of the youth as well as by the religious education that he received.

2. **Paul "is born several times . . . ."** (Brunot)

When we pass from the Gospel to the Letters of Paul, we are detoured. The more we felt at ease in the Gospel where everything is single, "evangelical," the more uprooted we feel in Paul: his reasoning seems so complicated, frequently labyrynthine. The impression we get is the same as we experience when we return from a weekend of basking in the sun in the peace of nature in the country and find ourselves right in the middle of the city with its business, bustle, and baffling bickering of politics and labor. This impression is not false: Jesus was a "country boy," and all the imagery that he uses is drawn from life in the fields or village, from the peace of the fireplace. Paul is a "city boy," all his companions are drawn from the town. Jesus is born in the midst of the "poor." Paul is the son of a rabbi. Jesus is a country worker, Paul is a theologian, and by trade or profession a tentmaker.

Paul is a city boy. He has the feel of the city, the facile repartee, the relationship to crowds. He has an open spirit, insofar as Tarsus is a university town whose schools of philosophy are on a par with the schools of Athens and Alexandria.

Tarsus is a stamping ground for civilizations; Athenodoros, the master and the friend of Augustus, teaches there, and a century earlier, Cicero was governor of the province. The Cydnus River flows there, which had cost the life of Alexander the Great, when, still sweating, he wanted to bathe in it. The young king remained in Tarsus only as long as it took him to be cured, but the hellenistic civilization was implanted there. They speak Greek here as in the entire Middle East, and Paul easily handles this "koine" or "common" Greek into which the Bible had been translated. The port of Tarsus, very near at the time, opened on Egypt (Cleopatra landed there one day disguised as Aphrodite to seduce the heart of the Roman, Mark Antony), on Greece, Rome, Marseille. And yet Tarsus never forgets that it is an Asian town, marked by centuries of Semitic civilization. Aramaic is always the national language. They learn Hebrew in school and Paul has, also, the name Saul.

Finally, Tarsus developed in the midst of a world on the way to urbanization and socialization. The Roman empire with its network of highways and communications on sea and land, its division of the territory into provinces, its police, gives rise to large cities, business and trade, exchange of ideas. Paul, a convert knows how to look directly to the vital centers of this civilization, the capitals and ports: Ephesus, Corinth, Rome.

So we see the depth of the human conditioning of Paul. But he depends even more on his religious education.

3. Pharisee

This name has a pejorative sense for us. This is too bad! Paul was proud of this title.[3] As a Pharisee, he is one of these saints who is violently in love with the only God, upon whom he has built his life. This God who created everything and who manages the world, this "completely other," who has deigned to enter into a relation of love with men, through the mediation of a people. And Paul, because he is a descendant of Abraham, knows that he is a member of this people, called to live now in the presence of the Holy God, to serve him in justice and in love. As a sincere believer, he knows that living in the presence of God is terribly demanding. And since God has transmitted his law to Moses, Paul bears for it the immense respect he has for him. The law, with its thousand-and-one rubrics invented by customs or traditions, to ensure that it be well kept, forms the framework of his daily existence. His entire life is a listening to the Word of God: "My life is the Law."

Paul is a reassured believer, sure of himself. This is the prevailing failure of the sect of the Pharisees. Since God has made a covenant with his people, it is sufficient for each believer to keep the law in order "to effect his salvation." Holiness, "justice" in the language of the Bible, is acquired by the works they perform. Paul knows that he is saved "by his justice which comes from the Law." It remains only to await the end of history, this moment in which God, through his Messiah, will re-establish his people; and all those who will accept becoming a part of the people, in its leadership over the world and through it, finally establish this messianic peace where there will no longer be "cries, nor tears, nor death."

This religious conviction, Paul has drawn from the heart of his family. He deepened it in Jerusalem where, as a young man, he studied at the feet of Gamaliel, one of the most famous rabbis. He will now teach as a rabbi himself. And he will defend this conviction, for a man like him could not be a theologian sitting in his room.

4. Committed theologian

Did Paul personally know Jesus? This is not very probable. He must have been absent from Jerusalem when this unknown stirred up the enthusiasm of the lesser ones and the fury of the great by proclaiming: "The Kingdom of God has arrived among you."

When he comes back to Jerusalem a few years later, he hears a gathering of poor people, sinners and publicans, proclaim that this Jesus is the Messiah, that God has raised him from the dead and made him "Lord," which means "God," since Lord is the biblical equivalent of Yahweh! Paul is stunned. In the name of his faith and his love for God, he has to struggle against this Church of Jesus. To him there is no doubt: Jesus is a false messiah and these are blaspheming.

Jesus cannot be "the Christ," i.e., the Messiah. He does not correspond to the person announced by the Scriptures.[4] He did not re-establish in a glorious way the Kingdom of God. He is opposed to the law as the leaders of the people teach it, and he would have provoked, if they had let him do it, the destruction of the nation by the Romans. He proclaimed himself the equal of God before the Sanhedrin, and they condemned him to death. Paul approves this execution with all his faith. It is the logical outgrowth of the blasphemous teaching and life of this man. The law condemns him. Moreover, does not God himself ratify this judgment, since he allowed him to die on the Cross? And "cursed is he who hangs upon a tree," states Deuteronomy (2:13).

And yet the leaders of the people allow this to go on. Even his master, Gamaliel (Acts 5:34-39). It is true, Judaism admits of a certain diversity of opinions, for example, the teachings, at times contradictory, of the Sadducees and the Essenes. But in this there is no longer a question of opinions: the very heart of the religion is under attack. "To preach Jesus as the apostles do is to put a man in place of God, is to profane the monotheistic holiness of the Jewish God so as to fall into the idolatry of the Gentiles"; it is the destruction of Judaism (L. Bouyer).[5]

Paul sets himself totally against the sect, without hatred, but with a deliberate and unchangeable decision. He took part in the killing of Stephen. Now he is almost to Damascus: soon he will lead back the Christians to Jerusalem in chains. If they are put to death, he will rejoice.

There, Christ is waiting.

5. **"I have been seized by Christ Jesus"** (Phil. 3:12)

"Certitude, Feeling, Joy, Peace."

Pascal, Nov. 23, 1654

The Risen Christ who appears to him is the one who hanged upon the Cross. The entire theology of St. Paul is based on this contrast.[6]

We have all experienced these sudden flashes, a hope that crushed, a friendship which gave meaning to our life and then suddenly we noted that it was of the wind. The appearance of Christ was, for Paul, something similar, but infinitely more dramatic. His entire life is totally turned back. Imagine a cloistered Carmelite who, at the moment of her death, would learn that the God for whom she had sacrificed every instant of her life did not exist! Paul, because of his faith and his love for God, struggled against Jesus, an impostor accursed of God. By appearing to him alive, Jesus reveals to Paul that God accredits him. Jesus is indeed what he claimed to be, what his disciples proclaim: the Messiah.

Then the Messiah has come! And it is a Messiah crucified, condemned by the law. . . . The entire meaning of his life has been crushed. Paul felt in a terribly painful fashion this upheaval of his entire being. At the actual moment in which we perceive a danger, a reflex saves us. After it is all over, then we begin to shake or tremble. On the road, Paul had the saving reflex: "Lord, what do you want me to do?" But afterward, for three days, he stays in Damascus, prostrate, blinded, unable to eat. He is attacked by Christ who overthrows everything that made his life. Three extraordinary days to make an inventory of everything that he had to get rid of. "Every conversion is an immense suffering." Paul feels poor, empty, vanquished. But into this great painful void, Jesus installs himself. Jesus, into whom his **faith** cast him on the road, Jesus to whom his **baptism** received from the hands of Ananias, a poor man but member of the Church of Jesus, has united him sacramentally.

Paul has found the center of his existence. "My life is Christ." The vision of Damascus has been, for him, bluntly, emptiness and fullness. In his life there is a **before** and **after.** And this will have profound influence on his thought. For the apostles, for John, for example, the discovery of Christ is made progressively. John, "the disciple whom Jesus loved," will discover in amazement that his friend Jesus, whom he followed as a prophet, then as the Prophet, the Messiah, that his friend is God! His theological reflection will consist especially of meditating on this marvelous friendship of two years. For Paul, zealous persecutor of Christ, who became his apostle in an instant, everything is arranged into "before" and "after." Everything on the plane of being as well as thought takes place in an instant. The synthesis of Christianity which he has given us and which had such a deep influence on Christianity, Paul received at this moment, not as a mass of new knowledge, but as a new light on all that he already knew. And this enlightenment is the Person of Jesus. With him he received everything at Damascus, but it will take his whole life and the events that make it up to become conscious of its full significance. For Paul, like each of us, will have to progress in his faith.[7]

Let us attempt in the light of all his teaching to learn at its source the heart of his theology.[8]

"My Good News, I received through the Revelation (Apocalypse) which is Jesus Christ" (Gal. 1:12). Only after the event do we understand. Only at our death will our life unveil its mystery. At the end of the world, only, will the meaning of history become clear for us. And, Paul tells us, in Damascus it is the Christ of the end of time who appeared to him: This was for him an "apocalypse" (OT, p. 173). Hence from this final point where Christ leads him, Paul discovers the plan of God as it is unfolded in the history of the world, and understands also how he, Paul, and every Christian, all of us, are inserted into it.

Paul is a Jew. His "conversion" leaves him fully a Jew. He remains "possessive" of his unique, only God. He knows that he is embarked on a holy history whose term and fulfillment will take place when the Messiah comes to establish the Kingdom of God definitively.

But nothing is taking place as the Pharisee, Paul, was expecting it: this Messiah has already come and hence we are at the term of history. This glorious Messiah has passed through death. And this completely upsets the notion which Paul had of salvation and the means to acquire it. God comes to plant in his heart the Cross of Christ. From now on, Jesus, dead and raised, will be at the center of his thought and life.

"Folly for the Jews, scandal for the Gentiles." Why a Messiah on a cross? It cannot be because of his sins. Was it not then "our sins he bore"? The mysterious figure of the Suffering Servant of Isaiah will clarify the figure of the Son of man (Dan. 7).[9] They were waiting for the Messiah under this form of the glorious Son of man, coming to fulfill history. It would be the symbol of the people; better, it would reunite really in his person all the members of the people had been condemned to death, since God had found no other destiny for his Messiah. Therefore the people and the entire world were corrupt, destined for death, not recoverable. Then rereading the first chapters of Genesis, Paul sees all the drama described in advance, but at the same time the announcement of salvation.[10] Because he spontaneously thinks in contrasts, an image will immediately come to the fore in the Letter to the Romans:

The Christ is the New Adam. The "second first man." Since Adam and in him all mankind was sinful, radically cut off from God, this world could be saved only by being put on the Cross, by passing through death and through creation. In Jesus Christ, God made this world of sin die. In him he has recreated it anew.

We shall come back to the role that the law played in this history. For the moment, it is enough to grasp this fundamental insight of Paul: **in Jesus, and in him alone, we are saved.** We are saved not by what we do, our works, the law; we are saved by letting ourselves act through Jesus by adhering to him, in life, in death, **through faith.** Faith is the total adherence of the entire being to Jesus. Faith, and baptism the sacrament faith, plunge us with Jesus into his death, in order to make us live again with him in the resurrection. They make us pass from this world enclosed in sin to the world of God in which Christ lives now in the light of the Father. From now on, Paul and each of us knows that by baptism, our being of sin is dead; a new being has come up out of the waters of baptism. I know myself first as a sinner favored, I receive myself from the hands of God as the most beautiful of gifts. For my principle of life is no longer mine! "It is no longer I who live, but Christ lives in me." And in all this, I am nothing. God does everything in me by uniting me to Jesus Christ. Everything is grace. There is nothing else that counts: "I am no longer trying for perfection by my own efforts, the perfection that comes from the Law, but I want only the perfection that comes through faith in Christ and is from God and based on faith" (Phil. 3:9).

Paul thus discovers the principle of **Christian morals.** The moral law is to conduct oneself according to one's nature. But my nature has been changed in baptism. Morals then is to live according to this new being received in Christ. There is no longer a question of performing "works" in order to be saved—our being saved is a gift—but since we are saved, it is a question of performing the works of faith, of living "in Christ."[11]

6. The telescoping of two worlds

"All this is magnificent: I am a new being, I live in Christ . . . but I know also that I am a sinner as much after my baptism as before." The paradox of Christianity, difficult to understand and yet a key to the entire New Testament and Christian life. Let us try to clarify it.

For the Jew, everything was simple: he was waiting for the Messiah, which would be the end of time. A final point of history: **Before:** a world on the road to God, but sinful; **After**: the Kingdom of God. The coming of the Messiah coincided with the end of this world and the beginning of the new world.

For the Christian: the Messiah has come and **therefore everything is done**. But the end of the earthly world is still to come and **therefore everything is still to be done.** Instead of a simple "before" and "after"; there is a "before Christ," and "after the definitive coming of Christ at the end of the world," and a "between-the-two" in which the two worlds "telescope" where everything is done in Jesus Christ but only in "Sacrament," i.e., the image in sign, but in a sign which causes what it represents, which bears in it and always engenders what it signified. The end of time is already realized[12] but the "final point" (**eschaton**) which the Jew was waiting for is extended or stretched through the length of history that remains to be lived.[13] The paradox of Christianity: fundamental optimism—Christ is the victor, evil is conquered; the ardent desire or longing for the Parousia, for the definitive coming of Jesus.

7. "Jesus, whom you persecute"

To his disciples, during his lifetime, Jesus had to explain this at length and on many occasions: allegory of the vine-stock (John 15), the judgment scene: "What you do to one of these little ones, you do to me" (Matt. 25). For Paul who persecuted the Christians, one word was enough: "Why do you **persecute me?**" The lesson took root. Paul, throughout his lifetime, will contemplate in his Christians the "Body of Christ" being built. The union into Jesus through faith and baptism is not to be an individual act. Grafted on him we form with him only one body, the personal body of Jesus thus growing, through the contribution of all generations, till the end of time, when it will finally have reached its perfect structure.

Is Paul Founder of Christianity? At one time it was the fashionable thing to oppose Peter and Paul. Paul, they claimed, falsified the true message of Christ by adding his own personal ideas, by transforming it according to "the mystery religions" of the Greek world. Paul a forger? A founder of a Sect? He certainly had all it takes for this: intelligence, education, personality, language of a tribune. Especially, did he not receive his gospel directly from Jesus? But this revelation reaches him at the moment when he is persecuting those who are already preaching Jesus, and he perceives in the "Why do you persecute me?" the identity of the Jesus who appeared to him with the one whom "those who were apostles before him" proclaim (Gal. 1:17). Rather than make him the leader of a school, his vocation makes him **enter a tradition**. He sets himself to preaching in Damascus only after he has been instructed by Ananias. At the end of a few years, he will come down to Jerusalem to meet Peter and James, the pillars of the Church "in order" to expose to them the gospel that he is preaching, lest he has run or is running" in vain," i.e., lest he have preached a message which did not correspond to that left by Jesus to his apostles. We know throughout his letters the care which he took "to hand on what he had received" and to watch over the unity of the Church.

But though he enters the Church as a "servant," he is also very conscious that he enters it with a special vocation.

8. Paul, apostle of the Gentiles

"It has pleased God to reveal his son in me that I

might announce him to the Gentiles . . ." he writes to the Galatians. We saw above how much difficulty the Church had to break away from Judaism and to turn toward the "world." Stephen and the Hellenists had played a determining role in this evolution. Paul, who will be their disciple, was specially predisposed by his whole human formation to grasp the universalist character of Christianity: if we are saved by Christ, gratuitously, without the works of the Jewish law, how could this salvation be preserved for Jews alone?

9. A saint who has his faults

Everything I have just written scares me a little: Never will my readers dare launch into the reading of the letters. "It is much too complicated for me . . . ." Paul certainly has obscure passages. When he preaches, he does not bother to give the "pabulum" of doctrine but he goes directly to the most difficult. The author of the second Letter of Peter says simply; "Read Paul: he is not easy to understand but he is good." And the Letter of James will take at times, apparently, the opposite viewpoint: "Beware, this is dangerous!" Looking beyond these difficulties, we find the reading of the letters enjoyable and inflaming, because we discover here a man of flesh and bone, who gives himself entirely. A man like you and me, who has his faults but is sincerely in love with Jesus Christ and who teaches us that our faults must not be so much removed as transformed from the inside to put them at the service of God and others. Paul is a complete character. In Judaism, this was an "all-or-nothing man" an "integrist." He is not always easy to live with when his mission is at stake. Peter learned this the hard way: "I opposed him to his face since he was manifestly in the wrong" (Gal. 2:11). Mark also, the unwilling cause of the break-up of the apostolic team Barnabas-Paul: "After a violent quarrel they parted company," says Luke simply (Acts 15:39). A leader who does not like to have others discuss his decisions, as the Corinthians soon learn. Someone who speaks all the time about himself, to discourage all our modern existentialists. At the same time, a weak, feeble person, dependent on others: he needs the affection of his followers. We could continue the list. . . . In the heart of this man Jesus is installed and thus he gives himself over to the love of God. His entire character is found in his love for Christ: this Christ he will implant in all the capitals in the midst of dangers, persecutions, hunger, prison, shipwreck, betrayal, and scourgings. Does he speak of himself? Pauline humility: he is not ashamed of his weakness for "he knows in whom he trusts." "When I am weak the strength of God can be revealed in me." "By the grace of God, I am what I am and his grace has not been barren in me. Rather, I have worked more than all of them; yet really, not I; but the grace of God in me." His affection could have been possessive. It made him "everything to everybody," giving his letters an impassioned accent: "who is weak and I am not weak . . . ." "My little children, for whom I suffer the pains of child birth . . . ." "I would like to give you even—my life." We resist the desire to make an anthology. Read Paul. You will become his friend. But note, his friendship is demanding. He risks planting in your heart "The knowledge of the love of Christ Jesus, his Lord."

"When love is carrying you, do not ask where it is going" (St. John of the Cross).

B. On the World Highway

Before you begin the actual reading of Paul, which is an occasion to visit a certain number of Paul's communities, get a sort of over-all view of his apostolic life.

It lasted thirty years.[14] In the thirtieth year, the sword of the executioner will complete this conformity to Jesus Christ which Paul was seeking to reach, at home and abroad, about three thousand miles on land and nine thousand miles on water. It is possible to divide his life into two parts.

A.D. 35-39: In search of his method of Apostolate: From his vocation to the "council"

35-36 (?): While on the road to Damascus to arrest the disciples of Jesus, Paul proclaims that this "Jesus is the Son of God!"

For three years, he **preaches** (where did we get this idea of a retreat) in Arabia, i.e., in the kingdom of the Nabateans and the area of Damascus. The Jews have soon had enough: they want to kill him. During the night he is let down over the wall in a basket. He goes to Jerusalem to meet Peter and James. He is there for fifteen days.

Then he returns to Tarsus and "preaches the Good News of the Faith" in the region. Six or seven obscure years follow of which we know nothing except that the churches of Judea praise God for his apostolic success (Gal 1:24).

43: The young community in Antioch is in full expansion. According to Luke, the apostles delegate Barnabas for this (Acts 11:19-26). He comes to realize that by himself he cannot do the work. As he sees it, the man for the job is Paul. He goes to look for him in Tarsus and for a year they form a team of leaders. "One day, while they were offering worship to the Lord and keeping a fast, the Holy Spirit said: 'I want Barnabas and Saul set aside for the work to which I have called them.' So it was that after fasting and prayer, they laid their hands on them and sent them off" (Acts 13:2-3). A decisive action from many points of view: in the course of this mission, the Spirit definitively launches the Church toward the conquest of the world. Paul acquires his opportunity to set his own pace and style—at the beginning, they speak of the team, Barnabas and Saul. On the return they speak of Paul and Barnabas—finally, Paul discovers here his method in the Apostolate. Until then, like all the apostles, he begins by preaching in the synagogues: through the mediation of the Jewish people, the bearer of the promises, the Gentiles are to count on reaching them. His lack of success, the clearsightedness of Barnabas, and the boldness of the Hellenists lead him to change his method and he adddresses himself directly to the Gentiles. His discourse at Antioch of Pisidia undoubtedly marks "the great turning point in his life and his method" (Cerfaux). From that time on, he will preach first to the Gentiles, and through their conversion he hopes to touch the Jews. Struck by jealousy and envy at seeing the Gentiles pass before them, will they not wish to be converted too? Read the account of this mission in Acts 13-14. At that time "the Spirit opened the door of the Faith to the Gentiles" to us, the non-Jews (Acts 14:27).

49: The return to Antioch is a source of the greatest joy to the Christians. There is one shadow in the picture: a famine is raging in the world, and the brothers in Jerusalem, whose communism, which was complete, is a wonderful example and always an appeal to us but was a fiasco from the economic point of view, are in need. They take up a collection. Paul and Barnabas bring the fruits of that collection to Jerusalem.[15]

End of 49: As they passed along, the two missionaries told everyone what God had done with them. They arrive at the Holy City and bring great joy to all the brothers. Then some "literalists," disciples of James whom they understood poorly and whose position they forced, arose and said: "A Gentile cannot become a Christian without becoming a Jew. First he must be circumcised." There is a long discussion. The question is very important and extremely basic: Is a person saved by Jesus Christ or by the law? Then follows a summit meeting, and the wonderful discourse of Peter. The debate is closed (Acts 15:3-12).

Paul returns to Antioch. Peter joins him there and in keeping with the decisions of the "council," looks upon the Gentile converts as completely Christian and eats with them. Some of the disciples of James arrive and they have not given up their previous position. Peter, who is noted more for his big heart than as a theologian, runs the risk of giving in. Paul stands firm and refutes him. This is called the "Antioch incident" (Gal. 2:11f.). The stake here is very important. The debate is brought back to Jerusalem where James, in the absence of Peter and Paul, makes a decision for his "diocese" of Syria-Palestine.[16] Paul sets out again on mission.

A.D. 50-67: "You know the knowledge of the Mystery of Christ that I have . . ."

Since the road to Damascus, fifteen years have rolled by: filled with meditation on the mystery of Christ, preaching, the founding of churches. Paul still has fifteen years to complete his mission. An important period for us, for the circumstances lead him to **write** to his communities, to put down in his letters the understanding which he acquires progressively of the mystery of Christ. We shall pass quickly for the moment over the details of his life: the study of his letters will lead us to take it up again. A simple bird's-eye-view (the dates and landmarks in the progress of his faith), which you will find again in the pages that follow.

50-52: "Second mission" of Paul: (Acts 15:36-18:22).[17] Accompanied by Silas his secretary, he visits the churches he has recently founded. In Lystra, he is joined by Timothy. Then a long, zigzag course through Asia Minor, a beautiful example of this collaboration between the Spirit and the apostles; Paul thinks out his mission and organizes it with all his human intelligence, and unceasingly the Spirit seems to put the spokes in the wheel until the apostle comes to think like the Spirit.[18] He opens up the Hellespont (Dardanelles); Christ arrives in Europe.[19] In the midst of persecutions and imprisonments, he founds the communities of Philippi, Thessalonica, Berea. In the course of his letters to the Thessalonians, we shall discover the enthusiasm of these young churches living in the expectation of the definitive coming of the Lord Jesus. Paul stops in Athens: an attempt at evangelization which seems to end in failure. Will the Greek thought refuse Christ? Alone, fatigued, discouraged, Paul arrives in Corinth. The slaves and the dock workers welcome him with open arms. As a working man in the house of Aquila and Priscilla, Paul stays there for two years. In this contact with the lowliest of people, he comes to an ever-more-living consciousness of the bankruptcy of human wisdom and the law: "during my stay with you, the only knowledge I claimed to have was about Jesus, and about him only as the crucified Christ" (1 Cor. 2:2). With them in their day-by-day living, he will "find" Christian morals.[20] From there he writes his two letters to the Thessalonians. Finally he sets sail for Ephesus, lands at Caesarea (and perhaps in Jerusalem), stops in Antioch long enough to get a change of linen and take off again.

53-58: "Third mission": This time he makes his long stay in Ephesus.

Because of the Acts, we can reconstruct one of his days.

He arose early, dedicated the morning to the making of tents for Aquila's account (who had followed him to Ephesus). Throughout his whole life he makes a special point of working with his hands to support himself. He does not wish to take any help from anyone so "the Word of God may be announced with complete freedom" (How could the Church have forgotten this first principle of Pauline Pastoral?). From 11:00 to 4:00, "the time given over by students to sports and leisure, he occupies the school of a certain Tyrannos": public conferences to a varied audience. At the end of the afternoon, there were numerous visits. Paul has a personal concern for each of his Christians (cf. 1 Thess. 22:11). "Finally, at night, there are Bible readings and the rites of the breaking of the bread with the community. There are the reflections and the correspondence!"[21]

Ephesus, capital of Asia Minor, a port open to Greece and the world, is the ideal place for General Headquarters. Paul is in contact with all his churches there, with Corinth especially, who causes him so much anxiety (he will make a lightning-visit there and then a stay of three months during the winter, 57-58. The "Great Epistles" date from this period: the letters to the Corinthians, Galatians, Romans, and Philippians.

He came back from Corinth through Macedonia and made port at Miletus. To the elders of Ephesus who came out to greet him, he made some touching goodbyes in a discourse which is his spiritual testament.[22] He arrives in Jerusalem. In the course of a riot stirred up by the Jews he is arrested.

58: Now begins the long captivity. After two years in prison in Caesarea, it brings him to Rome: "You appealed to Caesar, and you shall go before Caesar."

End of 60: Departure for Rome, the storm, shipwreck in Malta.

61-63: Two new years of captivity which end undoubtedly with a dismissal of the case. The accusers do not even present themselves.[23]

An important period for the thought of Paul. Matured in this enforced reflection, stimulated by the "heresies" of certain communities, he elaborates his most beautiful synthesis of the mystery of Christ: the **captivity letters:** Colossians, Ephesians, and the short note to Philemon. (Some place the Letter to the Philippians here.)

63-67: We have some trouble in following Paul. Only the allusions in the three Pastoral letters written at this time allow us to imagine him in Greece, Asia Minor, Rome, and perhaps Spain. These are the two letters to Timothy, and the one to Titus. They could also have been written after his death by a disciple from notes or letters he had written. It is a rich period in which he establishes solidly his churches by assuring his own succession. It is a painful period in which defections and betrayals begin. His end is near. The Lord completes his putting-off of his old self.

67: The executioner's sword unites him definitively to Jesus his Lord.[24]

II. The Yes in the heart of the believer, each day

Letters to: Thessalonians, Corinthians, Galatians, Romans and Philippians

"The New Testament Begins"

With this solemn title, "Beginning of the New Testament," Holzner shows us Paul in Corinth sending Timothy to buy ink and papyrus to write to his Christians in Thessalonica.[25] "Thus began the New Testament, whose first page was a letter dictated by the needs of the hour in the poor workshop of Aquila."[26] It is the year 51. Fifteen years later, the first Gospel, the Gospel according to Mark, will appear. By that time Paul will have ended his work, and completed his life.

When Paul takes up his pen, it is not to retrace tracts of theology. He is not a professor, but a shepherd who is writing letters of spiritual direction. All his letters are dictated by the circumstances and needs of one or another of his communities. This brings about a lessening of clarity. He does not say everything on the subject, because his Christians would not understand it, or he himself has not yet sufficiently worked out his own thinking. He repeats himself. They grow as they live: his thought, even the most abstract, will always start from facts. This does not mean that we will not find any theology here. In fact, his letters generally have two parts: a long doctrinal exposé followed by a "Parenesis": this means, an application and exhortation to bring this teaching into life. This is significant. We have transformed Christianity into a code of morality, and the God of Jesus Christ into a policeman-God, guardian of good order. For Paul, morality is definitely in second place: first he has to instruct, to revive the faith and clarify it. Morality will then be a conclusion: Live according to what you believe, according to what you are. This desire to educate the faith rather than to enact some rules or string up some barbed wire seems to me to appear in a way of thinking proper to Paul, which the specialists at times call "outline a-b-a" and which appears to me truer to call "a stencil for the reviewing or revision of life."

The stencil for the revision of the life of Paul: See—Judge—Act

The formula "a-b-a" diagrams this fact often enough in his letters: Paul breaks the development begun (a) to pass to a completely different subject (b); immediately everyone speaks of the incoherence of his thought: then suddenly he come back to his first development (a). Rather than incoherence, is this not the Christian way of reflecting on an event?

(a) **See:** Paul recalls the concrete fact that has come upon the community, upon which he wishes to reflect or some question that has been put to him.

(b) **Judge:** At first he seems to cut off completely from reality and present a point of doctrine which actually seems to be a digression.

(c) **Act:** Then he comes back to the concrete fact. Then we note that the doctrine, rather than being a digression, was a lamp turned very high, forcing us to understand the fact by not remaining on the ground level of the event but by lifting our eyes to Jesus Christ. Coming back to the fact, we note that he has now presented it in a completely new light.

Then, in a short sentence, Paul gives a precise directive: "Live according to this."[27]

We shall meet many examples of this. Let us take a simple example of it now: 1 Cor. 5.

(a) **See:** The fact: a Christian is living a morally bad life in Corinth; he is living with his mother-in-law as his wife. One fact of immodesty among a thousand others. Paul stops especially on the reaction of the Christians in the face of this fact.[28]

(b) **Judge:** The doctrine which apparently has nothing to do with this fact: "Christ, our Passover, has been sacrificed. You are bread without leaven" (at that time they used some of the old dough as leaven).

The concrete case in this light: through the celebration of the liturgy, the entire community has become a consecrated bread, the body of Christ. A sinner, from the old, mildewed dough, in this bread, can make it rise entirely in sin. And you do not react! You tolerate a conduct so out of harmony with what you have become.

(c) **Act:** "Expel this evil-doer from your midst."

When you recall again that Paul is a very intense man, then you must expect lightning flashes, accents of anger and tenderness; that he is a rabbi, then we shall grant him a few passages rather obscure for our morality. And now you are ready to read the letters. . . .

Letters to the Thessalonians

"Christian, who are you?"

Thessalonica, capital of Macedonia for two centuries, a place of passage where all races and all cults meet and mingle. Its port is the outlet for the province toward the Aegean Sea. The Via Ignatia, which crosses it, joins Rome to Byzantium. In a colorful account, Luke describes for us the arrival of Paul, accompanied by Silas and Timothy, his preaching, his success with the "well-to-do women" of the town, but also with the simple working people. The sly intrigues of the Jewish party soon force him to leave. Having left his companions in Berea and knowing the failure of Athens, he now preaches the Good News in Corinth. When Timothy rejoins him it is almost a year since they left Thessalonica. The news of his community is good and relieves Paul of his anxiety. "Now, we live again, since we know you stand firm in the Lord." However Paul, who has laid among them the bases for an authentically Christian life, does not have time to ground them solidly. Some questions had risen, especially on the subject of the afterlife, on the moment in which the Lord would appear for his second and final coming (Parousia). Some did not think it was imminent.

Paul decides to write to them.[29] These two letters are

overflowing with affection, which make known to us this young, fervent, and happy community. At the same time they tell us what Christian life is and introduce us to the heart of Paul, minister of the gospel.

A theology of Christian life

To be a Christian means to enter, willingly, "with all its human design," into the plan which God formed in his heart from all eternity. This plan, he brings into reality through Jesus Christ, so that we are sanctified in him, consecrated by the Spirit.

God has a plan of love

From all eternity, each of us is "chosen," is in the heart of God as a call. The choice of God in love is the beginning of our life. From the beginning we are sinners, this choice becomes a call to salvation.

God realizes the call through Jesus Christ

This plan of God's love reaches me at the moment in which his Word is proclaimed to me. This Word of God has a content. The "Kerygma" in its original form is: the Lord Jesus has been put to death by the Jews, for us. Therefore this death is a sacrifice which delivers us from death, for God has raised him. But even more, it **is** what it proclaims; it "works" in us, it is in us an active presence of Jesus Christ (1 Thess. 2:13; 2 Thess. 3:1).

When it reaches him, man is obliged to make a choice: the refusal—the sin of unbelief which places the rebellious sinner under the wrath of God (2 Thess. 1:8-9; 2:10-12); the acceptance of the Word—Faith. We detail this aspect.

(a) **Christian life is acceptance of the Word.** The moment in which the hearer of the preaching recognizes in it the Word of God and receives it as such is capital. It is the moment in which he hears the call of God, in which the faith is given, in which is realized the election of which he is the object in Christ (Masson), (1 Thess. 2:13; 2 Thess. 2:13). Faith is first of all "a conversion"; this movement of the entire being which turns us away from idols (whatever they are in our period of time) to attach us totally to God who gives us life (1 Thess. 1:9-10). Faith cannot be dissociated from hope and love. A total gift, it is perfect from the very start and yet it will have to be constantly readjusted in order to remain.

(b) **Christian life is a march forward.** It obliges us to progress constantly in order that our life be always in accord with this gift of ourselves which is faith (1 Thess. 4:1). Why does the Jerusalem Bible translate "to live" where Paul writes "to walk" or to "march"? This is the object of the prayer of Paul (1 Thess. 3:11-13).

(c) **Christian life is an expectation, a hope:**[30] An intense desire for the definitive coming of Christ. A certitude of sharing one day in the glorious "entry" (in Greek: Parousia) of Jesus coming on earth to judge the world and to establish his reign (1 Thess. 4:13-18).[31] We Christians too often give the impression of being a flock without joy, pushed from behind by the Shepherd already come, while we are really people on the march tending, or stretched out, toward Christ who is coming! The motivating force of Christian morality is our hope, which presupposes vigilance (you are sons of the days) and constancy, **hypomone**; this word, untranslatable and specifically Christian, which describes the attitude of him who "stands steady beneath the blow" because he has put everything in the hands of God.

(d) Finally, this Christian life brings with it a passage: death which has lost its tragic character because it is lived with Jesus. The dead: "those who sleep through Jesus" (1 Thess. 4:14).

And then "we shall be forever with the Lord." With

Christ, "in Christ," means, first of all, according to the Jewish expectation, the sharing in his Glory, but also, indissolubly, the intimacy with him. The more the thought of Paul is confirmed and strengthened, the more he will insist on the second idea without ever forgetting the first: from now on we are with the Lord.

God carries out his plan by consecrating us in the Holy Spirit

Paul speaks little enough of the Spirit in these two letters, but he has already said the essential. "God chose you for salvation in the sanctifying Spirit and by faith in the truth" (2 Thess. 2:13). Spirit, faith of man, two agents united by the same proposition. This gift to God which is my faith, the most personal and the most active movement that it is possible for me to accomplish, is also supreme passivity: the Spirit, in me, earnestly begs me to adhere to the Word of God and brings me to do it.[32] The Spirit dwells in our heart, foundation of our joy, of our purity, of our holiness.

Life in Church

The individual call of each of us is a community call. The **klesis** (the call) has as its purpose to form the "ek-klesia," the Church, the community of the called. "Within the Church, by means of belonging to the Church, the person of the Christian is reached by grace and salvation and laws in the midst of his brothers and in relation with them."[33] This ecclesial life is of itself missionary (Is this true in our parish community? Our team?). It must stir up a holy envy in those outside to become Christians (1 Thess. 4:12). Then will be realized that for which it is done: "to give glory to God and to Jesus Christ."

A priest. Why?

"The Word of God heard through our mediation . . . ."

Through these letters, Paul gives us, without thinking about it but because he lived it, a first outline of what the apostolic ministry is for him. The Word of God and its efficacy are at the heart of these letters. Thus he envisages here the ministry of the preacher of the Word.

He lets us glimpse his role through the numerous verbs that he uses to describe it. He "cries out like a herald" the Good News of salvation in Jesus Christ. He "exhorts" his hearers to accept him; he knows that he is elbow to elbow with them, on march with them, he "encourages" them (literally "speaks aside"); he "adjures" them.

He sums up his attitude in two words, his **overflowing "assurance"**: this security "of men brought by a power superior to them, filled with the uplifting sense of being workers with a work that surpasses them" (Masson)[34]; his fidelity (cf. 1 Thess. 2:1-12). He presents himself as a model. He does it in a spirit of adoration and thanksgiving for the God who tests him, gives him confidence, and works in him. (To marvel at seeing God work through us for the upbuilding of his Church, is not pride but adoration of God at work in us and in spite of us: "For the Almighty has done great things for me, Luke 1:49). He gives two signs of his fidelity: the authenticity of his preaching and his unselfishness. What does he want to accomplish? To win men for God, not for himself. He works with his hands so that the Word of God may be proclaimed without obligation to anyone.

First Letter to the Corinthians

The "finding" of Christian Morality

In ancient times they talked of living "à la Corinthienne." Corinth was an enormous city (600,000 men, of whom 400,000 were slaves), a port of international trade, famous for its universities, its games, its temple of Aphroditus with the thousand prostitutes (**hierodules**). Paul arrived there one evening in the year 50, tired, discouraged by his failure in Athens. He had left the wise men in the Agora and signed as a tentmaker in the house of Aquila. Lost in this immense city, he will yet find here his most beautiful experience. To the heart of this crowd of sub-proletariats, with its corruption, he will preach Jesus Christ crucified! In his eighteen-month stay, he succeeds in this impossible work of implanting definitively the Cross in the very heart of this pagan city. In this sort of low sport, a young Christian community, jolted by the heady wine of the Spirit, comes to the strong experience of the presence of the living Christ (Brunot). With these "terrible children" they do not pass smoothly from one day to the next, from the closed house to the Church—Paul will "devise" Christian morality: concretely, what does it mean to be faithful to the demands of his baptism when the person is a stevedore or a dockhand, a merchant or a sailor, slave or free, married or celibate? This is the manner in which these letters to the Corinthians become so intense and filled with feeling and so near to us. At the time of his writing, Paul has been gone from the Corinthians about five or six years. After a two-year stay in their midst, he departed and stayed for a short time in Ephesus. From there, because of the frequent communications between them, he can follow the life of his community. There is need for it! He writes them at least four letters.[35] We have two. The first is a reviewing of life starting from concrete facts. Four chapters: the Corinthians have profited from the "family of Chloe" passing through to pose some questions of the deepest spirituality. But Paul has learned from other sources that all is not well in the meetings of the community, that some Christians have difficulty in believing in the resurrection from the dead. And above all, the family of Chloe did not know how to hold their tongues:

Paul learns through them a series of facts which the Corinthians had kept well hidden when they wrote their letter. Here Paul begins.[36]

The family of Chloe did not know how to hold their tongues!

First Fact: Quarrels rising from the narrow-minded provincialism in Corinth. They pick for themselves leaders. (1:10-4:13)

(a) **See:** "I am for Paul, I am for Apollo, and I am for Pastor So-and-so."

(b) **Judge:** The Corinthians have not reflected on the full implications of this simple fact. Paul leads them to realize that they have such disputes because:

- they have not understood the true role of their shepherds, and more profoundly
- they have not understood what it is to be a Christian.

1. What does it mean to be a Christian: **Christian "wisdom."** A Christian does not attain his salvation by physical force, through intelligence, by his own qualities or "merits," which Paul calls "human wisdom" (the wisdom of the Gentiles—the Greeks; and of some believers—Jews), but by accepting the salvation that comes to us in the Cross of Christ: **Christian "wisdom."** It is not the rich man sure of his strength, but the little one confident in his Father.

Human wisdom: Paul does not condemn philosophy or humanism, but a philosophy which would claim to be self-sufficient, to find its God completely alone. This would be a "religion" perhaps, but not Christianity (cf. p. 60). He also condemns the religion of some believers, the "Jews." They have succeeded in this amazing feat of transforming their meeting with the true God into an automatic means of being saved: they do everything they must do (they go to Mass and confession), they accumulate merits by their good works and their mortifications, they have earned their salvation. They save themselves by their own merits, by their own "justice," as Paul says it. . . . Eternal temptation! This human wisdom cannot lead us to the true God.

Divine wisdom does not reach God by physical force, but by accepting one fact in faith: Jesus Christ on the Cross! This is folly for the Gentiles (to pray before someone who was hanged), a stumbling block for the Jews (they are waiting for a glorious Messiah). But for the one who accepts him in faith, the Christian, he is the power and wisdom of God. A power at work in you, Corinthians, who were not such outstanding people: "immodest, drunkards, thieves, adulterers. . . . This is what you were, at least some of you"; a power at work for me in my weakness; Paul: beaten, imprisoned, blocked out at Athens. . . . But how is this wisdom possible? Through the Spirit, who is the heart of the Trinity and who becomes your heart. To receive him, we must have the humility to welcome God. What is the proof that you have received him? Love. . . . And if you love, you are not divided. Are you Christian?

2. **The true role of preachers:** They are not masters who give themselves. There is only one Master: Jesus. They are only servants, servants of this Temple in which God dwells, i.e., the Christian community.

(c) **Act:** (4:1-8). Do not judge your preacher: God does this.

Thus is ended this reviewing of life. But because this small fact has revealed the mentality of the Corinthians, Paul leads them in putting their entire life in question. He does this with an irony that is proper to him by setting up a sharp contrast between the apostles, the true "wise" men, who have the folly of the Cross and bring it into their lives and the Corinthians, enriched, sated with their poor wisdom (4:9-21).

Second Fact: An unscrupulous Christian (ch. 5, cf. above p. 82.

Third Fact: Some Christians who are bringing each other to court (6:1-11).

(a) **See:** Some Christians, to regulate their differences, hail one another into the Gentile, pagan courts.

(b) **Judge:** Always the same manner of acting, according to Paul. He does not say that it is good or bad. He brings them back to what they have become by their baptism (6:11). If you have been washed, made holy, justified by Jesus and by the Spirit, live accordingly.

(c) **Act:** It is better to undergo an injustice than to attack one's brother.

Fourth Fact: Some Christians are so holy, that they are beyond morality (6:12-20).

(a) **See:** Paul has frequently insisted on the freedom of the Christians. Some of the enlightened have concluded: therefore everything is allowed! Provided they love God, they can do anything they please: drink wine or water, lie with their own wives or the wives of their neighbors, take advantage of their neighbor, or exploit their workers (the entire relation between faith and daily life is at stake here).

(b) **Judge:** We are the body of Christ, the temple of the Holy Spirit. Therefore all our bodily conduct has an extreme importance.

(c) **Act:** Glorify God in your body.

Here are the answers to some questions which are posed by the Corinthians. Their questions should have been more elevated or refined. Paul takes them up now.

Two questions asked by the Corinthians

1. Must we not **all** keep virginity, for is not marriage bad? (ch. 7).

(a) **See:** In a pagan world which gives free rein to their passions, the Corinthians who love Christ ask themselves if they must not all live as he: live a celibate life. Paul refuses to answer this question simply by looking at virginity, he wants to relate it to marriage.[37] Hence he takes up the ensemble of the question: virginity remains the ideal (he agrees with these Christians) but marriage is the law for all. He profits from this to recall a few principles: the equality of man and wife; this is a revolution in a world (but has it changed so much?) in which woman is considered inferior (judge his realism in his practical advice). "Celibates, you have the choice. Married men, you no longer have the choice: marriage is indissoluble. Husbands or wives bound to an unbelieving partner: your marriage is a means of apostolate." With the question better placed, Paul takes it from the height.

(b) **Judge:** Conversion is an interior transformation, and not an external upheaval through force. The call of the Lord has completely changed the meaning of our life, whatever may be this concrete life. To be a Christian does not mean that we depart from this world and every difficult situation, but rather, we stay in the world and keep the commandments.[38]

(c) **Act:** Paul personally thinks (this is not, as above, the command of the Lord that for those who are called to is; it is better to remain celibate, for this is an anticipation of the definitive world; cf. OT, p. 223), it is an exclusive love of Christ, a love which takes the entire being.[39]

2. Is the Christian condemned to the ghetto? The problem of meat that is offered to the idols (in Greek: Idolothytoi), (chs. 8-10).

(a) **See:** The Gentiles offered sacrifices to their gods. These meats immolated in sacrifice were eaten by those who offered them. The rest was sold. Hence every Christian was exposed to buying these meats on the market, or of seeing himself offered these in the homes of friends. Is it necessary then, in order not to form a pact with the false gods, to refuse from now on to eat meat, and to accept no more invitations to dine with others? Under this small problem of food the entire attitude of the Christian in the world is at stake: Must the Christian, to remain Christian, leave the world where he is living, this world in which money is tainted, life situations are ambiguous, business rarely completely honest?

(b) **Judge:** The light that clarifies everything: Charity, or love, is the only thing that counts. Love "builds" the kingdom of God.[40] Judge everything according to this. This principle is difficult to handle. Concretely: there are three qualities: **Freedom of the Christian:** because he loves, the Christian is the most free of men; idols do not exist. **Fraternal charity:** some Christians, weaker than ourselves, can be scandalized when they see us eating these meats. It is better to deprive ourselve of the exercise of this freedom than to scandalize a brother.[41] **Prudence:** No presumption! You think yourself a perfect Christian so led by love that you can permit yourself everything. Pay close attention! You are weak and you would do well to take a few precautions. Look at the example of Paul. Even though he is Paul he is not sure of himself. As long as we have not actually arrived we must still struggle. The example of the Hebrews: they were the People of God. All passed through the Red Sea and saw the marvels of God . . . and they have sinned and died.

(c) **Act:** There is one spiritual attitude to keep in every situation: you live in the world as people who communicate in the body which is Christ. Each Christian is then the body of the Christ living in the world. Thus Paul can give some practical solutions for the case of food offered to idols (they are easy to transfer into our lives). "Whatever you do, do all for the glory of God." We are free but we are members of the body of Christ which is the Church.

The Corinthians did not ask any more. But Paul has learned different small points about which he wishes to say a few words.

Good order in the meeting of the community

1. Must women have their heads covered in the Church? (11:2-16).

A small and commonplace problem which certainly has no importance. But there is nothing without importance, for a very small fact is revelatory of an attitude or mentality. And Paul discovers under this attitude a disturbing mentality. We admit that we no longer know what this was because we do not know enough of the custom of the time (in any case, the customs have changed and Paul would no longer be bothered today about the hat). We keep only the light with which he enlightens this fact. He states two things at the same time: Woman is subject to the man; woman is the equal of man (11:11-12). To understand this paradox, we must certainly refer to what marriage represents in the Bible (cf. OT, pp. 218ff.). The man and woman who love one another in marriage are the image of God and man who love one another. When the couple is thus seen as symbol, as "sacrament," man represents God (he who has the initiative, who manages the game), the woman symbolizes the creature—man and woman—who responds to this love with all its activity. On the human plane, it is quite evident that man and woman are equal. On the plane of the image," the "sacrament," man represents God and therefore if the woman wanted to be equal to man, she would be the symbol of the creature wishing to be equal to God.

2. The Lord's Supper (11:17-33).

An extremely important text, the first writing we have about the Last Supper.[42] Paul recalls here what he had already taught in the year 51-52, and which he himself had received. Hence, with this text we are very near to the event itself. And what he received is identical with what we believe now: in this meal, we represent the death and resurrection of the Christ, we render them present again; it is not only a recalling, but a real presence, and we communicate in it, in order to be involved in it "until he comes," and to live by it.

(a) **See:** In the community, some Christians lack nothing while others suffer from hunger.

(b) **Judge:** The point of reference: all, rich and poor, eat the same consecrated bread which is the Body of the Lord. If then you do not love one another concretely, it is the sign that your Mass is not true. (How demanding it is to communicate at the same table with one's patron, or employee, one's professor, or one's fellow student.)

3. Is the Holy Spirit responsible for the disorder in our communities?

(a) **See:** The ancients easily entered into a trance or ecstasy during their cult (consider these phenomena in some religious and especially the emotion-centered spirituals). When this happened in the Christian communities, should it be seen as an action of the Holy Spirit or a phenomenon of collective hysteria? We who no longer really believe in the Holy Spirit would quickly have cut it off, but Paul believes too much in the power of the Spirit to decide a priori that it is or is not the Spirit acting.

(b) **Judge:** Basic Principle: Every believer is under the action of the Spirit. If we believe, if we can say, "Jesus is Lord," it is the Spirit who gives us the power to do so. How are we to discern the true "charisms," the special spiritual gifts which the Spirit gives to Christians?[43] If their origin is in the Spirit, they can only "construct," "build up" the Church. Before passing them in review, Paul recalls to our minds that love comes before all the extraordinary charisms. Note the beautiful "hymn to love" in chapter 13. Paul attempts therefore to put a little order into the different charisms of his time: the criterion for classification: How far does this charism serve to "build up" the Church?

(c) **Act:** Practical rules for the "discernment of spirits" (as the specialists say): Everything is to take place in such a way as to "edify" (build up) the others; everything is to be in accord with the teaching. Advice for all the reformers of all ages, beginning with our own: whether there is extreme left or extreme right, there is always the teaching of the Church.[44]

"They will rise from the dead . . .? This is not possible" (Ch. 15)

This question must inevitably be asked one day in this Greek milieu for which the ideal of life is to depart from it to join again the "world of ideas." How Greek we have become! Paul answers from two points of view:

1. **We shall rise.** The proof? Christ is raised. If the resurrection is impossible, Christ has not been raised (yet we know that he is raised).[45] Hence we also shall be raised.

What difference does it make whether he is raised or not? In a few verses (15:20-28), Paul makes a luminous summary of the meaning of history. The world was corrupted by sin. Christ came, took this world into himself, he died and the entire old world with him. But he is raised. And with him a new world is born. This world is in process of being made by us the Christians in whom Christ works. When this work is completed, Christ will take up this entire world remade to offer it to the Father. Our whole present-day work of struggling against sin in us and in the world (injustice, hatred) is the work of the construction of a new world which is the body of Christ glorified, his "mystical body."

2. **The manner in which we shall rise.** Paul explains it according to the mode of thinking in vogue in his time, but this is gone. However, the teaching remains: this resurrection will be the total taking possession of our being by the Holy Spirit. In the image of Christ we shall be "spiritual"; the Spirit will be our principle of life.[46] And this starts as of now insofar as we allow ourselves to be led by the Spirit: already we are being raised.

Thus Paul can end his letter with a victory chant on life. "Death, where is your sting? Thanks be to God who gives us victory through our Lord Jesus Christ."

Conclusion

Particular points of advice and then "the polite formula" for closing a letter which for Paul is much more than mere words: "The grace of the Lord Jesus be with you all. I love you in the Christ, Jesus."

Second Letter to the Corinthians

The Diary of the Pastor of Corinth

Paul has undergone with his "enfants terribles" one of the longest struggles that he has had to undergo with any of his communities. For almost a year they have been a source of suffering to him (cf. note 35 on page 160). Now it is ended. Corinth has found peace and Paul writes to them. Reproaches? When a person suffers through someone else and they have found themselves again, they do not reproach each other; they speak of what they have suffered, it is true, that they are happy now, and that finally this suffering has been productive. The principal theme of this letter is composite.[47] It is the **communion of saints** and more precisely, since it is Paul speaking in a very personal manner, the communion of the pastor with his parishioners, this kind of mysterious osmosis which makes the suffering of one become the source of the peace of another.

Let us run through the letter before stopping at more length on the central passage:

Thanksgiving: for this suffering which has come from his Christians (1:3-11).

It is exactly the same suffering as Christ, which has flowed over to him. And now God has consoled him in order that this consolation may flow over to the Corinthians.

The apostolic ministry (1:11-7:16): A reviewing of life starting with past events.

(a) **See:** The fact: the difficulties he has had with them (1:12-2:13). If the apostolate is a service of the truth, Paul is conscious of having been authentic in the image of Christ, who is only Yes.[48]

(b) **Judge:** The light in which to judge this fact; consider the true meaning of the apostolic ministry (2:14-6:10). We shall come back to this immediately. Return to the concrete fact: "I, Paul, am conscious or having been a true apostle with you, so open up your heart to us. And this is indeed what you have done, you have found this attitude of the Christian before his apostle again." The joy of Paul, Titus, and the Corinthians.[49]

The collection (chs. 8-9): Two sermons on charity, parallel and yet independent.[50] Paul asks for help in his churches for the Church of Jerusalem. This is exceptionally important for Paul. It is not a charity, but a "liturgy," a religious service. It is the sign of the communion among the new churches that have come from paganism and the mother Church of Jerusalem. The mother church has given supernatural life and they have helped her with their material goods.

The "great apologia" (chs. 10-13): "When the curtain rises on chapter 10, we note immediately a complete change of scenery. Titus and the Macedonians have disappeared, as well as the plates intended for the collection. The apostle himself, alone before his parish, plays a quite different role: it is no longer a father reconciled with his children (as in ch. 7), but an irritated leader who defends himself by attacking his opponents" (Héring).[51] Behind this intense and impassioned apologia we must try to discover the heart of Paul and his religious experience. He is not an ambitious man: he is pursuing only the love of Christ and the holiness of his Christians, for he looks upon himself as the best man, i.e., the friend of the bridegroom, and wishes to present the Bride to Christ as the pure virgin. He is unselfish: "I have received nothing from you and I want nothing!" Do they prefer other self-styled apostles? "I shall speak foolishly: I surpass them all by my weakness, my work, and my missionary trials, by my strength which comes to me from God, and by this grace which God has given me by introducing me a bit into his unspeakable intimacy."[52]

With this rapid survey finished, let us come back to the central passage of the letter.

The apostolic ministry

This is the light by which Paul wished to enlighten his Corinthians. But Paul is so identified with his mission that for him to speak of the apostle in general becomes always an exposition of his own heart.

A heavy responsibility (2:14-3:4)

He recalls his apostolate in Macedonia, in Greece—and in the eyes of a human observer, this was not brilliant. He leaves Ephesus stealthily, runs aground in Athens, arrives trembling in Corinth, and does not dare to return there for fear that they will take their anger out on him. But suddenly, in his eyes as prophet, these events take on the appearance of what they are in reality: a triumphal procession of the victorious Christ through all these countries which he has conquered. The apostle is a part of this procession. His role: as a perfume reveals an invisible presence, he must spread around him the perfume of the knowledge of Christ. This perfume is the paschal sacrifice of Christ, pleasing to God. The apostle is so identified with this mystery that he becomes this good odor. Paul is conscious of his responsibility: to walk in the world while being and spreading this good odor, and thus to force those who breathe it to take sides for or against Christ. Men are "saving themselves or losing themselves" according as they accept or do not allow themselves to be united to this sacrifice. To be united to Christ, especially as is the apostle charged with preaching him, is heavy with consequences for those with whom they live!

Paul feels even to the point of anguish this task of being "the instrument of such a discrimination" (Allo), but he is conscious of having been well prepared for this. He does not need, as do others, letters of recommendation; the letter which recommends him before the entire world is his community. The image which at first was only a figure of style gives progression to the thought of Paul. Jeremiah and Ezekiel had already used this symbol: the law, the new covenant will one day be inscribed on hearts. Christ is this New Law which the Spirit, through him, Paul, has engraved on the hearts of the faithful. Paul then sets about describing this apostolate.

Grandeur of the Apostle (3:5-4:6)

His consciousness of fulfilling the role announced by Jeremiah and Ezekiel stirs him to describe this marvel by contrasting it to the ministry of the Old Covenant. The Christian apostle, servant qualified by God, no longer hands on the law, the letter of the law, as knowledge inscribed on tablets of stone, but as a living law inlaid in hearts by the Holy Spirit. His ministry surpasses that of Moses as far as the spirit surpasses the letter of the law.

This antithesis between the ministry of the "letter" and the "spirit" is the first outline of the long developments of Galatians and Romans. The law: an external code which imposes commandments without giving the strength to fulfill them and therefore necessarily leads to sin and death. The new law: an interior dynamism, the Spirit who in our hearts tells us what he must do and what he leads us to do. What a difference between the glory which Moses could draw from his ministry and the glory of the Christian ministry!

Overcome by enthusiasm, Paul finds himself again a disciple of Gamaliel, and to establish a contrast between the situation of the Jew and the Christian, gives us an example, disconcerting and magnificent, of rabbinical commentary. Moses, the Bible tells us, wore a veil on his face so that the glory of God which he radiated would not kill his interlocutors. Paul makes of this a veil which kept Moses and the Jews from understanding the Scriptures! "Each time they turn toward the Lord, the veil is lifted." The Spirit of Christ alone can give understanding. He is drawing on Exod. 34:34, a magnificent image of the conversion of a believing Jew to the Christian faith. A Jew does not have to be "converted," but to be turned toward the Lord Jesus; the Spirit removes his veil and he can then read the Scriptures and see the Christ proclaimed. The Christian reads them with "face unveiled"; there he discovers the Christ upon whom rests the glory of the Father, and, in this contemplation, this glory invades him and transforms him into the image of God (cf. note on Rom. 8:29). In his turn he reflects this glory, radiates it upon his brothers. This glory of Christ has shone in the heart of Paul on the Damascus road, in our hearts on the day of our baptism; the creation of light on the first day, the only image that suggests a little light.

But, a truly Pauline contrast, this glory we carry in vessels of clay (our body) in order that we may see that it does not come from us.

Weakness of the apostle

For the Christian and more even for the apostle who is as a child in the life, it is Good Friday and Easter all the time (4:7-5:10).

Christian life is nothing other than living one's baptism daily: death and resurrection with Christ. The paradox of Christ: he was the most effective when he was the most powerless on the Cross! God can act in us and through us only beyond our powerlessness accepted and offered. And then there is a community of life between the apostle and those for whom he is responsible, even if externally his apostolate seems ineffective (4:7-12). Faith brings us to contemplate the Risen One in the "one hanged upon the

Cross." Faith brings us to see even from within our suffering and death life at work.[53]

Christian death is the moment in which our baptism is completed, in which it becomes true. We abandon this "carnal dwelling," our earthly body with its debt of sin, to put on, to become the body of Christ Risen, our "heavenly dwelling." Our baptism has already united us to him. Blessed be our death which, definitively; established us "with Christ" (5:1-10).[54]

The Apostle, Ambassador for Christ, charged with the ministry of reconciliation (5:11-6:10)

Only one thing weighs upon the heart of Paul: the love which Christ has for him. Unity of doctrine and life: the whole Paul is there. This desire to be united to the Lord is not an escape from the world, but the desire, today, to do his will in the world.

God has remade us anew, has reconciled us with him, "we are a new creation," and he entrusts the concrete realization for each man to the apostles. To justify us, God has destroyed sin in his Son whom he "made sin for us," Jesus, who identifies himself in some way with all our sin in order that life may leap forth from his death. It is sufficient to turn yourself toward him in order that he become the Spirit in us, the dynamism of life.[55] And "where the Spirit of the Lord is, there is freedom" (3:17).

The freedom of the Christians: this will be the theme of the letter which Paul will write to another community during this same period.

Letter to the Galatians

The Christian: A free man under the dynamism of the Spirit. Free to love

"I hate you because you are not free."
A. Camus, **Caligula**

Communication media have popularized, if there was a need, the figure of the old-fashioned big-spender. But he has "penetrating and living intelligence" (Themistius), "endowed with a great mobility of spirit, eager for all new opinions, making rapid decision of which he must quickly repent" (Caesar) who "since he was a child has had an untamable character, the need to feel important, the taste for quarrels, the absence of judgment, continuous prattling, inconstancy of desires, and powerlessness in discipline"[56]; but who above all other things has an immense love for freedom. Such were the grown children, German cousins of "our ancestors the Gauls," to whom Paul writes.[57]

Before Paul came among them during his second mission, 50-51, these pagans served idols, the Greek gods whom they had adopted, but also the stars and the cosmic powers. Paul freed them from this slavery "by depicting before their eyes the traits of Jesus Christ on the Cross." Toward 53-54, he comes to them again "to strengthen them in the faith" (Acts 18:23). And two or three years later, from Ephesus or Macedonia, he learns "they have allowed themselves to be hindered in their obeying the truth." "Are you Galatians mad? Has somebody cast a spell on you?"

Who? Former Jewish converts and pseudo-disciples of James whom we have already met have persuaded them that to be saved they (the former pagans), must keep the Jewish law and be circumcised, this carnal rite which marks the entrance into the Jewish people.

Paul is completely overcome. These children in the faith have not seen the great evil in this: some further practices, this can only do good. The apostle sees full well the seriousness of this matter. (Has he not already fought hard for this in Jerusalem?) By this conduct they give the impression that their baptism is not sufficient for them to be saved, since they still wish, after being baptized, to be circumcised. It is not enough for them to accept gratuitously the salvation of Jesus Christ in the faith. They wish "to do something else," to obey the Jewish law. For the theologian Paul, the very foundation of Christianity is at stake: it is no longer Jesus Christ alone who saves us by means of our faith, it is we who save ourselves by our works, our "merits," by what we are doing, through obedience to the law. And this has a fearful consequence: to be saved, we must become again a slave of the law, even though Christ has made us free. We can understand why Paul acted in a very blunt manner.

His letter is polemical, difficult because it is written under stress of emotion, but very intense because he puts himself entirely into it. "The most Pauline of the letters of Paul" (Augrain). In a few months, when his calm has returned and his emotions are in check, when he has had time to mature his arguments which he is using here, he will write the Romans a course in theology on the very point. This will be clearer, more developed, but there will no longer be the same life. Here he is concerned with snatching these fools, the Galatians, from their mistake, and Paul puts himself right into the middle of the fight.

He does this with all his resources:

With his theology: We find here a certain number of very deep doctrinal exposés (too many for our taste).

With his knowledge of the Scripture which he reads as a rabbi: He wishes to prove, according to the procedure of the explanations usual at the time, but disconcerting for us, that to be faithful to the law, we must abandon the law. God gave it for a time, this time is passed. If we come back to it, we are faithful to the law and to Scripture, as the adult who wanted, because of infantilism and to please himself, to return to the discipline of the tutor.

With all his heart: And this is undoubtedly the most solid point of his argumentation. Intense appeals to the experience of the Galatians: "recall what Christ has brought you to become through your baptism."

Do not these intense appeals of Paul still reach right into the midst of our twentieth century? "Are you Christian? Are you really what you have become through your baptism?" Certainly we do not have the desire to become Jews (the law and circumcision), but we are always tempted to pass from faith to the law, to think, at least practically in our everyday life, that we are saved because of what we do (what Paul called the "law"), and not only by what Jesus Christ has done and always does in us, by means of our faith.

Let us attempt a rapid reading of this letter.

An opening that is fully alive. The only letter of Paul (with 2 Cor.) which does not have a thanksgiving. He does not have time. He cries out his indignation: "You are going over to a new gospel!" There is only one: the gospel of Jesus Christ."[58] "This Gospel which he preaches, Paul will defend on three scores."

First Point: Whence comes the gospel of Paul? (1:11-2:21)

It comes from God alone and not from men. He himself was a Pharisee intensely loyal to the law, and he was turned back by Christ on the Damascus road: he knew then that there is no salvation except in Jesus Christ. This is what he has preached from that time forward, and this was directly revealed to him by God (1:11-24).

He was acknowledged by the "pillars" of the Church, the apostles. He is a soldier, as a preacher he was chosen directly by God, he is not a sniper. His vocation was entrance into a Church which already had its traditions (2:1-10).

He defended it even against Peter who, unconsciously, seemed to stand against it, at the time of the "Antioch dispute." Paul gives us here a summary of a short sermon which he addressed at the time to the head of the Church, but which he now addresses to all Christians looking beyond the head of Peter. An extremely forceful summary (too forceful!) of his "gospel" (2:11-21). It serves as a very skillful transition.

Second Point: What does the gospel of Paul contain? (chs. 3-4)

Paul develops his thought in a doctrinal exposé (3:6-4:10) centered between two "appeals to the heart" of the Galatians (3:1-5; 4:12-20). He ends with a parable drawn from the story of Abraham where he sums up, in an image, all that he wished to say.

Appeal to the heart of the Galatians (3:1-5): They have received the Holy Spirit through faith and not through the practice of the law. They have received him not because they had kept the law (they were pagans) but because they welcomed Christ through faith. And the proof that they have received him: the activity of the Spirit who manifests himself even in them through "charisms" (cf. 1 Cor. 12).

Doctrinal exposé (3:6-4:11): Let us try first to discern the thought underlying this entire ensemble by taking one image. A man plans to adopt a son. He brings him into his home and promises to make him his son. He gives him his love (everything begins with this gift) and the child responds with confidence, faith, love. The relation between them is not defined in terms of a contract. There is no contract, but only a promise on the part of the father, a response of love on the part of the child. Now, this child begins to refuse this love and wishes to abandon his benefactor. The father, because he truly loves the child, will keep him near himself with an iron hand until he is capable of responding again in love. Of course, during this time, the nature of the relations will have changed between them. This will no longer be the rapport free and confident in love, but the commandment (a "law") on the part of the father and an obedience on the part of the child.

This is almost the exact picture of the history of mankind as Paul reads it in the Bible. In the beginning God is "completely alone." He has only this marvelous plan of making mankind his "son." This can be realized when his own Son, Jesus, comes to gather all men in himself in order that with him and in him they may become the Son of God. God thinks before all on this moment. But he must begin by educating mankind.

He chooses Abraham, and while giving him his love, "promises" him that he will one day be his People, and that he will be happy with him in the Promised Land. God gives himself in love to Abraham and Abraham responds through faith, total confidence. Between them, there is no law, or contract, only a promise, an exchange of love.

But the people that come from Abraham refuse this life. They sin. Then God changes his manner of acting. Through the mediator Moses, he imposes a law, the law of Sinai, which obliges them to remain in relation with God. But these are no longer the free relations of the time of Abraham. This law imposes many obligations but it does not change the heart of man. It only keeps them in relation with God. But by imposing commandments without giving the strength to fulfill them, it multiplies the occasion for sinning. Thus this law succeeds only in multiplying the failures. And since men are obliged by this contract to obey under pain of death, this law in the end leads men to death. It could be compared to a railing which keeps us from going off the road, or to a tunnel in which God encloses men to be sure that they will not wander. But as man cannot depart from his sin, and as he continues to heap up his failures, the tunnel empties out into death!

Thus God, in some way, is taken in a contradiction of which he himself places the terms. To Abraham he promised unconditionally to give happiness to this people. He has to do it since he is "just," i.e., "faithful" to himself and to his promise. Through the mediator, Moses, he makes a bilateral contract with this people: He will give them happiness on condition that . . . . And the people enclosed in this tunnel of the law, do not respect the condition. The "justice" of God, like the dignity of man, demands then the death of this people (cf. OT, pp. 34f.). Then God has an original idea of love. The law was a tutor in preparation for Christ. At the end of the tunnel, God willed (and had promised) to make this people his adopted son by uniting them to his own Son. In fact, in the end, this people has to die.

Then God places at the end of this tunnel the death of his own Son! And man coming out of this tunnel passes indeed through death, but he undergoes it through the death of Jesus, so that in this very death which marks for him the departure from the tunnel, the liberation from the law, he becomes the son of God, being united in the death and the resurrection of the real Son of God.

Such is, it seems, the thought underlying these difficult chapters. This thought Paul develops on two planes. A "historic" plane: he takes up the history of Israel stopping on three strong points: Abraham—the law of Sinai—the Christ; then on a "cosmic" plane, more adapted perhaps to the mentality of his Galatian, readers who were formerly the slaves not of the Jewish law but of "the cosmic powers" which they obeyed.

First exposé: the historic plane (which he will develop in Romans).

If we consider the result which faith or the law attains in man, we see: **First** that Abraham was "justified" not because he was a Jew, but because he believed.[59] Hence to be a "son of Abraham" and heir to the promise which God made, faith is sufficient (3:6-9); **Second** that those who are under the law are cursed because they cannot keep it, and Scripture moreover declares "it is through faith that the just man lives" (3:10-12); **Third** that Christ in order to take us out of this impasse, has taken our place and has liberated us by giving us the Spirit, the fruit of the promise made to Abraham (3:13-14).

Now as we compare for ourselves faith and the law, we note: **First** that the promise was made to Abraham and "his descendants" (i.e., the Christ of whom God was thinking before all else), a promise which the law, coming a long time after, cannot modify; **Second** that the law was only an "interdict" (a prohibition) of the way that leads to Christ, a prohibtion "spoken between" the two ends of the road; and then **Third** that now that we have arrived at the terminus, the law is destroyed, faith in Christ makes us sons of God.

Second exposé: The "cosmic" plane (which he will develop in Colossians 2:8-23).

You Galatians, you were not slaves of the Jewish law (nor you Christians of the twentieth century). But this is something like it: You were under the law of the cosmic powers which you adored (the stars, power, progress, pleasure). You were under them as children subject to a tutor. Christ by his Spirit liberates you from this tutorship, confers on you adoption. The proof? The Holy Spirit in your heart brings you to pray as a son.[60] You are no longer slaves but sons. By grace, you do not become again slaves (4:1-10).

After a new appeal to the heart of the Galatians ("Recall that I loved you as a mother, and you loved me so well . . .") (4:12-20), Paul, in order to be more clear (for his Jewish readers) sums all this up in one image which he draws from the Bible: The story of Sara and Agar (4:12-31). Sons of Abraham through faith be free! This is the conclusion to draw from these exposés.

Third Point: Where does the gospel of Paul lead to? To the freedom of the Spirit, in the faith, which is manifested through love (chs. 5-6).

Choose freedom! (5:1-12): "We must choose between Jesus Christ and the Law. . . . Would that you would run so well in this way of freedom by being obedient to the truth . . . ." This is the doctrinal conclusion of the entire letter. Paul is not stating anything new here. He is summing up the theme of freedom and slavery to bring out everything that he wants to say to the Galatians. This summary is not a demonstration, it is an intense appeal to choose freedom (Bonnard).

Free to love (5:13-25): For a Christian there is no longer a law or commandments. There is only a dynamism in his heart which makes him sense what he must do: The Holy Spirit. This is infinitely more demanding than a law which we can always twist. More uplifting also. The Spirit in our heart is a principle of love.[61]

Concrete Applications for the Galatians (6:1-10): "See what large characters I trace for you with my own hand . . . ."

In taking up the quill to sign, Paul feels the need to return to a word which is closest to his heart: "You are a new creation." Not merely men who have been made better, but from slaves, sinners condemned, created anew. The new creation is not for the end of the world. From the time of baptism, we are of this new world, of the world of the Spirit.

Letter to the Romans

Saved in Jesus Christ, through Our Response of Love

God "saves" us. Close your eyes for an instant: What do you think about when you pronounce the words "salvation," "to be saved"?

"Do not enter here without a desire." The word of Valéry engraved in letters of gold is valid not only for the Museum of Man: Paul speaks to us of "salvation in Jesus Christ." Have you a desire to be saved?

This desire can be born only if we experience the feeling of "being lost." Would you like to examine this desire a little? To see the picture clearly it seems to me that we could group the men according to their desire for salvation into three categories.

1. **Those who do not experience this need:** Happy men . . . or unconscious. Everything is going for the best in the best of worlds. Their loves are only in the world. Rousseau . . . Giono . . . Nature is good—it is enough to abandon oneself to nature. The self-satisfied. Or the complacent optimist: "Tomorrow, scientific technique will settle

everything." Every one of us, on one day or another, finds ourselves in this group. And then comes failure or setback to awaken us to our naïve unconsciousness. Failure in the world around us, suffering everywhere, hunger. When I pass a little girl with disfigured face in the street, this friend handicapped for life, when I see children who suffer. . . . These are the days on which I can only weep with the anger of despair before my powerlessness. Failure also in my own interior life: Loss of appearance, "I no longer know where I am in my own personal history; formerly everything was clear, now . . ." a rupture of community: "I no longer understand my parents; this love has vanished; this friendship is broken. Loneliness. The stranger among all the others," breaking of communion with myself: feeling of internal division, of alienation, "the good I want to do, I do not do, the evil I do not wish to do, that I do . . . ." And with Paul I would like also at times to cry out: "Alas! who then will deliver me from this world of death, from this self which leads me to death?"

Would this be God?

2. **A second group of men answers:** "I need to be saved. But this salvation I want to receive only from myself." "Here where the glance is stopped on every side, the whole earth is planned so that the face be lifted up, and the glance beg. Oh! I hate this world in which we are subjected to God. But I who suffer from injustice, they have not acceded to my request, I will not bend my knee" (Camus, **Le Malentendu**). "The anti-Christian expects and awaits his alleviation only from himself, he does not seek an appeasement, but a victory, a peace that is won" (Malraux). We undoubtedly feel ourselves in communion with the wonderful texts of Camus, for example,[62] of the Marxists: "We live and we struggle in order that beyond this double victory (over fatality of nature and the social

contradictions) man consciously continues the creation of man and his history" (Garaudy).

But however beautiful this may be, it is enough to fill up this "terrible hope that is so deep in man" (Malraux). We always run head-on into this stupid, definitive, total failure which is death. The death of each one of us: "man is a being for death," repeats Heidegger and many of the contemporary philosophers. "Life has never an objective purpose unless we thus designate death" says the priest Koruga in the Twenty-Fifth Hour. The death of history itself: that for which generations of men gave themselves, will perish also.

In the deepest part of our being as men, we know there is a need for total salvation, the definitive success of our life. This is the victory over death.[63]

3. **Those who accept the salvation of Christ:** "I am the resurrection and the life." Because God has become man, fully, bearing our suffering and our lowliness, because he has been the stranger among us, rejected on the Cross, murdered, because God had raised him, they know that in him death has been conquered, that with him they can conquer death.

But this time will it be only an "opiate" to lull to sleep our evil of being man? "There is higher faith: that which all the crosses of the villages proclaim. . . . It is love, and appeasement is in it. I will not accept it, I will not abase myself to ask of him the appeasement to which my weakness calls me" (Malraux). We are tempted at times by this religion-opiate[64] and a passing through certain atheism (in departing from adolescence, for example) can be allowed by God in order to lead us to meet him in the faith.[65] For Christ is not a "tranquillizer," a "happiness pill." He does not take us out of our condition of being man, but taking it on fully, he tells us that our life and our history, in him make sense.

Everything had been lost and God saved us in Jesus Christ. This is what Paul wishes to explain in his Letter to the Romans.[66] This is the only insight that Paul presents in the doctrinal part before he develops the practical consequences in his second part. There can be no question of giving a commentary on this entire letter. We shall attempt to point out the broad lines by taking our time over a few passages.[67]

Address and Thanksgiving (1:1-15)

Taking his inspiration perhaps from a profession of faith of the primitive community, Paul sings the praises of the Gospel, the Good News which is Jesus Christ.

FIRST PART: DOCTRINAL PART (1:16-11:36)

In two verses (1:16-17), he gives us the theme of his letter: the gospel is a power which saves those who believe, the Jews to whom it was first proclaimed, and then the rest. For in this gospel, the "justice" of God who is faithful to himself ("just") by punishing sin, but especially by saving gratuitously, is revealed to him who has faith, and a faith which grows, which through the length of our life makes us readjust constantly our concrete attitude, on our first act of faith. As the prophet Habakkuk wrote: the just man will live by faith.

Does this appear a little complicated? For Paul too! He will take it up three times to lead us into his thought.

1. Justification explained in a theoretic and historic fashion (1:18-5:21).

Paul attempts to make us conscious, by reasoning and the appeal to history, that we were lost without Christ.

He forces us to descend even to the bottom of this "unhope": Not only is there nothing human to which we can cling, but because we are sinners, it is not even possible to cling to God! And at this point, God has come to seek us: "scarcely would a person die for a just man . . . ." The proof that God loves us is that Christ, even when we were sinners, died for us (5:7). With Christ we are saved. Or rather—an important precision of vocabulary—we are "justified" and we shall be "saved." For Paul does not put under the word "salvation" the same thing as we do. For us "I am saved" often means "I have been extracted from some affair," "I am saved for the moment while knowing very well that this probably will not endure." When he speaks of "salvation," Paul means something total, hence definitive. Thus this salvation will arrive only at the end of the world.[68] The word "justification" designates the passage made once and for all (at the moment of the act of faith and baptism) from the state of sin to that of "holiness," "justice."

Let us follow his demonstration: he distinguishes three times in history:

(a) **The time of sin: before Christ** (1:18-3:20)

Sin of the Pagans: A terrible description of pagan society.[69] Paul writes from Corinth, so he has good models before his eyes. But he also uses some regular clinches. This sin carries within itself its own punishment: the failure to recognize God, which ends in scorn for man.

Sin of the Jews: (too prone to say, as does the Pharisee in the Gospel, as does each of us: "I am not like these men"). Paul destroys this security of the Pharisee: "what counts, is not the evil which we have not done, but the evil we have done and the good we have not done" (Leenhardt).

Hence the sin of all men: "Paul condemns mankind entirely in order to hand it over to the grace of God alone. He demands of us that we recognize with him that we are all poor men, sinners and incapable of freeing ourselves from the clutches of sin" (Augrain).[70]

(b) **The time of justification through faith: the present time** (3:21-4:25).

In a theological exposé that is very deep (and difficult), he sums up his thesis (3:21-31) and then explains it by taking the example of Abraham, justified because he believed in the living God and not because he "did" something (cf. what we said in reference to Galatians and also OT, pp. 100-101).

(c) **The time of salvation and glory: in the future world** (5:1-11).

Justified by faith, we have the hope of being one day definitively saved. This hope "does not deceive because the love which God bears us has been poured out in our hearts by the Spirit who is himself this love and who has been given to us."

Summary: The Christ "New Adam" (5:12-21)

To render his theoretic exposé more living and because he thinks spontaneously in contrasts, Paul sums up everything that he has said by an extraordinary contrast. He sets before our eyes the two "first men," the two "Adams"; the first Adam launched mankind into an existence dedicated to sin; the second first man, "the Christ," "firstborn" of a new mankind, carries us with him in the adventure of his holiness. Here Paul reveals to us perhaps the most exalting mystery of Christianity: **original sin.**

Original Sin. In this domain we have the unfortunate habit of reading Scripture "against the grain" and the naïveté to be surprised that this grates on us! Have you noted that neither Genesis nor the other books of the Old Testament, nor even Jesus himself in the Gospels speak to us of original sin as such? "See the sins that are forgiven you," said Jesus. God reveals our sins to us only after he has delivered us. Compare our reading with that of Paul.

We start with Genesis and enter thus, with head lowered, into an impasse because we take the Bible for a book of history or science in the modern sense of the word. All our legitimate questions thus become objections: How did the Bible know about this beginning of mankind (a tradition of a million years or more)? Who are "Adam and Eve": a single couple? a group of primates who arrived at the same time at becoming men? (monogenism or polygenism?). What was this sin? How could Adam commit an act which would have such consequences?

Paul, like all the Bible, has a **religious view** of history. He starts from Christ, and starting from his attempts to understand.[71] Jesus died to save **all** men; **therefore** all men need to be saved.[72] Starting from this truth, he has no difficulty in reading in Genesis the original drama of mankind, but always from the angle of **religious truth.** How did this take place concretely? I do not know and it is not up to the Bible to tell me, but it is the responsibility of science. Take, for example, what the Bible tells us about the creation of man. I find this objection very amusing: "Adam and Eve never existed." Unless we think that the world and mankind are eternal, we must admit that there was a beginning for mankind. This "beginning," in order to reveal religious history to us, the Bible calls "Adam," i.e., "Mister Man," and this is the right and privilege of the sacred writer. Now if science then puts under the label one or several couples, this will in no way change the religious vision of the history of the origins of man. The same is true for sin, with one important difference: it is not evident that sin began with the beginning of mankind. Here we are not in the domain of science, but in the domain of religious history, and only the Word of God can give us certainty. Genesis teaches us that God created man good and that "Adam," urged by the serpent, sinned. Paul, rereading Genesis in the light of the Cross of Christ, reveals to us the consequences of this sin: It has put mankind in a state of alienation from God: as Hitler in his folly created a historic situation of war which we had to take on, so the sin of Adam created a historic situation of alienation from God, a situation which we must take on by being born, a situation which each of us aggravates by his own personal sins. A desperate situation if we had had knowledge of it before Christ; an uncomfortable situation but one which now fills us with gratitude; Christ has saved us all; each of us is before God as a sinner who has been favored (graced).

Original sin, a revelation which fills with joy; a revelation of our solidarity with each other, and especially our solidarity with Christ. Paul has set the two Adams before our eyes and this sums up his entire exposé. But he points out to us that this remains a little complicated. Will we have to be an intellectual or a theologian in order to be a Christian? Fortunately not! Every Christian, even if he is not able to explain in skillful words what has taken place in him, yet has lived what Paul has just explained. Hence it is sufficient, to repeat the same thing more simply, to attempt to make him conscious of what he has lived: "Christian, you are baptized! reflect on what has taken place in you!"

2. Justification effected by the sacrament of baptism (6:1-7:6).

This development merely takes up the theoretic explanation in sacramental terms. It shows us that "justification **is** a death and a resurrection with Jesus Christ" (Bonnard). And he develops the consequences of this: the Christian must live in conformity with this new being which he has become. The Church has found this text so beautiful that she asks us to spend a whole night meditating on it: it forms the heart of the Easter Vigil. She helps us to savor it through some vivid images: the **light** (paschal candle) victorious over the darkness as Christ over sin and death; the **water,** whose destructive power (think of a dam that breaks, or a flood, or, in the Bible, the Flood and the crossing of the Red Sea) is exorcised to make it become a power for life: it can become the water of baptism in which we are plunged with Christ (and it destroys the sin), and from which we come forth (like Christ by his resurrection) for life.[73] We can then end the Vigil with the **eucharistic meal** which is at the same time a recalling of this sacrifice in which Jesus himself made, and we in him, this passage from death to life, and at the time time an anticipation of this definitive joy which we shall one day taste, "saved" at the table of God.

In this text, search out the images which describe for us baptism (some, unfortunately, are not perceptible in a translation).

"Baptize": the Greek word means to "plunge into." "One and the same being" (5:5), "sym-phyo" from "phyo," sprout or bud (is said of plants), to grow or to be born, and "syn"=with (cf. the meaning of "con-naitre" according to Claudel: "to be born with"). **Liberation** from slavery. **Death and Life.** Paul in his letters uses other images besides: the **bath** (1 Cor. 6:9; Tit. 3:5; Eph. 5:26); "burial" with Christ (Gal. 3:27; Col. 3:9); **"to put on"** Christ (Gal. 3:27; Col. 3:9); to be **marked with a seal** indicating the belonging to someone (Eph. 1:13; 4:30; 2 Cor. 1:21); **illumination** (Eph. 5:14).

This manner of explaining justification is more concrete, but it still remains a little complicated. One last time, Paul takes up the same idea in an existential manner.[74]

3. Justification lived in our "spiritual life (7:7-8:39).

As in a scene in a play on stage, there evolves a person in whom I recognize myself, Paul, in a dramatic turning back to existence before Christ, puts on the stage the "Ego" of every man, this Ego torn between the good he wants to do and the evil which he actually carries out, between the desire of life and the leap into death which he makes through sin. "Who will liberate me from this body which dedicates me to death . . .? Thanks be to God through Jesus Christ, our Lord!" The Apostle then calls on the most profound experience we can have in ourselves, that of the Holy Spirit received in baptism and who has made us children of God: "All of those who are animated by the Spirit, are the sons of God." And through them, the Cosmos itself finds its first ordination to God.[75]

(a) **The "ego" torn apart under the law of sin** (7:7-25)

This is one of the passages of Paul where our modern sensitivity attaches best. The underlying allusions to the history of Israel (earthly paradise and gift of the law) make the first verses a little complicated, but do not keep us from the understanding of the whole.

(b) **The "ego" reunified, under the law of the Spirit** (8:1-17)

Here is the great Pauline text about the Spirit. Through him, we become "sons in the Son" and we are able to with a familiarity which no man would ever have had the boldness even to imagine, this very familiarity which Jesus uses to call God "Father! Abba!" In us the Spirit speaks to the Father and involves us in his prayer.

(c) **The cosmos bound to the lot of man, destined with him for glory** (8:18-25)

In the very heart of this chapter dedicated to man reunified in the Spirit, here is a decisive text about the lot of the cosmos awaiting impatiently the liberation of man in order to be, with him, extended toward the glory of God. "I sense that I bear in the most secret part of my being the total effort of the Universe. . . . By way of my intention which is clean, the Divine fills the Universe insofar as it is centered upon me. Because I have become, through my consent, a living member of the Body of Christ, everything that influences me serves finally to develop Christ. Christ permeates me and **my cosmos**." We have to resist the temptation to quote Teilhard further: has he not finally, and magnificently, organized and orchestrated this intuition of Paul?

After a beautiful summary of the plan of salvation of God (8:28-30), just as he had ended his first part with a poem on the New Adam, so Paul concludes here with a **hymn to the love of God** (8:31-39). There is no comment for such texts where poetry, the bearer of life, becomes a prayer.

The mystery of Israel (chs. 9-11)

After having breathed this uplifting atmosphere of the high peaks, we get the impression, with these chapters, of falling back into the confining corner of the ghetto. The reason for this is that Paul is not a disembodied idealist; the most beautiful ideas have to be justified in history and he has to respond here to a serious objection: God had chosen the Jewish people to carry out his promise. But this people seems rejected. Was God unfaithful to his promise? (This is a serious question for us also: if God is unfaithful in this case, who guarantees me that he will not be unfaithful in other instances?) These three chapters are important also from another point of view: Paul states that God will one day put an end to the "primordial schism." More serious even than all the divisions between Christians, Protestants and Catholics; the division between Jews and Christians. One day, the people of Israel, as a people will recognize Jesus Christ as him whom they are expecting. This promise makes us and the Jews even more brothers, and invites us to do everything to find this brotherhood in our hearts and by our acts, hastening thus the day of its realization.

To answer the objection, Paul shows that the promises of God do not take away from man his freedom of choice (9:1-20; cf. 1 Cor. 10 and Heb. 3:4). Moreover God is not unjust in rejecting Israel, for Israel is guilty for not having accepted Christ (9:30-10:21). Above all, this rejection is not total, since the Church is the true Israel, receiver of the promises; nor is it definitive: the people of Israel, as a whole, will one day accept its Messiah.

This terminates the first, the doctrinal, part of the letter in which Paul tries to make us conscious of what we were without Christ, and of what we are to become with him. But Paul would no longer be Paul if, after **seeing** this, he did not urge us to **act**. He does this in his second part, which is easier to understand.

SECOND PART: EXHORTATION TO LIVE AS "SAVED MEN" (chs. 12-16)

The true cult of the Christians, the true "victim," which we must offer to God, the only sacrifice which can please him, is not the bread and wine of the Mass, it is **our very person,** our daily life. But for this to be possible, this offering must pass through the offering of Christ: bread and wine are the image, the summary of our life, and in them our life is "consecrated"; like them and in them, our life becomes the body and blood of Jesus Christ. Our true offering is an interior attitude, "obedience," submission of our will to the Word of God, an interior offering which is expressed by an exterior attitude: the gift which we make of ourselves to others, in love. Why did we have to wait for these last few years so that we, Catholics, might rediscover this "royal priesthood of the baptized" which the first Christians lived so intensely? Paul did not invent this doctrine. He takes his inspiration from the baptismal catechesis, i.e., from the basic instruction of the baptized, as he will do it again in Phil. 2:14-17; 3:3; and elsewhere; and as Peter, and James, and the author of the Letter to the Hebrews do also. This is so important that we shall give the next chapter to it.

After he has recalled this principle in two verses (12:1-2), Paul can trace "the broad lines of an authentic Christian conduct: the spiritual worship consists essentially in a charity recapitulating all the aspects of moral and civil life" (Lafont), (12:3-13). He takes time out for a concrete example: Let the "weak" (those who are scandalized for nothing) and the "strong" (those who are solid in their faith . . . less solid perhaps than they think) imitate the charity of Christ (14:1-15:6). Here he develops some principles already given in 1 Cor. 8:10. Note in passing this wonderful definition of man: "A brother for whom Christ died" (14:15).

Epilogue: 15:14-16:27

Some personal news and plans for a trip (15:14-33). Here (15:16), Vatican II found the best definition of the **ministry of the priest: (Decree on the Ministry of Priests,** No. 2).

In chapter 16, Paul greets all his friends and collaborators (for some, this chapter would actually be a note addressed to the Church of Ephesus). He completes his letter with a prayer in which he takes up his principal themes.

Letter to the Philippians

For the Sake of Jesus and the Gospel

> "They do not possess joy, but joy possesses them"
>
> **Le soulier de Satin**

A letter written for no special reason! There is no crisis, no heresy in Philippi. It is written simply because Paul, a prisoner, is possessed by the joy of communicating in the suffering of Christ; simply because he loves his Philippians dearly. We have all known these moments, in which, without knowing why, community is established between friends, in which, without hesitancy, we can expose everything that is inside, these fleeting moments in which we can be no longer a student or worker, a parent or child, a professor or priest, but be simply our own self. There is nothing to uphold, promote, forbid, or explain, only to share. The Philippians are not lacking a title for glory: their town, founded by Philip, father of Alexander, became a Roman colony in 42 B.C., was heaped with honors and privileges by Augustus. When Paul arrived there in A.D. 50-51, with Silas, Timothy and Luke, they were given an enthusiastic welcome. But their greatest glory consists in having been the only church among the churches of Paul with whom he felt himself one day sufficiently in communion to unburden his inner self.[76]

For the sake of Jesus and the gospel. The secret of the life of Paul and his joy. We listen to it. Here are a few notes merely to help you.[77]

For the sake of Jesus . . .

"Father de Foucauld is teaching and tenderness," said Father Peyriguere, "teaching that blossoms forth in tenderness and tenderness that bursts forth from teaching." This letter is permeated with tenderness for him who "seized" him on the road to Damascus. "Jesus," "the Christ," "the Christ Jesus," the "Lord Jesus" . . . this name, like a spellbinding chant, resounds in each phrase and blossoms forth once in perfect accord—the only time, I think, in Paul—"the Christ Jesus, my Lord" (3:8). His existence is a life "in Christ." "My Life is Christ." This tenderness for the "well-beloved brother and Lord, Jesus Christ," as Father de Foucauld liked to call him, is not sentimentalism. It bursts forth from the teaching. And we are amazed to discover by chance in reading, said as if in passing, one of the most moving expressions of the mystery of Christ: the Hymn to Christ the Lord (2:5-11);[78] twenty centuries later, theology is still searching out its riches and the Latin Church uses it as the theme and meditation chant for the three days in preparation for Easter. There is perhaps no more beautiful commentary than the Gregorian melody: grave and sober as a ballad (Good Friday and Holy Saturday), triumphal as a Te Deum when it declares to the world the joy of Easter.

This magnificent poem carries also quite a few difficulties. The word "condition," for example, translates a Greek word which can mean "nature" (an impossible translation: Jesus did not abandon the divine "nature"); here it has almost the same sense as "resemblance" of verse 7 (or "became as"; "being as") but with something more interior and more durable; the radiating of an intimate state. "Did not cling jealously," or better, "did not look upon it as a prize that could be taken by force" is difficult: Jesus possesses by nature this "divine rank"; he cannot take it by force. There is certainly an allusion here to the drama of Paradise: Jesus, by his voluntary abasement, redeems the failure of the first man who wished to "take by force" this equality with God. There is an allusion also throughout the text to the Songs of the Suffering Servant who voluntarily gives his life as atonement. A painful abasement which reverberated to the inmost depths of the free consciousness of Jesus: reread the accounts of the test of Christ or even Heb. 5:1-10. But from that time Jesus is "Lord," "God" (since Kyrios is the Greek equivalent of Yahweh), but "God-with-us" (he has been God forever), or better "we with God": through his exaltation, Jesus has become Lord of mankind and the cosmos, and leads us with him into the glory of the Father.

And this teaching again blossoms forth into tenderness. "My God," prayed Father de Foucauld, "I do not know whether it is possible for some souls to see you poor and to remain voluntarily rich . . . not to want to resemble you in everything. . . . But for me, it is impossible for me to understand love without the search for resemblance, without the ardent desire for conformity of life and without the need to share all the crosses." Conformity, communion, words which spring spontaneously from the pen of Paul: "To know him with the power of his resurrection and the communion in his sufferings, to become conformed to him in death in order to arrive at being raised from among the dead:"[79] Conformity to the death of Christ which is at work in him, Paul—his chains, his struggles; in his disciple Epaphroditus (3:25-30). Must we then, to be a Christian, have a morbid taste for suffering? The opposite notion is too common even to pause on this question. In this desire for death, as it is given to us, there is a double grievance: the sense of sorrow and pain and the sense of being set free.

Sense of being set free: Alongside his brothers who are struggling for a human happiness, for more justice and love, the Christian is said to be in "exile," awaiting the moment of returning to his true "fatherland," heaven;[80] death is the "great friend" which will finally liberate him from this earth to permit his soul to rejoin the world of ideas. Actually we could cite many a text for this. This is a sign that a certain Christian piety is no longer Christian but Platonic. I purposely wrote "world of ideas," rather than "heaven." For how many Christians and spiritual writers is heaven no longer the heaven of Christ, but the heaven of Plato? The doctrine about the immortality of the soul has too often destroyed the expectation of the resurrection of the dead. Cullmann[81] in an extraordinary contrast opposed the death of Socrates and the death of Christ. Socrates, in the greatest peace, drinks the hemlock whicle discoursing on the immortality of the soul; Jesus cries out in the face of suffering and dies with a loud cry. For him, death is the "last enemy" (1 Cor. 15:26) that he has to overcome. God is life, and death destroys life. We aspire to heaven, it is true, but not to an ethereal place outside the communion of men. Heaven is communion with Jesus, and, what comes down to the same thing, "heaven is the others" (read Phil. 1:21-26). If Camus could have understood this—but he sees it now I hope—that while it is a rendezvous with his brothers, it is to the rendezvous with God that he is going.[82] This love of God, far from withdrawing us from the world, engages us more deeply in it by keeping us from resting in what is transitory, in order to force us to pursue in it that which is eternal. This gives us a "refined touch" (1:9-10) which leads us to discover true values: "Finally, brothers, fill your minds with everything that is true, everything that is noble, everything that is good and pure, everything that we love and honor, and everything that can be thought virtuous or worthy of praise. Keep doing all the things that you learned from me and have been taught by me and have heard or seen that I do. Then the God of peace will be with you" (4:8). This "eternal map of Christian humanism" (Gilson) is in harmony with the other texts we have already seen (1 Cor. 3:21-23; Rom. 8:19-22). We must "communicate with God through the world" (cf. OT, pp. 182-183).

But then, why this desire for death? Is it a form of delight in the midst of pain for the sake of pain? No. It is a love of life. It is a love of all that is true and eternal in life. At the time of our baptism, our "old man," all that there is of the old man in us, of that which is not able to be recovered by God, has been destroyed. But this is in image only. But it is in an "effective" image, in a "sacrament." That which has been done at that time, we still have to do, we have to let Christ do it in us throughout our lifetime. Our carnal death is the completion of our baptism, the moment in which it is finally true. This desire for death is, finally, an appeal—though painful—for the total appearance of God and our brothers, for this lived "mutual sharing of consciousness" which the personalist philosophy seeks, and in the communion of love.

Hence we see that this letter more than any other praises the conformity to the death of Jesus, and at the same time is the most magnificent hymn to joy.[83]

Hymn to joy

If you have gone through the whole letter, as we suggested, and underlined all the words which express joy, you know now what it is that makes up the joy of Paul, what it is that must make up the joy of the militant Christian, of a priest: the joy of Paul, of Epaphroditus, of the Philippians are so intermingled that we no longer know which is which! (2:25-30). Joy of the unity of Christians: an important theme of this letter which deserves that we take time out to consider it.

Is it not as an appeal to unity that Paul sings the hymn to Christ the Lord? "In your minds, you must be the same as Christ Jesus." The specific joy of the priest (2:17-18): as priest, his proper role is not to construct the earthly city, but to help men to make their lives a spiritual sacrifice, to make sure that their lives are built on the eternal. He does this by his preaching, he does this by the sacraments, he does this by his own life: "and then, if my blood has to be shed as part of your own sacrifice and offering—which is your faith—I shall still be happy and rejoice with all of you, and you must be just as happy and rejoice with me" (2:17-18).[84] The libation was the most solemn moment of the Jewish evening sacrifice; without it, the sacrifice was not complete. Hence Paul expresses, it seems, his joy as priest of enabling, by offering his own life, the spiritual sacrifice of his Christians to be "accomplished," liturgical, pleasing to God. Thus, in his prayer for his parishioners, he tells God of his joy (1:4), for the "joy of their faith" (1:25), (these "faces of the risen ones" which Nietzsche sought among Christians in vain). But before all else, his joy is the proclaiming of the gospel (1:18).

For the sake of the gospel

The gospel: to announce the Christ, to proclaim the Word, to serve the cause of the gospel, I have for a mission to defend the gospel, my struggle is for the gospel—an obsession for Paul. The gospel is Jesus Savior proclaimed to men: Jesus insofar as he reaches me today, insofar as he asks of me my response of faith and love. The peak of the mystical life for Paul, apostle, the moment in which he is most intimately united to Jesus, is when he is preaching him. The supreme happiness is not to contemplate him, but to "seek out his interests" (2:21), to put oneself at the service of others (1:21-26), or, rather, by doing this he contemplates him and is united to him: "To know Jesus

Christ we must build the church," said Paul. Paul lived this: "the understanding that he has of the mystery of Christ," and his love for the churches are very closely bound together. We know that Vatican II wanted to give the apostle Paul to priests as a model by recalling to them that their holiness has for its primary source their "pastoral charity," their ministry performed with love.[85]

Leon Bloy said: "There is only one sadness, i.e., not to be among the saints." St. Paul can teach us how to be, in our world of sadness, "sources of light by presenting the Word of life" (2:15). "Joy is always the sign that life has succeeded" (Bergson).

Note on the Biblical and Pauline Anthropology

The manner in which Paul speaks of man and the different parts of which he is composed should appear to us as terribly complicated. He borrowed it from the biblical (i.e., Semitic) mentality, but gave it Greek names (which settles nothing). Let us attempt to understand it here by simplifying it very much (but without falsifying it at all).

Two evidences, extremely important:

The biblical thought is not metaphysical but historical, it is not interested in man "in se" (his "essence"), but always in man "in a situation" before God.

Our thought, coming from Greek philosophy, is instinctively "dualist": man is composed of **two** principles, soul and body; the biblical thought is "monist": man is not a composite but a unity, he is one "person," one "ego," one "creature of God." Just as we do not say I "have" a person but I "am" a person, so the Bible does not say I "have" a body, a soul, but I "am" a body, a soul. The body, the soul, the heart designate not a part of man, but one aspect of the entire man, of the entire person, the aspect under which I am considering him. If I want to speak of man especially insofar as he is perceptible to the senses, insofar as we can touch him, that he is external, I would say: He is a body. To designate him insofar as he is interior, open to God and to others, they say: He is a soul. It is a little complicated but very modern.

A practical consequence: When you see these words in the Bible: "body," "soul," replace them generally, mentally, with "person," "I,"

Let us consider now this person in the history of salvation:

Let us start by expressing the things in our everyday language. "I was a sinner and Christ redeemed me." I was a sinner: "I," "Me," not my soul, or my body, but me entirely, my person. Christ redeemed me: that which in me was a sinner, the sinful "part of me" has been destroyed and the "part of me" that was open to God has been sanctified.

Paul says the same thing in language filled with imagery, but very real. He takes especially four words (I am simplifying it); two which designate man especially insofar as he is exterior, "body" and "flesh,"[86] and two which designate man especially as interior: "soul" and "spirit" (**pneuma**)[87]: "I am a sinner." Paul translates: Evil has entered into me, laid hold of me in the most vulnerable part (man as exterior). The "sinful part of me" he calls "the flesh" (myself as not recoverable by God); it is in me, a source of corruption which then touches the body (especially it), the soul, the spirit. "The flesh designates every man as sin has made him" (Prat). "I am redeemed" Paul translates: The Spirit of God enters into me and takes hold of that "part of me open to God," my spirit. This Spirit is then in me a source of sanctification. It will replace my "soul" and "spiritualize" my body. The "flesh," not recoverable, is evacuated, destroyed, "nailed to the Cross"! (Gal. 5:24). "The Spirit designates every man as grace has remade him" (Prat).

Let us try to outline this by placing ourselves in three moments of our history:

1. Sinful man, before Christ
2. Man definitively saved by Christ (at the end of time)
3. Man saved: in the "interim," this time in which everything is done and everything is still to be done. Already my "flesh," the source of corruption, is destroyed. But it still acts in me. Already the Spirit permeates me. My baptism will be "completed" in its aspect "death," at the moment of my carnal death; in its "life" aspect, at the moment of the resurrection of the body.

III. A Love of World Dimensions

Letters to the Colossians and Ephesians

Paul's way of the Cross: First Station. Caesarea

April, 58: Luke sets aside his quill. He has spent the day in editing his diary of the trip,[88] and, seated on the balcony of Philip, his friend, he reviews these forty days of event-filled voyage. At his feet, the port of Caesarea is bathed in bluish water. Over there where the sun is setting, is Corinth. More to the north is Macedonia. He was in Philippi when, shortly before Easter, Paul arrived from Corinth with seven companions. They were expecting him by sea. At the last moment, in order to spike a conspiracy, he had to take the land route. When the paschal festivities were over, they had left for Troas, in two groups (as they had to do almost the entire voyage) to elude the ruses of enemies, whose hatred is not abated. Troas . . . what a memory! Sunday.[89] The Eucharist at night. A night passed listening to Paul. And the young Eutyches who fell asleep on the edge of the window on the third floor in the middle of the sermon and was killed when he fell out. So that he would lose nothing of the sermon, Paul first revives him and then continues on into the morning.

Then there was Assos, Chio, Miletus. The elders of Ephesus had been waiting for them. Disturbing goodbyes of Paul: "You shall no longer see my face. . . . I trust in God and in his world who has the power to build the building . . . ." And then, Cos, Rhodes, Cyprus. Everywhere marks of affection, also fears: "Do not go up to Jerusalem . . . ." But always Paul continues on toward the Holy City. Tyre, Ptolemais, and Caesarea. The peace of the evening finally in this friendly house where the somber presentiments disappear. The friendship of Philip is solid; engaging is the delicacy of his four daughters. All these fears would perhaps be empty. . . . But what is this? They hear the murmur of a voice in the room below.

Agabus, one of these men who speak in the name of God, has arrived from Judea. In the silence which reigns, he takes Paul's cincture and binds himself hands and feet: "Behold what the Holy Spirit says. The man to whom this cincture belongs, the Jews will bind like this in Jerusalem and they will hand him over to the pagans." Are these the exact words of Agabus? Luke, afterwards, would not swear to it. At that time he was editing his Gospel and the words of Jesus have come back to his memory: "Behold: we are going up to Jerusalem and the Son of Man will be delivered to the pagans, beaten, and put to death (Luke 18:31-33). One thing he has understood well in any case: today a long Way of the Cross begins for Paul. And Paul, like his Master, freely gives himself to it: I am ready to die in Jerusalem for the name of the Lord Jesus. "May the will of the Lord be done. Let us go up to Jerusalem."

Second Station: Jerusalem: From the house of James to the pretorium

Why is it necessary that our Ways of the Cross always

pass through the house of brothers? Some influential Christians from around James have not disarmed themselves against Paul. They accept the fruit of his collection and, while listening to him recount what God has done among the pagans through his ministry, they are obliged to give glory to God. But they bind him in chains immediately: "Thousands of Jews have been converted and they have all heard you speak on your subject . . . ." "It is almost the same as if a missionary, well known, came back to his own country after long years of work for conquest in Christ in the heart of Africa," writes Holzner in a pleasant vein, "and was listened to by an ecclesiastical synod: God be praised! However, brother, they tell us that you have not made the black people sing the plain chant according to the Vatican edition! And for this they give him the fatal advice: 'Show openly that you are a Jew. At your own expense fulfill the vow of the Nazirite with four of your brothers . . .' A heavy penalty, financially for sure," an even greater humiliation in appearing to make concessions to the extremist party. Paul accepts because his mission is not at stake. Fatal advice: the seventh day, a well-ordered riot breaks out in the temple and Paul, scourged, trampled under foot, could not have saved his life except for the Roman soldiers who led him out, in chains, to the Antonian fortress.[90] From the steps which overlook the court of the temple, Paul gets to speak to his brothers by race: No, he has not betrayed his fathers by becoming Christian, he has only remained faithful to the law, a tutor in reference to Christ (Acts 22:1-21). His discourse is quickly lost in the howling of the hysterical crowd. The tribune, who understood nothing about the matter, will ask Paul the question Roman fashion—by scourging. Humor of the saints! Paul understood that the entire human mechanism for his arrest had been set in motion, that there was nothing more to do. He who "learned to be at ease in all circumstances" now finds or sees the humor of the situation. When they have already raised the scourges to begin the punishment, an innocent question throws the tribune into the greatest anguish: "Are you allowed to scourge a Roman citizen?" He is led to prison with some excuses, and the next day they bring him before the Sanhedrin. Pharisees and Sadducees are violently opposed to each other on certain points of doctrine, especially the resurrection. Paul knows this well. A simple statement, and then he has only to sit back and watch, ironically, the respectable leaders of the two parties as they dispute. Some of the Pharisees even come to the defense of Paul. But concerning the night in prison, humor is no longer in possession.[91] Jesus, who experienced this solitude himself, comes to strengthen him: "You must still render testimony of me in Jerusalem." And the following night, to offset a conspiracy which his nephew has engineered, Paul is led under armed guard to Caesarea.

Third Station:

Prison in Caesarea . . . "Jesus was led before Herod"

"Cruel and sensual," writes Tacitus, "Felix exercised power with the soul of a slave." This is the man who will keep Paul in prison for two years. Right in the current of the Jewish religion—Drusilla, his wife, is the daughter of Herod Agrippa I—he enjoys listening to Paul, except when Paul starts to talk of justice, temperance, or the judgment to come. Felix knows Paul is innocent, but he is hoping to pick up a cash settlement.

Festus, who replaces Felix in the year 60, is an upright man.[92] He goes right to the roots of the case. A new appearance before the Sanhedrin. Understanding that he is treating of a religious affair, Festus proposes to Paul to transfer it to the jurisdiction of the Sanhedrin. This would be death for him and Paul knows that well. He pronounces then the word that removes all other jurisdiction: "I appeal to Caesar." During the few days that precede his departure, Agrippa and his sister, Berenice[93] come to visit Festus: this is a good occasion for Festus to get the help of these experts of Jewish law to draft the report that he must send to Rome. You do not know a great deal about the quibbling of Judaism, do you, Festus? You had better! Because you are a straightforward man, you have grasped the heart of Christianity from the start: "It treats, he sums up for Agrippa, of the controversies about a certain **Jesus,** who is dead, and whom Paul declared is **living.**" The next day, Paul speaks before Agrippa and Berenice.

The Fourth Station:

Toward Rome . . . And Herod sent him back to Pilate

Now he is enroute for Rome. It is a long trip with many ups and downs: the storm, shipwreck, despair of the sailors, calm and authority of Paul, wintering in Malta. . . . The warm welcome from the brothers in Rome, who have come into his presence, gives him his courage again. Years 61-63: a prisoner, but in a manner quite free to receive visits, Paul at the heart of the empire, proclaims boldly and without obstacle, the Kingdom of God and the Lord Jesus.

Four years in prison! Who will ever know what these years represent in the life of a man: periods of seclusion, voluntary or forced, reduced to exterior silence, the thoughts must go back on themselves to their very source, as in geometry a section of a pyramid flows toward its point and comes finally to concentrate on one, single point from which the whole comes. In the letters that Paul writes at this time we certainly find the theologian of the Letter to the Romans. The thought is basically the same. But the center of interest is slowly displaced, to be fixed on this unique point from which his thought flows from that time on: **the Lordship of the Christ.**

Two letters: Colossians, Ephesians, and the note to Philemon. Theologians for 2,000 years have been searching out the wonderful doctrine in these letters. Shall I tell you here why I love them? "The Kingdom of heaven or the kingdom of the earth? History or a ghetto . . ."? From the beginning of this book (cf. OT, p. 1) I kept calling to mind this conflict which every believer some day experiences, "between this carnal world which he loves intensely and his faith which, he thinks, obliges him to give it up," this crucial choice between the meeting with God and the meeting with his brothers. And now these letters give rise to the deep conviction, beyond words, to this fullness of joy in knowing that my love of Christ does not in any way destroy my human love. The Yes spoken to Christ is not opposed to the Yes spoken to his bride.[94] Christ is not jealous of human attachments, he fulfills them. Never will the meeting with him cause me to fail in the meeting with my brothers. One can die in the peace of the human brotherhood;[95] Jesus died for it also. Intense love for the world does not oblige me to a choice against Christ. In fact it casts me into him.[96] Paul, unified by suffering, solitude, can finally teach me how to become again a brother with the world and with men. In the Church, this Church, disfigured by all our sins and all our fears, this virginal bride of Christ, is the place to meet men because she is the body of Christ.

But you do not have to accept what I think. Let Paul speak for himself.

Letter to the Colossians

"The Universe takes the form of Jesus."
Teilhard de Chardin

Colossae. Today a mound of earth, very near the modern village. The natives call it "the hill" as the Arabs call it "the tell." It had its hour of fame in the time of Xerxes and Cyrus. It had become only a secondary town when Epaphras, a Colossian disciple of Paul, implanted Christ there. Its title to glory? A heresy: A happy heresy of the Colossians which marks a stepping stone in the thought of Paul. The years of seclusion have matured him. This crisis in Colossae—Epaphras has come to Rome to tell him about it—sets forth the central point of view which he was seeking perhaps, which in any case, allows him to organize his thought. He throws it out in this letter like a cry of alarm. Soon, calmed down, he will be able to take it up again, as he had written the Letter to the Romans after the Letter to the Galatians. This will give rise to a sort of encyclical letter, a wonderful synthesis of his thought, the Letter to the Ephesians.

But were the Colossians really heretics? This has been frequently stated and the writers based their statements on what Paul himself says. But this means that they forget the genius of Paul to go straight to the root of the trouble and to draw out the consequences of which his Christians certainly have not seen. Recall the case of the Galatians. Rather than "heresy," it would be better to speak of it as danger of doctrinal deviation. Its origin? The Jews were numerous in these areas and Judaism was alive. It was a natural for tempting "the religious or superstitious curiosity" of these young Christians (Benoit), especially if it was accompanied, as seems to be the case here, with some clarification on the Almanac and the powers of the sky that rule the course of history.[97] In practice this "tendency to deviate" is manifested externally by additional observances: abstinences, feast days, the Sabbath (2:16-23), perhaps by circumcision (merely advised, 2:11); more profoundly, by the importance given to certain intermediary beings between God and men. Is Christ then not in danger of being merely one among many or below all these cosmic powers?

In this letter, Paul accepts the field of battle which his Christians offer him: He starts his attack with the "powers" and this will lead him to deepen thought or make it explicit on three scores:

The Powers: "The angel of the rain has not performed his service": a simple pleasantry which for us is nothing more than this. But it unites with the problematic of Paul and carries with it a deep truth. Opposite to our logical and "lay" minds, the ancients were naturally "religious": in the presence of any thing or event, we seek the cause or the essence and we find it in natural laws. The ancients had a deep sense of living in a world inhabited, "haunted," by the Divine, and they gave everything a spiritual cause: the power of the storm, for example, came from the god of the storm. There was the god or the power of the streams, of each people, or love . . . . The astral and cosmic forces are so many "powers" (think of the atom), but where we know how to control them and put them to our service, the ancients felt that they were controlled by them and worshiped them to get them to be of service to them. Paul is a man of his times and has the mentality of the times. But he knows well that there is only one God and Father, hence he continues in the line of that which the Old Testament had already begun (cf. Ezek., OT, pp. 91ff.): he likens these "powers" to the creatures and servants of God who are angels. In doing this he brings them into the plan of salvation of God and puts them in their true place, in relation to Christ.[98] This leads him by contrast to give greater stress to the cosmic supremacy of Christ.

"THE UNIVERSAL CHRIST . . . peak of the world" (Teilhard).

Granted, admits Paul, these cosmic powers, the angels, since he must call them by their name, have received from God a role to play before Christ, in the government of the world as well as in the transmission of the Word of God.[99] But now this role is finished, Christ has come and from now on he has taken in hand the direction of the cosmos. Thus we are present at a broadening of the framework in which, until then, Paul had thought of the mystery of Christ. The simplest way to see this is to compare the two great hymns on Christ in the letters to the Colossians and to the Philippians. The center of interest is exactly the same: **union into Christ.** But the perspective is enlarged.

Hymn of the Philippians: Paul considers **Christ as Redeemer,** as Savior. He does this in the two successive states of Jesus: **The state of the Suffering Servant:** become like to men and resembling them in himself, he makes his painful "passage" to the Father. **Glorious state:** from now on "Lord," he can present to the Father the ensemble of men in him by anticipation.

Hymn of Colossians: Paul considers **Christ as Creator.** The backdrop of his mystery is the cosmos. This poem is made up of two parts well constructed (1:15-16 and 18b-20). The central verse sums up the teaching (vs. 17 is the summary of the first part and vs. 18a is the summary of the second part). The two stages of the mystery of Christ are now: the pre-existent Christ, "image of God," and the Christ "Lord,"[100] "Image of the invisible God!" An absolute paradox: the Christ for human thought: in him we see the invisible, he is the infinite become individual.[101] The word "image," which Paul uses only in a religious sense, is faithful to a biblical theme represented by Gen. 1, Wisdom, and Daniel, and indicates origin and likeness. He has undoubtedly borrowed it from Wisd. 7:26, which remains the best commentary on this passage (OT, p. 186). Everything has been created **through** him and **for** him. He is like the foyer in which are bound together and coordinated all the sons, all the daughters of the universe. Anyone who would like to have an instantaneous point of view on the total universe, past, present, and future, will see all beings suspended ontologically on Christ, and in the final analysis, intelligible only through him (Huby). Therefore, because he has created everything and because everything was created for him, Christ is the center of the world from the beginning. But he had to become this effectively by becoming "Lord."[102] This second stanza sums up the second point on which the thought of Paul has made progress: the Church.

THE CHURCH: a body of which Christ is the "head."

How are we to conceive the relations between the earthly Church and the heavenly Christ? This is a really difficult question, and attempts at a solution are being constantly made. Vatican II attempted this recently when reflecting on the relation Church-world. In the language of imagery, we can say: The Church is the Body of Christ. He is in heaven, it is upon earth. To explain their relation, Paul tries two ways. At times he pushes to the end his paradox of "already made": the end of time (the "eschatology") is already realized, already we are seated in heaven with Christ (Col. 2:12; Eph. 2:16). Sometimes in a more realistic way, he accepts the distinction between the heavenly Christ and his body, but, to maintain the relation, explains that Jesus is the "head" of this "body," which receives its flow of life from him (he had already made this discovery).[103] As Christ is the Lord of the cosmos, the body of Christ which benefits from his life is no longer merely the ensemble of the Christians, the Church, but also the ensemble of beings visible and invisible and the entire universe which is his "pleroma" or "his fullness." This then is the final statement about the reconciliation between ourselves and the world, which makes Paul stand in amazement in the face of what he calls from now on the "mystery."

THE MYSTERY made known by Paul.

"In biblical theology, one mystery does not mean the unknowable, but that which God has kept to himself to make known (at the end of time) through his Christ. First of all, we are not treating of the secrets of the divine nature considered in itself, but of the **mystery of the conduct of God in reference to man:** the eternal plan of salvation" (Augrain). That which he had in his heart from all eternity, God makes known to Paul so that he may pour it out upon the world as a festal song: salvation is for all men, pagans as well as Jews, for all creation.

Now take a look at this letter. You will recognize the basic themes which Paul always develops, but taken up in a new way and especially with an accent on the marvelous, which rises to a crescendo and shines out in the Letter to the Ephesians.

Greeting and thanksgiving: This is terminated with the hymn which forms at the same time the doctrinal exposé of this letter (1:1-20). Paul immediately applies this doctrine to his faithful (1:21-23).

Starting with 1:24 the explanation of the doctrine becomes polemic. Under two forms:

1:24-2:5: Speaking of pagan converts, Paul restates his authority: as "apostle of the Gentiles" he hands on to them this mystery which God has entrusted to him for them. But as a model for every preacher and every soldier, before proclaiming it, he bears it in his own flesh.[104]

2:5-23: Here is his head-on attack on the errors of his Christians. He has only one thing to say again and again: Salvation comes only through Christ, this Christ, who is superior to the angels and who communicates to us his life, to whom we have been united in baptism (2:11-13). This Lordship he acquires through his suffering on the Cross.

3:4: All that is left is the application: live in keeping with this teaching! "From the moment that you are raised with Christ, seek the things from on high, where Christ is found" (3:1-4). General advice: refuse to sin, and establish the universal brotherhood (3:5-17). Particular advice: all the daily life lived "in the Lord," husbands and wives, parents and children, slaves and masters, And live all this in an apostolic spirit: pray and let your life be a call to those outside (3:18-4:6).

PHILEMON

One person who had to listen to everything that Paul has to say on the master-slave relationship is Onesimus. He had fled from the house of his master, Philemon, a Christian of Colossae, and sought asylum near Paul. Paul converted him and through baptism "has begotten him in his chains." Now the apostle sends him back to his master, but accompanied with a note which remains "one of the masterpieces of all literature" (Benoit).

"The Note to Philemon" reveals to us a Paul full of tenderness and cleverness, who could have commanded but preferred to make delicate suggestions instead. Beyond what it teaches us about Paul and his affections for the members of his communities, we have a great interest in the solution that the apostle gives to one of the most dramatic problems of the hour: slavery. Some are surprised that Paul does not demand immediate abolition of the custom. He does not do it, it seems, for two reasons. He thinks that the Parousia is near: then it will be of little importance what social class we are in. The essential is to be united with Christ who comes to save us. "The Christian does not focus his attention on the immediate, he focuses on the real" (Preiss). Christianity is not bound to this precise structure. In it Christianity joins the real man in that which he has of the true: united to Christ (cf. 1 Cor. 8:10). And especially it does better than to regulate a precise problem, no matter how grave it is, it recalls the principle that will lead men to settle all problems, and in this it traces for the Church its line of conduct: as such the Church is not to be mixed in social or political affairs; human organizations (political, union) will do this, but the Church is to recall unceasingly the principle which should guide these organizations. This principle is respect for the person of the other, no matter who he is, because he is a man (and hence an equal, even though a slave), because he is a son of God. It is surprising too that a note treating of a strictly personal matter between Paul and Philemon, "a case of tact and professional secrecy par excellence," begins and is completed in a letter associating the whole community with Philemon. A precious instruction: "In the Body of Christ, personal affairs are no longer private" (Preiss); personal life and reactions of each Christian involve the entire community.

The human community: this is the theme which Paul develops so magnificently in the great synthesis which he now sets out to write and of which Colossians was only the outline.

LETTER TO THE EPHESIANS
"All that you bear of mankind . . ."

> "Everything that you bring to a sacrament, the sacrament takes on, except sin. Your body in the Eucharist, your will in Penitence. . . . Why not, in baptism which is the very sacrament of the reunion of man with God, everything that you bear of mankind, beyond your individuality!"
>
> P.-A. Lesort, **The Wind Blows Where It Wills**

The sunrise on "Great Paradise." A long ascent in the night, disturbed only by the grating of the nails of the hobnail boots and the metallic click of the pick. A fairyland of ice, cold wind which gives color to powdery dust of the snowy ridges in bare but perfect lines. A little rock glazed over. The peak—the Alps offer us 4,000: turning Italian from the chain of Mont Blanc in the hard and abrupt lines; so many friendly peaks recognized in passing: the Oisans over there, where the Barre des Ecrins is gradually set on fire by the yellow sun. A sense of wealth, of definitive fullness. So many other paths incomparably more difficult: this permits us to gather them all in the rich offertory of a "Mass on top of the world": "Accept O Lord, this total Host, which Creation moved by your attraction, presents to you in the new dawn . . . ."

A sentiment analogous to that which I experience in starting on this encyclical that Paul sends to all the Christians in the valley of Lycus.[105] After we have labored through the wanderings of his thought, in the slow or blunt rhythm of the letters, which we have suffered in the abrupt division of his theology, happily interspersed with so many notes of tenderness, on coming out on this peak, we experience a sense of total fullness. Vast horizons in unending lines are enkindled before our eyes. Everything becomes transparent in the light of God. It takes real effort to snatch yourself from it.

This is the unique peak where everything takes its origin: the glorious Christ, triumphant in heaven, completing the plan of God which is to unite all men in him.

Paul sings out this plan from the beginning in one of the most beautiful poems that he has written (1:3-14). History is oriented, or rather attracted, toward this ultimate hearth from which it already burns: the total Christ who "will recapitulate," will gather together all beings in himself. The purpose of our history which God placed from the beginning when creating it, when choosing each of us to be sons in his Son (cf. OT, pp. 7-9). Thus Jesus is the "alpha and the Omega," the beginning and the end of all things, the purpose or goal toward which we go, and the means whereby we are given entrance. The Spirit is given to us as the down payment of our inheritance, anticipating this definitive life in us, making us enter personally into the redemption which Christ acquired for us in his blood. Son in the Son through the Spirit, we shall be and always are, for the praise of the Father. The formula (as if we could reduce Christian living to an algebraic "formula") is almost complete: toward the Father, in the Son, through the Spirit. We have only to add one term, in the Church, which is not really added but develops the second term.[106]

In the Church: Paul's prayer (1:15-22; 3:14-21) has a single object: that God give us the "knowledge" of this Mystery of which Paul is the minister (3:1-13). "Knowledge," not only or first of all in intellectual act, but a tension of the entire being which casts us body and soul, with our entire plan of man, into Christ. Or better perhaps, a passivity, supremely active of him who allows himself to be borne entirely into the depths of this love. Behold: the Church, the union of all the men, forming the body of Christ, bringing with them the entire cosmos. There are three points here to be considered further:

1. **All Men: One in Jesus Christ** (2:11-22; 4:1-16)

> "I am sure that the grace of God transforms love into an image of the very love of God. The Church proclaims this by the sacrament of marriage. But friendship? What does it do to friendship? What it does do, will it do with the bond which attaches me to my close friends?"
>
> P.-A. Lesort

Paul starts the problem from its most difficult aspect, in which all the others will be solved: the union of these two parts of mankind: Jews and Gentiles. Jews and Gentiles remain for him a sort of symbol of the impossible unity. In Rom. 9:11, he had expressed the hope of this reunion even though he had some misgivings. Here, he considers it as realized in the body of Christ: "In his person, he killed hatred, creating the two into a single new man in his person." The human brotherhood is sought painfully through all the "internationales." Our sins raise up all the barriers: race, social classes, ideologies. But beyond these, all our human friendships are already begetting this brotherhood. And this brotherhood sees its own face in the face of Christ covered with our spittle, but transfigured by the resurrection. All human friendship is already a call and an outline of this unity in the Church which gives it its fullness.[107]

2. **The Church, "the Body of Christ, the Wife of Christ"**

Would you say that these two images are contradictory? No: really they are complementary. These realities are so complex that we can sound this mystery only by photographing it from different angles. To say that mankind is the body of Christ expresses indeed the identity that exists between the two. But do we avoid a sort of "pan-Christism," an impersonal dilution of men into the being of Christ? The image of the union between husband and wife maintains the personality proper to each of the partners. But do they not remain **two** in a single flesh? This was, I think, the genius of Paul, after he grasped immediately the complexity of this point, to present our union in Christ under this double image. For this, he had at his disposal two biblical themes: the Temple, and marriage.

The Church: The body of Christ

We have seen (OT, pp. 211-216) how God made his people pass from the notion of a material temple, a place where God dwells, to the notion of a spiritual temple, a people of believers, where he wishes to be present, to this reality finally of the personal body of Christ where God is visibly present and to the "mystical body." This mystical body of Christ is the personal body of Jesus dead and raised from the dead into which, through baptism, all the believers are "incorporated." Paul picks up here a traditional teaching, but develops it in view of the new perspectives which he has discovered. In one of the rare passages of this letter, a rather difficult one (4:1-16), he shows us how it is through his body that Christ exercises his Lordship over the world. After he has insisted upon its unity (4:1-6), he quotes Ps. 68 according to the rabbinical tradition and comments on only two words: "descent" and this "ascending" (the incarnation or the descent into Sheol and the ascension) affect the personal body of Christ, but it is "to fulfill all things," to create his body. And he does this in two ways, by two "gifts." The first gift is his Spirit:

"To each of us has been given grace according to the measure of the Gift of Christ."[108] The other gift—it is the "Gifts" which he has made to his body: the ministries, the services. "Christ gave the apostles, the prophets, the shepherds . . . in order to organize the saints for the construction of the body of Christ" (4:11-12). Hence beyond these functional differences, the Church is a unique body, structured from on high by the Spirit and the ministers (4:13-16).

The Church, the Bride of Christ (5:21-33)

Paul had already spoken of presenting his churches to Christ as a pure virgin (1 Cor. 11:2), but he had never reached this perfection in his thought: the Church.[109] Is this virgin pure and without blemish, to whom he has given himself as a nuptial bath, baptism which draws its efficacy from the faith that accompanies it? Thus cleansed, made holy, it can be united to him with bonds so intimate that the bonds of marriage are only an image. But they are really an image, and more than an image: a "sacrament," an "efficacious image." And here, given as if in passing is the very foundation for the spirituality of marriage: when a man and woman give themselves to each other, they realize, or make real, the union of Christ and his Church. Not only for us who see them—and have to see their tenderness in order to grasp the freshness of the love of Christ—they are an image of the tenderness of God for us; and again they make this real; they give to each other the love of Christ and they help to make this love of God for mankind more present in our world (cf. OT, pp. 61f., 151, 153f., 218ff., 225).[110] After he has opened such perspectives we understand that Paul has no trouble in passing over to the application. In fact, this applies first to Christian married people (husbands and wives, live in keeping with this teaching), and on the same score it applies to the lives of all the baptized, since marriage is an image of our life of love with Jesus Christ (application: 4:17 to the end).

However, the amazed glance of Paul before this "mystery" does not stop here either. The body of Christ is not only composed of mankind whom he unites to himself, but of the entire cosmos.

3. The Church: The "Pleroma" of Christ (1:23)

We have seen above that the term "pleroma" signifies for Paul the ensemble of creation giving to Christ his "fullness." And now he states that this very Church is his "fullness." Besides the Christians who are the "body" in the full sense of the word, the Church takes on in some way all these forces of regenerated creation in which the energies of the Risen Christ who fills the entire universe, pours out (4:10) as he is fulfilled by it (1:23). The Risen Christ is the initial cell of the new world: in him, God has recreated mankind (4:24) and "recapitulated" the universe (1:10), (Benoit).

\- - - - - - -

When he writes these letters, Paul is in prison, but his captivity is nearing an end: "Get a bed ready for me!" he writes to Philemon, "for I hope to come to your place, through your prayers." Undoubtedly it was a case of the charges being dismissed, since his accusers made sure that they did not appear.

63-66 (or 67): These are the four or five last years of Paul and it is difficult to establish the exact chronology. Only the indications from the letters to Timothy and Titus allow us to figure out his intense activity, by logging his trips here and there in the entire Mediterranean basin. Set free in the spring of 63, he may have set out immediately for Spain as he had planned in Rom. 15:23. Clement of Rome, in 96, implies this, and old authors state it. The Letter to Titus tells us that he founded some communities in Crete: he entrusted them to his disciple. He spent the winter in Nicopolis, in Greece. When he writes the first Letter to Timothy he has just left Ephesus for Macedonia, but is counting on coming back there soon. Finally his second letter shows him to us again as a prisoner in Rome. The captivity, this time, is severe. Onesiphorus had to look for him very painstakingly, just to find him. No one helps him during his court trial. Some of the brothers abandon him and make trouble for him. Only a few friends are present, and as with Christ in his suffering, humbly he begs for a little tenderness: "Timothy, hasten to come before winter . . . ."

At Tre Fontani, Paul is beheaded. What is happening? Everything is a grace or favoring.

IV. "Do Not Fail the Church . . ."

The "Pastoral" Letters

> "To suffer through the Church is nothing, we must suffer in the Church. And we owe our suffering to each other, it must circulate like blood in the very blood of this body which Jesus Christ has given to us to become members. Neuville is not failing the Church. There is so much which is failing him!"
>
> P.-A. Lesort, **The Wind Blows Where It Wills**

When I was a young boy, I stopped at times at the home of an old pastor in the neighborhood, a sturdy peasant of the class of the pastor of Torcy. He had had to give up an important post because of a dispute with his bishop and had spent his life as a priest, from that time on, in a small country parish. We spoke of everything and of nothing, and never did he know what a tremendous mark these rare visits made on me. The thing that struck me the most: he was happy. An old priest, in the evening of a long life dedicated to God, kept **joy**. This is the impression I get when I read the Pastoral Letters.[111] Paul planted Christ in the entire known world, he founded churches, he knew now that his end was very near, and so he wrote to two young men whom he had formed, whom he had ordained, and to whom he now hands on the torch. He gives them bits of advice for their ministry—and priests without end reread these letters to find here the best of their spirituality—but above all, despoiled of everything, abandoned, he expresses his joy. Less exuberant than in Philippians, this joy is first of all the serenity of him who "knows in whom he has believed," confidence in Jesus Christ of whom he sings, as in every other letter. An apostle of Jesus Christ, he contemplates in his hands, with full amazement, the only treasure that he has jealously kept: the faith.

Letters to Titus and Timothy

"Servant of God: Apostle of Jesus Christ . . ." (Tit. 1:1-4)

It is perhaps in this greeting of this Letter to Titus that he gives us his most complete definition of the apostolate. He places it first of all in the ensemble of the plan of God. This returning of a mentality of which Vatican II (**Decree on the Church**) marks the flowering forth, by treating first of the people of God before speaking of the hierarchy, Paul did not have to do. For him, before all, there is God who has chosen men, in Jesus Christ, in order to save them. This is the mystery revealed in the Scriptures[112] and especially to him, Paul, a mystery from which men can benefit only if they have the knowledge or awareness. Thus Paul (and after him, bishops and priests) is chosen by God as his servant to be the "sent one," the "apostle," of Jesus Christ. Hence what is expected first of him is that he be faithful: "keep the deposit which has been entrusted to you," he repeats to Timothy and Titus. They are to be at the service of God.[113] The Church, serving and poor! This service he fulfills especially by the preaching of Christ. The purpose of the apostolate? It is unique: being realized in three stages. He must engender **faith** in his hearers, bring them to turn themselves toward God with their entire being, but with a faith that is knowledge or awareness, i.e., which inaugurates with God a life of deep intimacy, "knowledge of the truth ordered to piety," this interior and exterior religious attitude which is born of a mutual affection. This faith will stir up **hope** that is unfailing because it is founded on only reality which cannot deceive: the fidelity of God. Thus they will obtain **salvation,** definitive union with God.

"Keep the Deposit . . ." I Have Ended My Course— I Have Kept the Faith" (2 Tim. 4:7)

Despoiled of everything, the only treasure that remains his, and to which he clings above everything else: the deposit of the faith which God has entrusted to him on the far-off day in Damascus, which he now transmits and which the Church will receive and will transmit. We have heard him proclaim this through the length of his life. There is nothing new in these epistles, except perhaps the entirely new value which is given to everything by the last words of a man who entrusts to you the truth of his life.

Meditate on these very weighted texts in which he sums up again the essential of the Christian life: (1 Tim. 1:12-17; 2 Tim. 1:6-14; cf. Tit. 1:1-4; 2:13-14; 3:4-6). Always the same key ideas: Love of God, Jesus Christ the Savior, and the "wonderful testimony he has given us before Pilate" (1 Tim. 6:11-16), baptism, salvation through grace and not through the law or our works,[114] the Holy Spirit. Two new stresses, at least through the insistence which he puts on them: the "humanity of God," his love, his "love of mankind" (Tit. 3:4-7);[115] the universality of salvation. "God wills that all men be saved and come to the knowledge of the truth" (1 Tim. 2:1-8; 4:8-10), a statement of extraordinary importance in that it permits us to hope that, even though there is a hell, there are no men who enter eternal death there.

For the Christian life you find the advice that Paul always gave to each group of Christians, basing it on their baptism. Note a strong summary of his thought: "For the clean everything is clean" (Tit. 1:15), and a surprising statement about the impossibility of separating faith and daily life in its most human aspects: "If anyone does not take care of his own, especially those who live with him, he has denied the faith: he is worse than a heretic" (1 Tim. 5:8). Who is there in confession who thinks to accuse himself of this "moral heresy"?

At the very hour in which his painful death is about to complete his baptism and render true and definitive the union which he has consecrated with Jesus Christ, instinctively Paul finds, to express his prayer, these hymns which undoubtedly he very often sang in the liturgy of baptism: 2 Tim. 1:9-10; 1 Tim. 3:16; Tit. 3:4-8; (cf. with 1 Pet. 1:4-5)[116] and the wonderful song Paul lived before he handed it on to us.

> Remember Jesus Christ raised from the dead. . . .
> If we die with him, we will live with him,
> If we suffer with him, we shall reign with him!
>
> 2 Tim. 2:8-13

[1]For this difference between John and Paul, cf. OT, pp. 136-174.

[2]Acts 22:15; 26:5; 22:25-28.

[3]Cf. what we said in OT, pp. 169-170.

[4]At least to certain texts of the Scriptures: it seems that the Pharisees had "forgotten" certain prophecies like the Songs of the Suffering Servant, or the poems of Zechariah, about the King who is pierced (OT, pp. 114-116).

[5]Without paradox we can say that Paul, already before his conversion, because he was a trained theologian, understood better than Peter the revolutionary novelty of the sermons that Peter was preaching. When he becomes a Christian, he will be more in a position to search out this mystery.

[6]We have three accounts of the conversion of Paul on the road to Damascus in the Acts of the Apostles. Then there is what could be called a fourth account in the letters of Paul. (We usually speak of the "conversion" of Paul. This is not really an accurate term. A Jew does not have to be "converted" because he already believes in the true God, just as we do. He merely has to go to the completion of his faith to believe in the true God who speaks to us in his Son, Jesus). Each of these accounts has a different point of view which explains their differences.

Acts 9:1-30: The only biographical account. Luke would have to collect his material in Damascus, perhaps from the lips of Ananias. In any case the event is seen by the persecuted Church.

Acts 22:1-21: Paul himself gives this account before the Jews and he speaks "in his own defense." He is especially careful to show that his change of attitude is not betrayal of Judaism, but fidelity to the religion of their fathers.

Acts 26:2-23: Paul is speaking before King Agrippa. This is the most personal account, in which he shows the place God has kept for him in the realization of his plan. We must add Gal. 1:11-17, in which, in a few technical words, he gives the theology of the event, and 1 Cor. 15:8-10; Phil. 3:5.

[7]An extraordinary event in the life of Paul. But an event as extraordinary as each of us has lived on the day of our baptism. In one instant, God has taken possession of us to make us his child. How, then, can we take part in a baptism or think of our own without feeling somewhat of this newness which so moved Gabriel Marcel? If the "orders" of Pascal are true, this passing from natural life to the life of the child of God is infinitely more important than was the passing from animal to human existence for the primate.

[8]Pardon the simplicity of this outline. It will be filled out and,

I hope, clarified by the reading of the pages given to the different epistles.

[9]Cf. OT, p. 176, and in this book, p. 9.

[10]We shall come back to this when we are reading the Letter to the Romans. For the moment note the importance of reading the Scriptures "in the good sense." Only by starting with Christ and by "coming back" to him do we get the entire meaning. To study original sin by starting with Genesis is to take things backwards.

[11]"In Christ": a formula specifically Pauline which will be met in different forms more than 160 times in his letters.

[12]In their own jargon, the specialists will speak of "anticipated eschatology." Paul merely explains in more technical terms what Jesus had said, and of which the original community had had intuition (cf. above p. 24.)

[13]A difficult balance to maintain: some sects (Jehovah's Witnesses) think only of this final or definitive end and refuse to live in our world. The temptation of Christianity is to be contented with what has already been done, to keep the faith while losing hope. And it is on the debris of Christian hope that Marxist hope could one day be born.

[14]The chronology of the life of Paul is not easy to establish. A certain number of the dates given here are only approximate.

[15]The history here is quite obscure and tangled. I follow the reconstruction proposed by Father Benoit. Cf. also the notes in the Jerusalem Bible on Acts 11:30 and 15:1.

[16]We are treating of the "peaceful cohabitation" among Christians come from Judaism, formed from their childhood to respect certain rules of ritual cleanliness (in matters of food and cooking particularly), and the converts from among the Gentiles who have no scruples in these matters. In this area where the Jewish converts are numerous, the friction is in danger of being increased and multiplied. To avoid this friction, James, very wisely, takes practical measures. In a different context, Paul will adopt a rule of conduct quite similar, except that he will not make any laws but will leave the matter up to the conscience of each one (1 Cor. 8:10; Rom. 14).

[17]We usually distinguish three missionary trips besides the captivity. Cf. the map in the Jerusalem Bible. Note especially

that the second is marked by a prolonged stay in Corinth, the third, in Ephesus.

[18]The very conduct of God with Abraham (OT, pp. 29-30) and with each of us. Guided by the Spirit, we do not become passive, but inventive, in all docility.

[19]The formula is beautiful but not very exact: the Church of Rome was already founded (by whom?). Starting from Troas, Luke is a companion of Paul.

[20]We shall see later in what sense, for there is already quite surely, in the community, a moral teaching. The appearance of Paul before Gallio, the brother of the philosopher Seneca, and proconsul of Achaia is one of the principal points of contact for establishing the chronology of the apostle.

[21]A. Brunot, "Tensions et unité de vie chez l'apôtre, Paul": an intensely moving article which appeared in *Vie et Tensions,* supplement to *Masses Ouvrieres,* 191.

[22]Acts 20:18-36. Look up the wonderful (and easy) commentary of J. Dupont: "The Discourse in Miletus. Pastoral Testament of Paul" (*Coll. Lectio Divina,* Cerf, 1963).

[23]Paul has brought Christianity to Rome. Hence Luke can complete his book here. The Acts of the Apostles have reached the heart of the empire.

[24]What books are to be consulted by anyone who would like to go more into depth in the thought of Paul? The bibliography is immense and varied. My favorite is the book by A. Brunot, *St. Paul and His Message* (Coll. "Je sais, Je crois," Fayard, 1958). Ch. Augrain, *Paul of Spiritual Life* (Fleurus, 1962), or A. George, *The Gospel of Paul* (Coll. "Foi vivante," Cerf) would help you in the reading of the epistles. L. Cerfaux, *L'itineraire spiritual de St. Paul* (Cerf, 1966) is good and will eventually be an introduction to the other more technical works of the author. C. H. Dodd, *St. Paul Today* (Edinburgh University, 1964) is at times contestable (ch. 7 for example), but so understanding and suggestive in the good sense of the word. For meditation: B. Lyonnet, *Initiation into the Spiritual Doctrine of St. Paul. Ten Meditations on the Text of the Epistles* (Coll. "Vie Chretienne"). A biography? Take J. Cantinat, *Life of St. Paul the Apostle* (Apostolate des editions, 1964) or the larger but more living, J. Holzner, *Paul of Tarsus.* But above all, read St. Paul.

[25]We have thousands of letters from antiquity. Writing was a

big work. Even the shorthand, at least the system invented by Tiro, the secretary of Cicero, did not go fast. They have estimated that writing a letter like the one to the Thessalonians, on papyrus, would take a week at least. Not less than a month for the Letter to the Romans! Silas (who edited also the first Letter of Peter) and Timothy wrote under the dictation of Paul. Perhaps, at times, they redacted freely on a theme given them by their master. In any case, the thought was really Paul's and he quickly acquired the habit of signing his letters in "large writing" to authenticate them and fight against the forgers.

The epistolary form has its rules, codified by the "manuals of good manners" of the period. The salutation: "To Caligula Alavacomgetepus, prefect of the Gauls, I, Gracchus Nengetepus, send greetings!" It could be in the good taste here to add a formula of thanksgiving to the divinity and a prayer for the one to whom you were writing, and friends. Paul gets into this literary form and yet he develops the formula to give them a very personal tone. The banal "greetings," becomes "Grace and peace" and the prayer will be at times very long (except when he is angry and is concerned with getting to the point!). As a closing he will wish his Christians: "The grace of the Lord Jesus be with you all," but he also knows how to free himself from sanctioned formulae: "I love you much in Jesus Christ."

[26]Unless the Letter of James was already written, which is very doubtful.

[27]It is true, this outline of schema is not always so clear. Set about finding it. A thrilling work: make yourself an anthology of the points of doctrine on which Paul bases himself. This would allow you to see what appeared fundamental to Paul and his Christians and to note if you base your life on the same strong points.

[28]A case of incest. How would we react? Undoubtedly: "This is not done, this is not good, this is forbidden." or, "This is contrary to the natural law."

[29]Paul wrote two letters within a few months' interval. They are so much alike we could easily put them in parallel columns. Thus we have to study them together. Rather than an ordered reading, I have attempted here a synthesis of their teaching. This likeness has made some people think that the second letter is

not the work of Paul, but a skillful forgery. The reasons given are not convincing.

[30]I do not like the word "return," "coming back." It is not biblical. It gives the impression that between the "coming" of Jesus, 2,000 years ago, and his "return," there is an interim in which he no longer is. Jesus came, he comes unceasingly through the whole of history, he will come one day definitively.

[31]Usually the only teaching retained from these epistles is the "eschatology," i.e., the teaching about the coming of Christ in the end. This is a betrayal of Paul. As a good scenario he tells us what he has to say but he wants to think. A Jew, nourished on the hope of his entire people, speaking to Greeks who are aware of this great holiday when they welcome their sovereign in a triumphal procession making his "entry" (Parousia) into the town, he uses Jewish and Greek expressions to which we must not give more importance than to some images. On the "when" of this coming (which bothered the Thessalonians so much), Paul tells us: it is near (he will develop this point), it will be sudden (therefore keep vigil), it is not immediate.

[32]Does this suppress my freedom? Here we are in the order of *love.* When an engaged man, or a married man, feels that he is "obliged" to do something *because he loves,* is he less free? Love does not destroy freedom but makes it rise higher.

[33]L. M. Dewailly in his wonderful little book, *Lajeune Église de Thessalonique* (Cerf, 1963).

[34]See the study of J. Dupont in his commentary already quoted, *Le discours de Milet* (Cerf).

[35]A possible reconstruction of the facts: in the course of his third mission (53-58), Paul writes a first letter (lost, unless it is 2 Cor. 6:14-7:1?). From Ephesus, following on the delegation of the family of Chloe, around Easter, 57, he writes our first letter. The calm that was re-established has been disturbed anew. Paul makes a lightning but painful visit to Corinth. He promises to come back and stay a longer time. After his departure: new intrigues. Disgusted, Paul puts off his trip and writes his "letter in tears," also lost, unless it is 2 Cor. 10-13. He sends Titus for the news. Meanwhile, he has stirred up the silversmiths of Ephesus, and he is obliged to flee. He departs for Macedonia where Titus rejoins him. The bearer of good news: the painful letter has had effect. Filled with joy, he sends Titus back to

Corinth; then from Philippi, he writes our second letter toward the end of 57. He then sets out for Corinth and here during his stay of three months, he writes to the Romans.

[36]In this letter more than any other, Paul utilizes the outline of the reviewing of life. In the reading of each fact, and before going further in the reading, try to find similar facts in your life and the life of those around you. You will see how up-to-date Paul is.

[37]He is not treating of marriage for itself in this passage. He will give the spirituality of marriage in his Letter to the Ephesians, ch. 5. Perhaps you may say that he develops in between. But we should stop tagging him a misogynist or a Jansenist!

[38]The ever present importance of this principle: we can and we must be Christian whether rich or poor, whether engaged in politics or trade-unionism to the right or to the left, single or married—in every situation we must be "servants" of the Christ who has redeemed us with his blood.

[39]Paul then considers two particular cases, and gives the solution for his times. The times have changed and the specialists have difficulty in seeing exactly what he meant.

[40]"To construct" or "to edify," a key notion to which Paul constantly refers and which recurs in his letters as a theme. But now this word "edify," and "edifying," has lost its meaning for us.

[41]Example of Paul: he had the right to be materially supported by those to whom he preached the Good News. He preferred to deprive himself of this right for the sake of the weak Christians who might believe that he was preaching just to make a living.

[42]The accounts that we have in our Gospels were redacted afterwards. Thus we have four accounts of the Last Supper which undoubtedly go back to two different liturgical traditions: Mark, followed by Matthew, transmits to us the liturgical account of the Judeo-Christian churches. Paul, followed by Luke, gives us the tradition of the Greek churches. Which of the two traditions, Mark or Paul, is the more primitive?

[43]Consider the charism of John XXIII launching the Council and opening the Church to the world, the charism of the writer putting his pen to the service of the truth, the Christian who has the charism to speak of Christ to his comrades, the art of revealing to others, by his love, that God is love.

[44]This is not to condemn the Church to stagnation. Each

Christian moved by the Spirit has the duty to bring it forward, boldly, always with humility, ready to submit to the teaching of the Church.

[45]For these first Christians, the resurrection of Christ, far from being a point that gives rise to difficulty, is on the contrary the solid base on which we can support ourselves.

[46]Cf. p. 131, the note on "anthropology."

[47]It is a combination, some think, of several short notes by Paul. 6:14-7:1 would perhaps be the first letter to the Corinthians, a lost letter. Chapter 9 would be a note to the Church of Achaia in general (doubling chapter 8 written for the Corinthians). Chapters 10-13 would be the "letter written in tears."

[48]Note the Trinitarian formula: a probable allusion to the Christian initiation: baptism and confirmation (1:21-22).

[49]6:14-7:1: this morsel outside its context would be perhaps a quotation of a text of Essene inspiration?

[50]Ch. 8: the note to the Church in Corinth; ch. 9 a sort of encyclical for the Church of Achaia?

[51]Perhaps this is the "letter in tears."

[52]To keep him from becoming proud, God has fixed in him a "thorn in the flesh." Some of the worst possible explanations have been given for this thorn. It treats almost certainly of this interior suffering of seeing the Jews, his brothers by race, refusing Christ. A suffering which is at the same time a handicap for the gospel: God prepared for himself a people to welcome the Messiah, and when he presents himself, this people refuses him. Is this not the proof that this is not the real Messiah? Think of the suffering of two missionaries, Catholic and Protestant, coming to preach the Christ together, but basing this on the "proof" that Christ is not God: the only proof that he has left us, is it not actually unity? (cf. John 17:21).

[53]The "outer man" is all that which is dead in us since our baptism . . . but we will need the whole of our life to put him to death. Always the paradox of "already done" and "yet to be done."

[54]It is important to understand well this desire of death. We shall come back to it in Philippians, p. 125.

[55]Did Paul have at this time as clear an idea of the Trinity as we can have, three distinct Persons? 3:17 could lead us to doubt

it. 13:13 however will make it clear for us (cf. Jerusalem Bible and the note e). His thought was still searching.

[56]Julius Caesar, *Histoire de la Gaul.*

[57]The original Celts of Asia were settled in Europe and in France in the sixth century B.C. In the third century, some tribes came down toward Macedonia (where they will be defeated) and into Asia Minor. Fixed in the northern region, they will be defeated by the Romans in 189 B.C. Cf. in Rome, in the Capitoline, the beautiful statue of the "Dying Gaul," a witness of the art of Pergamus, who will allow them a wide autonomy. In 25 B.C., their kingdom became a Roman province. Once, Rome will annex to their province other towns from the South, those which Paul will evangelize at the time of his first missionary trip. Some have said at times that these people would be the people for whom this letter was intended, the same people as those for whom the Galatians was written. Invented to settle the pretended literary problems (cf. introduction in Jerusalem Bible), this solution scarcely holds water.

[58]The criterion that he gives for recognizing it is important, for it is always the foundation for the infallibility of the Church: the "Christian sense," i.e., the deep or profound experience and life of the ensemble of Christians whom the Holy Spirit animates.

[59]"Justification" is the fact, realized once and for all, of being "past with Jesus Christ." It carries with it a negative aspect—destruction of sin—and another positive aspect—union in Christ for a new life which must grow unceasingly in order to blossom forth into holiness. We shall come back to this in the letter to the Romans, p. 112.

[60]To pray is not first of all to say something to God or to ask him something. It is not even "to lift up one's soul toward God." It is becoming conscious that in our heart, the Spirit is unceasingly united to the Father, is turned toward him, "speaks" to him; it is to allow oneself to be carried into this prayer of the Spirit in order that the vital attitude which he expresses in us may become ours: "Abba! Father!" It is to allow oneself to be carried along by "this living water which whispers in me and says within me: Come to the Father" (Ignatius of Antioch) (cf. Rom. 8:14-39).

[61]You must read the article by S. Lyonnet, "Christian Freedom and the Law of the Spirit," in the periodical, *Christus,* No. 4, 1954.

It is used again in the book by S. Lyonnet, *Vie selon l'Ésprit* (Cerf, 1965).

If we are free why are there still commandments—and especially the commandments of the Church? "Everything is done," we are free, delivered uniquely to the dynamism of the Spirit, but . . . "everything is still to be done," and insofar as we are sinners, certain restrictions are not only useful but necessary to keep us under the possession of the Spirit. But insofar as we do perform this act and refuse to perform that act, *only* because it is commanded or forbidden, to that extent we are no longer Christian.

[62]We cannot but cite this dialogue of the "just": "Do you know the legend of St. Dimitri?—No.—He had a rendenzvous in the steppe with God himself and he was hurrying to this when he met a peasant whose carriage was bogged down in the mud. St. Dimitri helped him. The mud was really thick and the pothole was deep. It took them an hour. When he was finished, St. Dimitri ran to the meeting. But God was no longer there.—And then?—And then there are those who always arrive late because there are too many coaches stuck in the mud and too many brothers to help" (Act 4).

[63]For those who would like to go deeper into this question: G. Martelet, *Victoire sur la mort, Chronique sociale de France* (1962).

[64]Some believe in God to keep a hope for living (the only "thing" to which they cling), for a "compensation" in the hereafter. Some come to confession because they have the "courage" to sin, but they do not have the courage to bear the weight of their sins.

[65]To see how a certain revolt against God can be one of the paths toward the true God, read again Job (cf. OT, pp. 138-145).

[66]The only community that Paul writes to without having founded it himself. Who did found this community? We do not know, but it was founded quite early. For a long time the Christians will be confused with the Jews, by the civil authority, which is an advantage for awhile but eventually brings with it some trials such as their expulsion by Claudius, 49-50. Paul, apostle of the Gentiles, wishes to crown his apostolate by preaching Christ in the capital of the empire. In this letter, he prepares for his coming.

[67]All the commentators note that this letter is remarkably well constructed. But their agreement stops there. Each one proposes

a different plan in which the main division remains noticeably the same.

[68]And already partly in our own personal death. But Paul, who always thinks collectively, who thinks "Church," scarcely considers this aspect.

[69]Paul knew good pagans. From this condemnation of the ensemble, we do not have the right to conclude the condemnation of each individual.

[70]It is characteristic that it is here that Vatican II (*Gaudium et Spes*) came to seek the biblical basis for original sin.

[71]If we want a comparison, we can perhaps consider Leverrier discovering the planet Neptune: by calculation alone and because of the consequences which he knew, he arrived by induction at the existence of this planet, which was then confirmed by observation. The evident difference here is that we are not treating of a human "induction" of Paul, but of "a revelation" which God makes to him as he meditates on the mystery of Christ.

[72]So also for us: it is not by mulling over our sins that we shall come to regret them, but by contemplating Jesus Christ on the Cross.

[73]The Church at this moment asks us to renew our baptismal promises, i.e., to become conscious of what we have been living with Christ until then and to declare that we are always in accord.

[74]For a first discovery of this letter, we could very well begin with this passage.

[75]Paul here returns to the past experience of the sinner and his justification. But something of this tragic turmoil remains in the Christian: insofar as he is not "saved," he is aware of this interior division in the "flesh" which struggles against the "spirit" (cf. Gal. 5:17-26). Note well the meaning of these words: "flesh," "carnal," for us mean "sensual." To the "sin of the flesh" we automatically contrast the "sin of the Spirit," pride. For Paul, "flesh" designates *our entire being insofar as it is opposed to God.* Hence pride is the sin of the *flesh* par excellence (cf. p. 131, the more technical note on Pauline anthropology).

[76]The only community also from whom he accepted financial help. This was the greatest praise he could give the Philippians. He was so sure of their love that would not run the risk of alienating his freedom. We shall always speak of "the" letter to the Philippians in order to make it simple. It is not impossible

that they combined three letters of Paul when they wanted other churches to benefit from what he had to say: 4:10-20; 1:1-3; 4:2-9; and 3:2-4:1. Where and when were they written? From Rome in 61-63? Or from Ephesus toward the years 54-57? The question remains open.

[77]If you may do this in your Bible, we suggest that you underline in different colors these three words: *Jesus, Gospel, Joy* or their equivalents.

[78]St. Paul undoubtedly gathered it partly from the liturgical treasure of the primitive Church (cf. p. 36).

[79]To get to the heart of this letter, and to the heart of Paul, one of the best ways is through the "Spiritual Writings" of Sister Elizabeth of the Trinity.

[80]When the Old Testament speaks of man as a "stranger" on this earth, it wishes to express only this magnificent conviction that the earth belongs to God and that man, on this earth, his home country, is not in his own home: he is the guest of God.

[81]In this very beautiful little book—all of whose conclusions the Catholic may not be able to accept—*Immortality of the Soul and the Resurrection of the Dead?* (Delachaux, 1956).

[82]Cf. Rom. 9:3. This is also what Moses thought: because of his brothers for whom he knew that he was "responsible," he refuses the happiness which God offers to him completely alone (OT, pp. 36-37) or again John the Baptist remaining at the gate of the Kingdom through fidelity to his Jewish brothers (Luke 16:28).

[83]We must remember, when we speak of St. Luke, that he was a disciple of Paul and founder with him of the community of Philippi.

[84]"If my blood must be poured out in libation" (Jerusalem Bible): in the Greek, this is a single word in which there is no question of pouring out his blood, but of making a libation, i.e., pouring out wine or oil on the altar or the sacrifice as an offering to God.

[85]We can show, starting with this letter, how the practice of the gospel counsels flows from the ministry. *Poverty:* 4:10-20: the supreme freedom of poverty, 1:12, in every situation—here he is in prison—he judges everything from the starting point of the proclamation of the gospel; 3:7. *Chastity:* his total love for Christ permits him to love his brothers with complete openness, without any selfish return to himself, 1:7-8; 1:23-24; 2:1-2.

Obedience: Vatican II (Ministry of Priests, No. 15) cites Phil. 2.; if all the leaders of the priestly team could praise their co-workers as Paul does Timothy (2:22)! The foundation of their pastoral team is the proclamation of the gospel.

[86]In the Old Testament, "body" and "flesh" have an equivalent meaning. Paul alone gives to the word "flesh" its pejorative meaning. Joy, for example does not do it. He declares: "The Word became flesh," i.e., man. Paul could not write this. For him, he became "body," and he carried the weight of our "flesh," of our "sin."

[87]I set aside certain more Greek elements as "interior man," "exterior man," "understanding," "consciousness." We keep this concern of Paul to "discern the best" in man with whom he enters into dialogue. Luke gives us an example in the discourse of Paul in Athens.

[88]Now read the end of the Acts (chs. 20-28).

[89]A witness that Sunday, the day of the resurrection of the Lord, replaced the Jewish Sabbath.

[90]The same, according to all probability, where Jesus appeared before Pilate.

[91]Consider the wonderful trial of Joan of Arc and the movie by Bresson.

[92]To locate Festus in the history of this half century, cf. later, p. 312.

[93]For the history of Palestine in this period, seen through the destiny of this woman, at that time mistress of her brother, before becoming the mistress of Titus, cf. the book by E. Mireaux, *La Reine Berénice* (A. Michel, 1951). It reads like a novel.

[94]"If you can say the two Yeses with one and the same heart (that of marriage and that of Jesus Christ), with one and the same clearness, how would I wish to oppose your baptism," writes Frances (an unbeliever), to Yves, her husband. Re-read *Le Vent souffle ou il veut.* P.-A. Lesort goes to the very heart of the mystery.

[95]"He died among those with whom he wished to live; he died like each of these in their sleep, because he gave a meaning to their life" (A. Malraux, *La Condition Humaine*).

[96]Dedication on a copy of *The Diary of a Country Priest:* "When I have died tell the sweet kingdom of the earth that I

loved it more than I ever dared to say." "The temptation of the Word too great, the seduction of the world too beautiful, where is it now? It is no longer. The earth can indeed, this time, grasp me with its giant arms. . . . Its charms can no longer harm me, from now on it has become for me, *beyond itself,* the body of Him who is and of Him who comes" (Teilhard, *Le Divin Milieu).*

[97]Father Benoit is thinking of Judaism as it was lived by the Essenes (cf. OT, pp. 170-171).

[98]Angels exist. Without any appeal to defined dogmas, this comes out too clearly from the entire Bible. It calls them "angels," i.e., "messengers," "ambassadors" of God. I am happy that we no longer believe in the troublesome imps of the Middle Ages or in those womanish beings with pale rose wings that haunt our churches. The angels are "spirits," and "lay" mentality is perhaps more apt than others to sense the power of the Spirit over matter. Teilhard, so profundly "materialist" in the sense in which, through scientific vocation and instinctive love, he stuck to the material world, does not find any mover for evolution than the *spiritual* energy of matter. God who is Spirit has indeed created matter. Why could he not act on it through these personal beings who are his servants, the angels? To refuse this, to refuse the influence on our world of angels and this angel in rebellion, against God, Satan, "the prince of this world, "is to condemn oneself to understand nothing of the history of salvation. It also means emptying the liturgy of part of its meaning or content: is it not sharing in worship that the angels render unceasingly to God, as we recall in the Preface and Sanctus at each Mass? Note the profound truth which Paul recalls to us. Can we give a more precise picture of their functions. It does not seem so. The functions which the Bible attributes to them have known developments bound to history, bound to the confrontation of Judaism and other religions, especially the Persian-Babylonian. They undoubtedly have only symbolic value. (Translator's Note: cf. *The Devil and His Angels,* by Timothy McDermott, O.P., *New Blackfriars* (Oct., 1966), pp. 16-25).

[99]A rabbinic tradition according to which God had given the law to Moses on Mount Sinai, through the mediation of angels. We shall find this in the Letter to the Hebrews.

[100]The mystery of the redemption: "the peace through the blood of the cross" is evidently present in this hymn (Paul could not

forget it), but only the evident truth which they recall in passing to be complete.

[101]We sing in the Christmas Preface: "Now we know God in him who rendered himself visible to our eyes." That which calls God to mind for the Muslim is the desert, for the Buddhist, is nirvana; for us it is the countenance of man! (OT, p. 228).

[102]"The more we reflect on the profound laws of evolution, the more we are convinced that the universal Christ could not appear at the end of time at the peak of the World, unless he was previously introduced into the course of the way, *by way of birth* under the form of an element. As truly as the Universe is kept in movement through the Christ-Omega, so from his concrete seed, the Man of Nazareth, the Christ-Omega draws (theoretically and historically) all his consistency for our experience" (Teilhard, *Christianisme et Evolution*).

[103]Here again the heresy of the Colossians has brought him to progress. The word "head" in Greek can have two meanings as the word "chef," in French (headgear). The Bible used it especially in the sense of "chef," meaning authority. The Greek thought more quickly of "head," this part of the being which gives out all the vital influence. Until then, when he spoke of the Church, "body of Christ," Paul thought of the "being" of Christ (without distinguishing between the body and the head which is only one of the members of the body). The Colossians have led him to speak of Christ as "head," i.e., "leader" of the powers. This has led to the normal transferral of thought to Christ as "leader" of the Church (biblical sense), then as "head" (in the Greek sense), which he uses here. For all this, see the footnote in the Jerusalem Bible on 1 Cor. 12:12.

[104]How could we not recall the well-known phrase of the curé of Torcy: "I simply claim that when the Lord draws from me, by chance, some word that is useful to soul, I feel it by the trouble it causes me" (*The Diary of a Country Priest*).

[105]"Paul to the Christians who are in . . ." This letter, destined to a group of churches, had to have a blank after the words "who are in . . ." to permit the adding of the name of each church to which it was addressed. We have kept the copy of the letter addressed to the church of Ephesus.

[106]Or "in Mary," the Catholic or orthodox Christian could say as

well. From now on, Mary is the image of this heavenly Church at the end of time (cf. OT, p. 225).

[107]Luke expresses it in his way in the parable of the Good Samaritan. This man is "moved with compassion" at the sight of an unknown wounded man. Compassion simply human. It is not "for the love of God" that he stops. But because it is true, fully human, his love is already of God: by loving humanly he loves "with a love of God." Luke suggests it by the use of this verb which he reserves for the love of God (the Father of the prodigal son, 15:20) and for the love of Christ (7:13). Certainly the unbeliever who loves his brothers will rise against this Christian "annexation" of his love. He is right. We do not have the right to baptize too quickly as a "Christian act" what is only human brotherhood. But faith reveals to us that in this act of merely human love, already the Spirit of love is sought, this love is already oriented toward the unity in Christ. Complex relations: "Church-world." In a sense, insofar as they are on the way to their goal, each keeps its autonomy in relation to the other, and the Church has the duty to respect the autonomy of the world. But seen in the light of God, at the end, Church and world will form only one, or rather, the Church disappears in this Kingdom of God which is the World redeemed and of which it is the anticipation.

[108]It seems quite necessary to identify this gift with the Holy Spirit, according to the parallel text of Acts 2: cf. Acts 2:38 and what we said above on pp. 22-23.

[109]This is the first letter where he uses the word "Church" to designate the ensemble of all the Christians, and no longer only the Christians living in a particular community.

[110]This gives baptism also an extraordinary dimension: if it is the "nuptial bath," it cannot be, less than ever, an act of the past. It is a first act which, to be true, must open out into the union of love with Jesus, in the Eucharist where this union is consummated, and in the mystical life, the daily life where it is lived and to which every baptized Christian is called.

[111]Are they written by Paul himself or by a pastor using, after Paul's death, the "spiritual testament" of the apostle?

[112]2 Tim. 3:16. Here theology picked up the word "inspiration" of the Scripture. Concerning this, cf. OT, p. 22.

[113]In these letters, the organization of the hierarchy as we

know it today takes its start: bishops, priests, deacons. Takes its start only: cf. the note in the Jerusalem Bible on Tit. 1:5. Until then the Word of God had been transmitted by the first witnesses who had received the charism, or gift (cf. 1 Cor. 12:14). Now that the revelation becomes a deposit which must be faithfully transmitted, becomes a "tradition," the different ministries, more stable than the charism, take it over.

[114]1 Tim. 1:8-11 sums up well what could be said about the role of the law: it is made for sinners, not for saints.

[115]This text which the Church meditates on in the liturgy of Christmas inspired Karl Barth with the title for his wonderful lecture of 1956: "The humanity of God"—*(Labor et Fides)*, a sort of "confession" in which the great Protestant prophet who has so marked the theology of our period sums up the evolution of his thought and gives it a new depth.

[116]1 Tim. 6:15-16 is undoubtedly a "Jewish hymn taken into the Christian tradition." For all this, cf. M. E. Boismard, "*Quatre Hymnes baptismales dans la première épitre de Pierre* (Cerf, 1961).

IV.

BAPTIZED TO CONSECRATE THE WORLD

FIRST PETER, JAMES, HEBREWS

The convent stands right next to the stadium.[1] One evening when I entered the chapel to pray, an old prelate was just completing a conference for the religious women. The more he spoke, the more I felt myself a stranger to this religion which preaches the scorn of the world, the necessity of suffering, the forgetting of the earth in order to pray. From the stadium we could hear the cries and shouts of happy delight. Below, in the town, there lived an enormous world of factories, stores, business offices, and games for young people. I tried to pray. I could not. To serve God in worship is the purpose of the life of Christians, the life of these religious women and my life. I had celebrated Mass in this chapel, I had consecrated the bread and the wine, symbols of the entire life of men, to make of them the body of Christ. To render this life "sacred," was it necessary then to destroy it as they burned the animals they offered on the altar in Jerusalem? I kept trying to pray. To my mind came only the words of the talk that I would like to give: This is not true, this is not **more** true, there is not a dichotomy of the "profane" and the "sacred." The "**profane**," **pro-fanum,** before the temple, outside the presence of God, which would form the quasi-totality of our life, and the "**sacred**," the domain of the sacraments, worship, Sunday Mass, the smallest part of our life. You have the chance, my sisters, to live near the stadium: you cannot pray if you close your ears to their appeals, and to those who come up from the city. The sacred and the profane, from the time of Jesus Christ, are no longer bounded by the cement cloister which withdraws you from the world, no more than by the massive portal which separates the weekday life from the Sunday Mass. The Mass is not beside the world, it is within it. The consecration of the Mass is not an aside of our life, it is the "sacrament" of our life, the "sign" of that which our life has become during the entire week and an "effective" sign, i.e., which returns our daily life just as it is celebrated in the Mass. And your life as consecrated women is like the eucharistic bread, a "sign" of this life of the world offered to God. If you empty this life that is offered of its very life, what is it that you are offering? The consecration is not "a snatching out of the profane" and a transplantation into the "sacred," but a penetration of the reality of the Kingdom into the very fibers of the reality of the world" (Ranquet). And to accomplish this consecration of the world and their life, every Christian has received the priesthood. Is it not painfully significant that we have reserved this title "priest" for a few men whom we imagine "separated" from the people of God? More significant still is that in French we do not have a word corresponding to "sacerdotium," or priesthood. To respect the thought of Paul, Peter, and the entire New Testament, we have to forge, as does the Italian, a word, "sacerdote," beside "prêtre," or priest. There is only one "sacerdote": Jesus Christ. And never in the New Testament does it say that the priests are "sacerdotes": all the baptized because they share in the priesthood (**sacerdoce**) of Christ, are the priestly people. Priests, as we use the term, are those who are set apart "in the bosom" of the people of God for a precise office or function.[2] The priesthood (**sacerdoce**) belongs to the people of God.

But rather than set up a course in theology, would it not be simpler to listen to Peter and to the author of the Letter to the Hebrews?

First Letter of Peter
A Priestly People . . .

Written in Rome, the "modern Babylon," redacted by Silvanus (his other name is Silas), this letter is a jewel too little known in Christianity. Peter[3] is not a theologian like Paul. Incapable of launching out into speculation, he prefers, to our greater joy, to go to a completely fresh source, the primitive liturgy, and particularly that of baptism. We already appealed to this letter in the second chapter where we were trying to discover the New Testament before it was put in writing. At that time we heard Peter citing the baptismal "creed" which was taken from this letter (3:18-4:6). Father Boismard[4] reconstructs three other hymns besides this creed. The one sings of the Father, author of our new birth, who has regenerated us through the resurrection of Christ, to make us heirs of salvation (1:3-5).[5] Another sings the praises of Christ, the Suffering Servant who has borne our sins in his body in order that we may live in his holiness (2:22-25).[6] The last text would be less a hymn than a kind of exhortation in the form of a hymn, inviting the baptized to renounce Satan and proclaim their faith in the Trinity (5:5-9).[7]

Baptismal hymns, renouncing Satan, proclaiming one's faith . . . . we would think we were assisting at a baptism! This is exactly what some of the specialists think. For them not only is Peter inspired by the baptismal liturgy, but he brings us to share in it by recopying even the summary of the homily. (This is an oversimplification, you realize!) But even if this solution is not entirely accepted, we must indeed recognize that this entire letter on the meaning of Christian existence in the world is centered on baptism. Before taking up the themes, let us outline the plan:[8]

1:1-2: Greeting: a magnificent definition of the Christian life. All that Paul has developed at length in his letters you will find summed up here in one verse. Note how the Christian life cannot and must not be defined outside the Trinity.

1:3-12: We find the same ideas in the great **Trinitarian Hymn.**

3-5: First hymn which Peter cites: the Father author of our new birth.

6-9: Jesus Christ object of our love and of our faith. Baptismal exhortation to support joyfully the trial in order to obtain glory. This theme, constancy in trial, will be found in Jas. 1:2-4; and 1:12 and Rom. 5:3-5.

10-12: The Spirit of Christ from a long time back and in advance exposed the mystery of Christ in the Scriptures.[9]

1:13-2:10: BAPTISMAL HOMILY: if we follow the hypothesis of Preisker, we can distinguish two parts:

1:13-21: Homily **before** Baptism: It is inspired by this extraordinary event which God formerly made to live in his people and in which he gave birth to them as a people: the exodus or the departure from Egypt. The blood of the Lamb who saves us is the blood of Jesus. Hence, be holy as God is holy and live on this earth as "strangers," as people on a march.[10]

1:22-2:10: Homily **after** Baptism: "By obeying the truth, you have sanctified your souls."[11]

1:22-25: You have been begotten by the Word of God (cf. what we said in reference to 1 Thess. 2:13). How could we, Catholics, have forgotten this dynamism of the Word of God which comes into our heart and is welcomed by us and makes us become children of God? This tragic forgetfulness has transformed, in the thought of very many, our sacraments into magical rites which act independently of faith.

2:1-10: The consequences of this new birth: you share in the priesthood of Christ, your entire Christian life is a worship offered to God, is a sign raised in the world proclaiming the marvels of "Him who called you from darkness into his wonderful light." We shall come back to this.

Until now, this was theological reflection on the state of the baptized person. Now Peter, in two exhortations, invites us to live it. He ends each of the exhortations with a "doxology" (as our prayers end with a "Glory be to the Father, etc.").

2:11-5:11: **Catechesis on our responsibility as Christians:**

2:11-4:11: The Christian and the Christian community involved in the world. Each social category, servants, women, husbands, in every human or ecclesial institution, must give this worship to God in the midst of the nations for whom it is a sign.

4:12-5:11: You must also render this worship within your community. Advice to the "elders" (we would perhaps now say "priests") and to the "young," the faithful, or more probably the other ministers.

5:12-14: Final greeting: You have been established in this grace.

After having outlined the **Formgeschichte** of this letter[12] and its plan, it may be a good thing to sum up the teachings.

The postal address of this letter is significant: "To the elect, the foreigners of the diaspora," just as later "I exhort you, beloved, as foreigners and travelers" during the "time-of-your-stay-as-foreigner" (the word which has become "parish" in English). Then we must have come right back to what we said before: the Christian "in exile" on this earth, freed of this world which holds no interest for him, the only important thing in his life being the goal toward which he is marching, heaven, in "an exodus." But before you say more, note the real meaning of the words: These are the foreigners of the "diaspora": the term designates the Jews installed in the entire world in contrast to the Jews "resident" in Palestine. Note then how well-defined is the Church to whom Peter addresses himself, the very same one which Vatican II has redefined: not a ghetto, but a church spread into the whole world, in a state of diaspora, of mission. Hence it is a message specially adapted to our time: it starts with the concrete situation of the Church, scattered among men, in the world without being of the world.

We are treating of giving to it the spirituality that is fitting to it. Peter finds this in the baptism whose meaning he brings us to understand by starting with the experience formerly lived by the people of God, the exodus, and he draws the consequences from this for today.

The exodus (OT, pp. 34, 107-108) is this fact that God "called" his people from Egypt, drawing it from the "house of slavery" in order that it might serve him with their entire life, a service culminating in this offering which is worship. The exodus was the birth of the people, consecrated by the covenant of Sinai, made in obedience to the commandments of God, ratified by the sprinkling of blood on the altar, representing God, and on the people (Exod. 19; 24). The purpose of this exodus was the entrance into the "heritage," this land promised to Abraham, and the notion will be spiritualized throughout the history of Israel to come finally to designate the sharing in the glory of God in the future Kingdom. Israel became thus a "holy nation," consecrated, separated from other nations, to be the domain of God, a "kingdom of priests" entirely consecrated to the service of God. "What the Israelite priests are for their brothers in the holy community, the entire Israel will be for the other people of the world. The priest-people of the other peoples. A charge, grave before God and men, which consists in adoring the Lord in the name of all, of assuring prayer, sacrifice, praise, intercession for the entire world!" (Auzou).

Behold, says Peter to our Church in a situation of diaspora, that which you have lived through baptism, which the exodus only prefigured, this is the spirituality which you must live.

The Church is a people "called" to make the true exodus, ratified by the blood of Jesus Christ through the "obedience" of our faith. But—and this changes everything—this exodus is "spiritual." We are no longer treating, as for Israel, of locally leaving one country for another. We are treating, while remaining in this world, of quitting a way of being, of being a foreigner to a certain world. You must "gird the loins of your spirit" for a completely spiritual voyage, for a new conduct. The passage from darkness to the wonderful light of God. Our new birth does not snatch us from our world and from "the friendship of companions," it does not give us any "assurance" about the beyond or hereafter, and does not free us from a certain tragedy of human existence;[13] it gives us only the gift to live this in the light of God. The purpose of this exodus-baptism remains the same: to make this people a "royal priesthood" that it may serve God. This priesthood carries with it a double aspect: "to offer to God spiritual sacrifices, pleasing to God through Jesus Christ" and "to proclaim in the midst of the nations the perfections of him who has called you." But before going into detail, Peter brings us to contemplate what the priesthood is: the Christ.

Jesus himself has accomplished this exodus in his paschal mystery. Peter sums it up for us with the help of images drawn from the Old Testament. He is the "rock on which God wishes to construct a new world and this rock has been rejected by the builders": He is the Paschal Lamb, he is the Suffering Servant, who freely offers himself to death for our liberation. By his resurrection, he has become "a living stone" and he renders all the stones living—every man—who is willing to be based on him through a total faith. Thus this spiritual temple is constructed, the true dwelling of God toward which the whole Old Testament tended (OT, pp. 51, 211-213), in which we "have" access to God (3:18).[14]

In this Temple, Jesus Christ, the Church exercises its priesthood, each Christian is "a priest," i.e., he is qualified to make his life a sacrifice, a worship of God. It is true, this worship will avail or be worthwhile only if it is offered with the sacrifice of Jesus, if it is consecrated in the Mass by the priest, but the consecration of the Mass will be worthwhile only if it consecrates something: this offering of the entire life. The importance that we have given to the Mass has led us, paradoxically, to make it lose all its importance.[15] We have cut off worship from life, to consider the Mass as the sacrifice all by itself. Let St. Augustine set us straight on this point:

"The visible sacrifice is the sacrament or the sacred sign of the invisible sacrifice. The true sacrifice is every work that we perform to unite us with God in a holy union. . . . Paul exhorts us to make our body a living victim, holy, pleasing to God, to render him a spiritual worship. . . . A sacrifice which we ourselves are. This is the sacrifice of Christians: 'All together are one and the same body in Jesus Christ.' It is this mystery which the Church so often celebrates in the sacrament of the altar, where it teaches that in its offering it is itself offered."

Baptism does not snatch us out of our concrete life and then leave us to human suffering. The word comes up frequently in this letter. Let us forestall an objection: There would be no difficulty at all—at the price of a gigantic misinterpretation—to define Christian morality as a "morality of slaves" (read, for example, what Peter says to the servants, 2:18-25). Peter's intent is not to make his Christians reflect on the manner in which they must act on the temporal structures in order that they become more human (he does this, in passing, when he recalls the great principle of brotherly love). He wishes to teach them how to live in these structures in a Christian manner, accepted for the moment as a fact, how to make a "sacrifice," an offering to God, of them.[16] For this, the Christian must be irreproachable, so that this suffering does not come from his own failures or be a just punishment on the part of others. And he must bear the suffering for the name of Christ. Then Peter can detail some specific situations: conduct in civic life ("Be free men"!); servants: let them remember that the Son of God willed also to become a servant; husbands and wives;[17] conduct with each other. A little further on, he will give advice very useful for priests.

The People exercises its priesthood in this living Temple

which is Jesus Christ. But this temple is not limited to the walls of our stone churches. This temple has the dimensions of the world.[18] As Vatican II has recalled, the Church is defined by its mission in the world. The apostolate is first that of Christian life, that which the wife exercises in the presence of her husband, by "winning him through her life, chaste and full of respect, without preaching at him," the life of "non-violence" in persecution, the life of the entire Christian, who by his conduct must lead those "farthest away" to glorify God. Peter here gives us the definition of evangelization. It begins first with the testimony of an upright life that is lived "by sanctifying the Lord in one's heart." Then when a question arises on the lips of those with whom you live: "be ready always with your explanation, but with meekness and respect, to anyone who asks you for the reason for the hope that is in you" (3:15). This hope is the glory of the Father given by the Spirit (4:14) to those who will be united to Jesus when he is finally "revealed" in his Parousia.

Before we go on to the Letter to the Hebrews, let us say a word about the Letter of James. Is Peter inspired from it?[19] Or do both draw from the same source of the liturgy? In any case, it develops with less freshness, similar themes.

Letter of James

"Sent to Bring the Good News to the Poor"

> "After twenty centuries of Christianity, thunder of God, it should no longer be a shame to be poor. Or else, you have betrayed your Christ! . . . Yes! I know that this subject is not pleasant. If it is true that the poor man is in the image and likeness of Jesus—Jesus himself—it is annoying to set up on the usher's table (in your churches), to show to the

whole world a mocking face on which after 2000 years, you have not yet found the means to wipe off the spittle. For the social question is first of all a question of honor."

G. Bernanos, **The Diary of a Country Priest**

Who is this James? When did he write? Many questions have been raised about his letter, which does not fall into the usual categories: a sequence of moral developments, not much doctrine, only two allusions to Christ. It is in the highest vein of the Wisdom writing of the Old Testament. Luther treated it as the "straw epistle" and the Catholics made it a trained charger against the Protestant doctrine of "salvation through faith alone without works." We have arrived at the best meanings, even if we do not know how to settle the questions. The author is undoubtedly the Bishop of Jerusalem who was killed in 62. We hesitate between two dates: the very archaic character of the letter leads some to see it as the first writing of the New Testament, before the Council of Jerusalem (in 49). Others think they see here a development of a Pauline statement in his Letter to the Romans which has been poorly understood. They would date the letter then from the year 60.

It "is situated in perspectives very close to those of the Christian communities of today when they gather together, on Sunday, to celebrate the Eucharist. St. James as many of the pastors of today exhort their believers to live the gospel better, in all its purity, on the level of their human and social relations, in the framework of the concrete difficulties of life" (Gantoy). A series of very diverse instructions which flow from a single source, the "Sermon on the Mount," and revolve around two themes: the poverty of the gospel, and faith that must show itself in works.

Poverty: The conditions of life that appear through these lines seem very like ours: among the Christians for whom these lines are destined some seem to be "little ones for whom life is hard, deprived of the opportunities given by material comfort" (2:5-8) (Gantoy). Some of the others, not too numerous, are rich but their attitude is not much like the gospel. To both groups James repeats, with the bluntness of the prophets, that they cannot serve two masters. May these words in all their significance find the path to our heart, in order that already in us the Church of Jesus Christ begin to find this look or countenance which is (or which should be) his: a Church that is "servant and poor."

A True Faith: It is certain that Paul and James approach this question from different angles[20] but it is very sad that Christians have fought with each other for such a long time starting from a mutual misunderstanding. As Catholics we believe with the Protestant that we are not saved except through faith and that faith is a grace.[21] And the Protestant, faithful in this not only to the thought of James but of Paul, maintains with the same force as we do, that there must be good works: if the faith which is the total gift of self to Jesus does not make us live as Jesus Christ in the concrete circumstances of daily life, is it still faith? James answers: it is "dead."[22]

Letter to the Hebrews

"Jesus Christ, Yesterday and Today and Forever"

(Heb. 13:8)

> "I am leaving because I wish to see God and to see him, I must die . . . ."

Then a spanking: thus undoubtedly ended the adventure for this time. Theresa was seven years old when she decided with her brother to leave Avila to seek martyrdom among the Moors. She was setting out that day for the only adventure which makes pain worthwhile, the definitive adventure. But perhaps she was wrong about the road. One day she will be called "Theresa of Jesus" and then she will find him: to see God, there is no other path than the humanity of Jesus Christ. "I am the Way."

"To set out . . . to see God . . . to die . . . Jesus." A single theme. Four key words. This, I think, is the heart of the Letter to the Hebrews.

This letter is not easy. That is true. Written in excellent Greek, composed with an art which astounds us, the author[23] breaks out into methods of rabbinical exegesis and quotes the Old Testament with disconcerting ease. But what power! When you enter a Byzantine church, and you see in the apse the Christ, the maker of all things (Pantokrator), you know that you will no longer be able to see anything else. The entire monument is full of this presence. When you suffer a little in the wanderings of this letter, may the same presence be imposed on your entire life.

"**I want to see God**." This is the essential request of the author: How see God? Or rather because he is not Greek but Jewish, how enter into the presence of God?[24] For this he must "leave." This going away is in fact a "return." Because we are sinners, in a sinful world, we must leave it. To leave to this extent that we must "**die**" to this world, not by the animal, absurd death, which is the final, tragic and inescapable moment of this life. But we must die by this death which is a **sacrifice**. How is this possible?

"**In Jesus Christ**": He is the only "means," the only mediator between men and God because he **is** man and God. God became man in order to put himself at the head of this people on the march and to effect this return to the Father. He died and he made his death the sacrifice which saves. Because he has offered the only true sacrifice, he is also the only priest, or rather, to be faithful to the author and to our new use of words, the only "sacerdote."[25] And sharing in his priesthood, the entire people of the baptized, now, following him and in him, can make their lives a sacrifice and have access to God.

The thought is simple and the perspectives magnificent. What complicates everything is that the author is Jewish and he is speaking to . . . . But to whom is he speaking? It seems that the people for whom the letter is destined are Jewish priests—Essenes perhaps?—converted to Christianity. And these priests are passing through terrifying spiritual crises, augmented by the perspective of persecutions near at hand. Until then the Jewish worship with its stirring ritual and ceremony had been the center of their lives. This cult had as its peak the liturgy of Yom Kippur, the solemn day of atonement and penitence, on which, once a year, the high priest alone entered the third part of the temple, the Holy of Holies, where in silence and darkness God was present. Carrying the blood of the immolated victims, he entered into the presence of God to obtain pardon for the entire people. This worship they had abandoned on becoming Christians and now they thought about it with nostalgia. The author of the letter, an old Jew himself, adapts his development to their mentality. He will start from the Jewish liturgy constantly, especially that of the atonement, while showing them with much delicacy and respect that they have lost nothing by abandoning it. This Jewish worship was in fact only an image, did not actually give access to God, but it was an image: what it prefigured is "fulfilled" in Jesus Christ. A double aspect: negative (the old worship had no value), and positive (it has value as a prefiguring) which is understood throughout this entire letter and comes back with regard to everything: the exodus, Moses, the Jewish priesthood, the sanctuary, the sacrifice.

Thus this letter is the most extended theological reflection of the New Testament on the priesthood of the faithful, this sacrifice of mankind of which St. Augustine spoke and which the Letter of Peter was already developing, or in other words, the most extended theological reflection on the **paschal mystery**. Let us try to see with the author how this Paschal Mystery was prefigured in the Old Testament, was fulfilled in Jesus Christ, and is lived in Christian life.[26]

1. The paschal mystery prefigured in the Old Testament

The People, the "assembly convoked" by the Word of God and founded on his promise to Abraham, truly became his people by entering into the covenant, on Sinai, a covenant sealed in blood (but this is only a "type" of the true covenant in Jesus). It is a people on the march, under the leadership of a leader, Moses, through the desert where God puts them to the test, the "temptation." The people sinned and thus missed the goal of their march, which was entrance into the rest of God. Then throughout the length of its history it will make efforts, and constantly remake them, to reach its goal: every year, the high priest enters the sanctuary, and every year he has to begin over again because it does not flower out truly to meeting God. Then comes Jesus Christ.

2. The paschal mystery "fulfilled" in Jesus[27]

He finally brings into reality this return to God. He enters into the sanctuary. He is qualified for this, for he is the perfect mediator: He is God (and no author exalts the divinity of Christ so much) and he is man (and the letter insists on the realism of the Incarnation). He did not play at being man. He took on our human condition in its most severe reality, "tested in everything, except sin," he is "surrounded by weakness" and with tears and cries he learns what it is to be man (5:1-10). Thus he has become completely "one with us his brothers" (2:10-18). Then only could he offer the true sacrifice, true because Jesus himself is the victim: This sacrifice is effective because the victim is God; it is unique because he offers himself and because he has only one death to give (9:25-28); it is perfect because it is interior: not victims external to himself, but the sacrifice of his will, of his obedience (10:5-10—a marvelous meditation on Ps. 40). This sacrifice is true likewise because Jesus is the perfect High Priest, eternal, chosen by God, without sin, capable of really suffering with us because he is man. And thus this sacrifice fulfills what those of the Old Testament symbolized. It cleanses us "once and for all" of our sins[28] and in the blood of Christ it ratifies the better covenant, the covenant announced by Jeremiah (9:15-17). The purpose of sacrifice is thus finally attained: Jesus enters into the rest of God, into the true sanctuary, into heaven itself, into the presence of God (9:24) where he celebrates forever the true liturgy (8:1-2; 7:26-28; 9:24-28).

3. The paschal mystery lived in the Church

The sacrifice of Jesus was a "sacrament" of ours, he lived it "for every man," in his willing offering of himself we have been made whole" (2:9; 10:10). We have become "sharers in Christ," our sacrifice is fulfilled within his. Christians have therefore in Jesus Christ access to the rest of God. This must be the foundation of all their spirituality.

They are the true people of God, called together by this Word of God, who **is** Jesus Christ (4:12-13), "heirs of the Promise" made to Abraham, introduced into the new covenant by Christ; the people who accomplish the true exodus in the footsteps of Jesus, the head and "the first of the chain" of whom Moses was only a figure or type in his exodus through the desert: "today, God puts us to the test" (3-4). A people "on the march": here undoubtedly is the best definition of the Church of Christ. It is only "as a people" that we can make this exodus, and anyone who separates from the caravan runs the risk of death. Hence we must support our brothers. And therefore the need of practicing the virtues: the three great ones first: faith following the example of the great marchers of the Old Testament (ch. 11); hope, love; but also "constancy," the specific virtue of those who march and struggle (10:32-39; 12:1-3); all the Christian attitudes (13:1-6). It is absolutely necessary to nourish one's faith. There is evidently a necessity of fleeing sin: this would be "crucifying Jesus Christ on one's own account" (6:6; 10:29).

Then, in the end, in Jesus, we have an openness (a franchise), a freedom to enter into the house of God and to be a cultic people in the state of an eternal offering. At the terminus, i.e., not at the end of the world or of our existence, but at the terminus of this participation in Jesus Christ through the sacraments, baptism effects our passage, our exodus with him; the Eucharist establishes each of our lives, right now, as an offering and a means of access to God.

Now we can undertake the reading of this letter. It is made up of three parts, and the central part has three sections. The whole is organized in such a way that the center section (which treats of the sacrifice of Christ) is at the high point of a parable which supports it and brings it out.

(1) **chs. 1-2:** The heavenly Christ

(2) **chs. 3:1-5:10:** A High Priest, faithful and compassionate

(3)
- **5:11-6:20:** Invitation to be attentive
  - (a) **7:1-28:** A High Priest according to the order of Melchizidech
  - (b) **8:1-9:28:** Arrived at the fulfillment by **his Sacrifice**
  - (c) **10:1-18:** Cause of an eternal salvation
- **10:19-39:** Invitation to put it in practice

(4) **11:1-12:14:** What this demands of Christians: to be like Christ (cf. 2, above)

(5) **12:14-33:** The fruits which the Christians gather: with the heavenly Christ (cf. 1)

Let us take up this plan a little more in detail.[29]

(1) **chs. 1-2:** The grandeur of Christ who, through his sufferings and his humiliations, has been introduced into the presence of God.

(2) **chs. 3:1-5:10:** Jesus the High Priest, faithful and compassionate:

FAITHFUL: 3:1-4:14: Moses was faithful, but as a servant. Jesus is faithful, as a Son. Take heed if you are not faithful, note what happened to your ancestors: they did not enter the Promised and, the image of heaven (beautiful text about the Word of God: 4:12-13).

COMPASSIONATE: 4:15-5-10: Definition of the High Priest and the magnificent text about the "weakness" of our High Priest who learned through his suffering how to become man.

(3) **chs. 5:11-10:39:** The Sacrifice of Christ:

5:11-6:20: Exhortation to stop being lukewarm and indifferent. They should be finished with "milk" that is given to babies, that is, the doctrine of the beginnings.

(a) **7:1-28:** Jesus the High Priest according to the order of Melchizidech. He was superior to Abraham and to the priesthood of the Old Testament. In this he is an image of Christ, who also is completely superior and eternal.

(b) **8:1-9:28:** Christ by his **sacrifice** has brought everything to fulfillment. Here is the central chapter, built on a contrast!

8:1-9:10: The ancient cult was earthly and only an image. The first covenant was imperfect and temporary. The cult was powerless to give us access to God: the High Priest was obliged to begin again each year, a sign that it was not succeeding.

9:11-28: The new worship (the sacrifice of Christ) is made once and for all because he succeeds (the Mass does not "remake" the sacrifice, it renders present for us this only sacrifice).
The covenant in Jesus is definitive because it is sealed in his blood.
The new worship is heavenly and gives us access to heaven: it establishes us in a definitive relation with God.

(c) **10:1-18:** Jesus is the cause of eternal salvation.

10:1-3: In the Old Testament, they repeated the sacrifices, uselessly.

10:4-10: They are replaced by the unique and only sacrifice of Christ which is an **interior** sacrifice, the offering of his will, of his heart.

10:11-14: The numerous priests bustling about are replaced by the only Priest.

10:15-18: There is no longer need for any other sacrifice.

10:19-39: The summary of what we have acquired in Jesus;

The exhortation not to lose it through sin.

(4) **11:1-12:13:** This demands that the Christian be like Christ (cf. 2).

FAITHFUL: ch. 11: A marvelous chapter on the faith of the patriarchs.

Persevering: In the face of suffering; 12:1-13.

(5) **12:14-13:25:** The fruits that the Christian harvests: he is brought in where Christ ends, in heaven (cf. 1).

12:14-29: A warning: do not sell your privileges as Esau did.

13:1-6: Christian attitudes: charity, conjugal fidelity, confidence in the Lord.

13:7-19: True and false notions of religion.

13:20-25: Conclusion and mission.

"Keep your hope indefectible . . . . You need constancy . . . . Support one another all the more as you see the Day approaching . . . ." All these pleadings take on a dramatic character from the historic context. This letter is written between 64-70: Nero has already unleashed his great persecution against the Christians and the troubles in Palestine already give a glimpse of the catastrophe of 70, one of the "coming" of the Lord proclaiming his definitive "Coming" on the "Day" of the Parousia.

The coming of the Lord in the year 70

Through one of the windows, a soldier hurls a flaming torch into the temple. The fire blazes up. Titus has time only to run into the Holy Place and save a few pieces of the sacred furniture which will be used as figures in his triumphal march in Rome. He had commanded them to spare the Temple. He now shouts orders for them to put that fire out. But who is going to listen in the midst of such carnage? Since the morning of this August 10, 70, they have been engaged in hand-to-hand battle in the Temple precincts; they kill, they burn, they cut one another's throats in the bloody mud that covers the pavement. . . . Since we know that we are bound to Israel by so many spiritual attachments, this almost unlimited slaughtering which marks the end of its history cannot but move us to sadness.

For a long time this war has been in the making. Israel never could accept this being enslaved by the Roman yoke, and the best among the Jews, the Pharisees, were the soul of this spiritual resistance to the enemy. Unfortunately, others quickly become the leaders, those whom the Jewish historian Josephus called the "bandits": the Zealots and the Sicarii (their name comes from their short sword). Animated by an implacable and blind hatred, fanning alive the popular instincts, and playing up the messianic picture, they will bring about the destruction of their people by pushing the Romans to the end.

They had done everything necessary to provoke the catastrophe. With the death of Herod the Great, in 4 B.C., his kingdom was divided among his three sons (cf. Luke 3:1). It took only a few years for Archelaus, who claimed Judea and Samaria, to make himself completely hated: Augustus exiled him in A.D. 6. His territory is then attached back to the province of Syria, and from that time one is governed by a procurator. Pontius Pilate was the procurator from 26 to 36. From 41 to 44, Agrippa I, the grandson of Herod, succeeded in refashioning to his advantage the kingdom of his grandfather. At his death in Caesarea,[30]

Palestine falls back under the control of procurators. After the first two, then upright Festus (cf. p. 136)—this was the most beautiful collection that Rome could produce in the greedy, brutal, unshamedly criminal class. It was too much. The Pharisees and the truly wise men among the people could no longer do anything. The Zealots, stirred up by the extremist outlaws, such as John of Gisgala, aroused the people. Incidents erupted everywhere: a riot broke out in Caesarea in May, 66, then in Jerusalem; the Roman garrison of Massada was wiped out. In September the Jews in Jerusalem were killing each other. The extremists attacked the moderates: nothing could now stop the wave of hatred that had been unleashed. At the beginning of 67, Nero named Vespasian the crisis-governor of Judea. The future emperor carefully prepares his operations. With his army of 60,000 men, he begins by reducing Galilee to impotence, then in the spring of 68, the Jordan valley.[31] The methodical encircling of Jerusalem does not bother the outlaws who are constantly disputing about power and authority and systematically kill thousands of priests and leaders. The death of Nero suspends the military activities for a year. Vespasian and his army are stationed in Caesarea. Titus, his son, is also there.[32] In 69, Vespasian is proclaimed emperor, and he leaves to his son the command of the army of the Near East and the job of reducing Jerusalem to its knees. At the Passover in 70, Titus begins the siege, after his efforts at negotiation failed. Siege, famine . . . July: the Antonia is taken. July 12: the offering of the daily sacrifice ceases forever. August 10: the burning of the temple, murders, carnage, booty. Then "the mopping up" of the city: executions, the sparing of prisoners to sell them as slaves, destruction of the fortifications. But it still took three years for the destruction of the last fortified places, especially Massada where the besieged preferred suicide to surrender. Israel is no more, at least as a nation.[33] But Israel does not die. In 68, some Pharisees and scribes, at least those who had escaped the massacre of John of Gisgala, obtained from Vespasian the authorization to withdraw to the Mediterranean coast, to Lydda and Jamnia. As had happened throughout its history, Judaism, purified by this trial, will reconstruct its patrimony[34] and set out for a new period of its life, an obscure period, painful or productive according to the times and of which the present Judaism is the heir.

The Church of Jesus Christ, the true people of God, bearer of the promise made to Abraham, has already left Jerusalem. The Word of God, departing from the Mother Church, has caused to spring up in the entire known world communities of Christians. At one time, Jerusalem had been the center to which every runner and every ship, touching port in Caesarea, brought the news of the "daughter churches" from Asia Minor, Greece and Rome. Then, gradually, the Church came to realize that it was "catholic," i.e. "universal," that it did not depend on one place, but on one person, Jesus Christ, whose body it is. Thus from that time Jerusalem ended the historic role that God had unfolded in it. The fall of Jerusalem in 70, sad as it was for Christians, appeared as the sign of the definitive passing to the new Israel. With the death of Jesus, the veil of the temple was torn from top to bottom, symbolizing in advance the destruction of this temple: the true sanctuary from this time forward was to be the body of this man hanged on the Cross. In 70, the prophecy is realized: the true temple is no longer a determined place on earth; it is everywhere that the "body of Jesus," his Church, is found.

[1]This example is dangerous: it could lead people to think that I am depreciating the consecrated life. I have insisted sufficiently on the value of virginity (OT, p. 223) to show that the opposite

is true. The life consecrated to God in virginity is nothing else than the Christian life of the baptized: it is simply carried through to its culminating point. It must help us understand our own life as baptized. The fact that we would no longer see the place of contemplative religious women in our world, or that we have difficulty in understanding their role, is this not the sign that our notion of the Christian life is not too clear or exact? We would be Christian in the Church, for the Mass, or in certain circumstances, a parenthesis in our lives, such as prayer, but this would have nothing to do with our daily life of work, leisure, family, etc. To those who want to deepen this aspect of their knowledge; I suggest the booklet by P. G. Ranpuet, *Baptismal Consecration and Religious Consecration* (Fleurus, 1965).

[2]Vatican II, in the schema on the *Ministry of the Priests,* gives fine precision to the fact that they are not separated "from" the people of God, but set apart "in the bosom of" the people of God for a determined office or function which leaves them fully men and Christian.

[3]At times objections are raised to the attribution of this letter to Peter. But these are not compelling. What is the date? The context seems to be very close to the persecutions. It could be between 60-64.

[4]M. E. Boismard, *Quatre Hymnes Baptismales dans la 1 épître de Pierre* (Cerf, 1961).

[5]The following were also inspired by the same hymn: Tit. 3:5-7; 1 John 3:1-2; Col. 3:1-4; Gal. 3:23; Rom. 8:18.

[6]We find it again in 2 Cor. 5:21; Rom. 5-8; Gal. 3:13; Jas. 3:1f.

[7]It is reproduced in an almost identical manner in Jas. 4:6-10. Note the possible counter-sense for the "humble yourselves," 1 Pet. 5:6. This is not the terrible meaning, "become stupid" of Pascal, but "become little ones," develop the spirit of "a poor man," walk toward your true childhood (cf. OT, pp. 196, 163-165).

[8]Here again I draw my inspiration from Father Boismard.

[9]One of the precious texts about the unity of the two covenants.

[10]A good occasion to read or reread. 1 John 3:1-10; Tit. 2:11-14; Jas. 1:26-2:13; Col. 3:5-13; Eph. 4:17-24.

[11]Cf. 1 John 3:9-10; Jas. 1:17-27; Rom. 8:14-17; 12:1-2; Col. 3:14-16.

[12]In Chapter II we explained this word, which means "history of the formation" of a text.

[13]Reread the magnificent cry of E. Mounier against this religion of the castrated which has too frequently become Christianity. In answer to Nietzsche, "The defiance of Christ," not the following of Christ has unmanned [devirilized] man." "St. Francis did not castrate the wild beasts, he tamed them."

[14]This is the basic theme of the Letter to the Hebrews.

[15]The suffering of the priest at Mass, because he too often has the impression of consecrating bread which is no more than bread, i.e., the symbol of the life which all these Christians bring as "offering." Reread the orations at Mass, especially the "secrets": most often they are an intense petition for those present to offer themselves.

[16]In present terms we could perhaps translate: the temporal involvement, i.e., the act of every man because he is a man. In a Catholic Action meeting of working people, for example, when they meet as Christians they are seeking how to be Christian in the different concrete situations of work and in their temporal involvement. The daughter who is working in servitude, the militant union member who suffers because of his temporal action, have to bind this suffering with that of Christ, have to seek to make this suffering "pure," i.e., that it is not the result of any failure on their part.

[17]Peter gives some excellent advice to young ladies on the beauty of their heart.

[18]"You who follow Christ and who imitate him, you who live in Word of God, you who meditate on his law night and day, you who are carrying out his commandments, you are always in the sanctuary, and you never depart from it. The sanctuary is not to be sought in a place, but in acts, life, morals. If these are according to God, if they are fulfilled according to his commands, it makes little difference whether you are at home or in the forum, or even in the theater: if you are serving the Word of God, you are in the sanctuary, have no doubt" (Origen).

[19]You surely noted the numerous quotes from James while we were reading Peter.

[20]The way in which they use the example of Abraham is typical. Is James, as is frequently said, struggling here against a misinterpretation given to the words of Paul? It is very probable

that they are independent. James does nothing more than take up the commentary given in Jewish milieux about Abraham. Paul, with all his rabbinical skill, makes the text say the opposite of what it seems to mean! (This is much in the line of paradox!) Cf. the Jerusalem Bible, the note on Rom. 4:2.

[21]In his thesis on "Justification," did not H. Küng show that the thought of K. Barth was in agreement here with the Council of Trent?

[22]Note among the other teachings the beautiful text about the Word of God which begets us into life and the invitation to call, in case of sickness, the "elders of the community" to pray and anoint the sick person "with the anointings of oil in the name of the Lord": the oldest witness we have for the "sacrament of the sick."

[23]Who is the author? For a long time this was listed as one of the works of Paul, though it has neither his style nor form. Was he Apollos, the Alexandrian Jew, "eloquent, versed in Scripture, full of fervor to preach exactly what concerns Jesus" (Acts 18:25) and who became a disciple of Paul (1 Cor. 3:4-11; Tit. 3:13)? This is the most probable of all the hypotheses. The date of the letter? Before 70 (it does not cite the fall of Jerusalem and its temple), after 64, the beginning of the persecution of Nero.

[24]Greek philosophy, which we inherited, is especially desirous of contemplating God (the Beatific Vision which we shall enjoy in heaven). The Bible is expressed more in dynamic terms than static: mystical life for the Jew is not "seeing God," but "walking with him" or "before his face."

[25]This nuance is important. Never does Hebrews say that Jesus is "prêtre" (the Greek root means elder, and is translated into English as "priest"). Jesus is the "eternal Sacerdos" and all the baptized share in his "Sacerdoce." (This word is also translated into English as priest but it comes from the root "to give holy or sacred things.") The letter is not a tract or treatise, as has been said at times, on the "pretrise," this priesthood of bishops and priests. Rather, it is a reflection on the "royal priesthood of the baptized."

[26]I refuse to give the references. Look them up.

[27]"To accomplish": one of the key words of the letter. The Jerusalem Bible often translates this by "perfect," but this does

not give a sufficient rendering of the nuance of completion or achievement.

[28]Note the deliberate contrast between this frequent "once for all" and the "without ceasing" of the old worship.

[29]I borrowed the plan—the best that I know of—from Father Vanhoye.

[30]Reread the dramatic account given by Luke: Acts 12:20-23.

[31]It was not without emotion that the archeologists of Qumran in 1951 found arrowheads of these soldiers imbedded in the walls of the old convent.

[32]They are guests of Agrippa and Berenice. She is thirty-nine years old and Titus is twenty-seven. This union was already a year old. One day, it will lead her to the steps of the imperial throne.

[33]The State of Israel was proclaimed in 1948. But its relationship with Old Israel is quite complex.

[34]At the synod of Jamnia in 90, these Jews will establish the list (the "canon") of their holy books, keeping only the books written in Hebrew, as opposed to the Alexandrian Judaism. For this double canon, cf. OT, p. 159.

V.

THE STORY OF A LOVE: THE FOUR GOSPELS

"By a single act we would be enriched with hundreds of moments, of events lived together and kept in our memories because they reunited us."

Anne Philipe

"The time for a sigh!" Such the upsetting confidence of a young wife after the death of her husband, Gerard Philipe. "The story of love is not written with the same ink when it is edited day by day and when it is relived in memory, after death has sealed everything. Time is needed —and perhaps even death—to interpret the riches of these 'hundreds of moments' of living together" (Chalendar).

Rich with hundreds of moments

Two years, the Church, through the first witnesses, lived the unique adventure of its meeting with the Son of God. Two years of unconscious happiness: "Can the friends of the Bridegroom fast while the Bridegroom is with them?" (Mark 2:19). Not the death, but the resurrection has sealed this marvelous story of love. The passage of thirty or forty years allowed the Church to evaluate, appreciate, and interpret the riches of these hundreds of moments. But then one period of its life is ended. One by one, the witnesses who lived these moments are beginning to disappear, and some Christians are disturbed by the silence into which their disappearance threatens to plunge them: "They beg Mark, writes Cyril of Alexandria, to leave them a written testimony of the teaching which had been given to them orally. Thus they bring about the writing of the Gospel called 'according to Mark'" (from the account of Eusebius). "The Gospel according to Mark"—the first of these four accounts in which the Church will gather all that she knows about Jesus Christ in order to live it for all eternity, these four accounts which are the final point put to a long period of maturing. Before studying them separately, it will be useful, so as to avoid repetition, to sum up the three steps in their formation (cf. pp. 51ff., the summary of the origin of the Gospels.)

First Step: In the years 28-30, the gospel, the Good News. You have noted, with surprise perhaps, that in this book we have not yet said anything about this. Only the first chapter was intended to situate the decisive fact of the resurrection. We shall speak of it in the following chapter.

Second Step: In the lengthy interview with Peter and John, and then Luke, I tried to suggest the importance of this step which answers to the magical name **Formgeschichte** (in English this is called, "Form Criticism"): the gospel before the Gospels. After taking a look at the work of Paul, Peter, and the other disciples (cf. above chs. III and IV), you have a better understanding of what we were talking about in chapter II: by building his body, the Church, the apostles learn to know Jesus. They do not know more now, but they know it better. They perceive gradually the profound meaning of his words and deeds. Only after his death do we really understand a man. I know Socrates only through the Western thought to which he gave rise, or Marx only through the enormous hope he stirred up in the hearts of many men. In the tree I "see" the dynamism of the seed. However, and this is an essential difference, Socrates is dead and the seed of the tree is no more; their work issued from them but is quite distinct from them. The work of Jesus, his Church, is truly **his** work, because, raised from the dead, he through his Spirit, lives in it and animates it. The Church **is** his body. Hence we know that while, and by, preaching, answering the questions of Christians, baptizing and granting pardon for sins, "building up" Jesus Christ, the apostles also came to a better understanding of this Jesus with whom they formerly lived. In the course of these years, in the various "life situations" of the communities, the words of Jesus, accounts of miracles, parables, are memorized and gradually put into writing. Around the years 60-80, the Church is like a vast photo-laboratory. In it are deposited "flashes" of Jesus, "sequences," and at times even some "series," from the four corners of the known world. All this is without a preconceived notion of a film to be made about Jesus: the Church does not recognize itself as this laboratory. This is learned when some men decide to gather these documents together to make a "mounting" of them.

Third Step: The "mounting" or, for the sake of clarity, the stage of the **redaktionsgeschichte** (redacting or editing). We have been seriously interested in this step for only about twenty years. For centuries we were concerned with the first step—or better—it is the only one we knew. We thought: the Gospels bring us into immediate audio-contact with Jesus (a "live and direct newscast"). About 1920-1921, the role of the community in the formation of the Gospels was discovered. The thrill of this discovery gave rise to two excesses. Some, like Bultmann, claimed such a "creative power" for this community that the "first step" was a product of the imagination: Jesus as "Messiah," "Son of God," is nothing more than a product of the creative faith of the community (reread note 8, ch. II). This is a serious objection and we shall come back to it in the following chapter. All, or almost all, played down the third step: the authors of the Gospels were nothing but compilers. They have merely gathered together the different episodes born in the course of these decades. Their role is as important and as impersonal as that of a machine classifying cards in a drawer. After some years,[1] this was seen as perhaps too great a simplification of things. Then, without losing anything of the previous acquisitions, they began to see the redactors (editors) as true "authors." In what sense?

Let us take up our comparison with the making of a movie again. What makes the film and gives the producer the right to sign his name is the "mounting," this moment in which he gathers together the film strips ("shot" perhaps by others), cuts off, adds on, removes, organizes. Before this operation, all the elements are present but they do not make a film because these elements have not yet found their relationship to each other: "The movie is not simply this collection of pictures, shots, sequences, series, strips. Rather, the movie is the relation of all these elements to each other" (Epstein). The pictures get their meaning only in this relationship, or even the meaning is actually changed. Let us relate our experience with two Russian movie producers: "They took from a film a substantial series of the actor, Mosjukin; then they shot a sequence presenting a table filled with tasty food, then a sequence of a young woman who had died, and finally a sequence of a child. Then they arranged the following mounting: the table—Mosjukin—the young woman—Mosjukin—the child—Mosjukin. All the viewers were enthusiastic about this actor who, according to them, succeeded with a single glance in expressing sentiments so different as pleasure over food, sadness, and tenderness. In reality, it was one and the same look: the look took its meaning only in relation to the preceding sequence" (Ch. Rambaud). Now let us take two examples from the Gospels, the one on detail, and the other on ensemble. Matthew and Luke both report the episode of the two (or three) men who want to follow Jesus: a memory is recounted by the apostles. It it kept in the community, who recall that to follow Jesus is demanding. Matthew and Luke have gathered it but have made a different mounting and the meaning is modified. Luke places it at the peak of his Gospel, at the moment in which Jesus turns "resolutely" toward the Cross and decides to go up to Jerusalem to die. Thus his response to the three men who wish to follow him is a warning: to become his disciple, you must loose all ties, without looking back, and go with him to Calvary (Luke 9:57-62). In Matthew this episode cuts off or divides the account of the calming of the storm which he has oriented toward the faith of the disciples (Matt. 8:19-22; cf. note 30, p. 57). Thus in Matthew, the two men in Luke become two **disciples** who have already abandoned everything for Jesus. The words of Christ are no longer the first call to leave everything, but a "second call" inviting the disciples of all times to progress constantly in detachment and in faith. Another example of an entire "sequence": Matthew and Mark recount for us the sending of the apostles on mission and the discourse in parables. But they reverse the position of the two collections and the general sense of the parables is modified. In Mark, Jesus speaks in parables before sending his disciples: they are a simple and imaginative way of presenting the message and are primarily an invitation to conversion. In Matthew, Jesus sends his apostles from the beginning of his ministry in Galilee and he preaches in parables only at the end of this ministry when the Galilean crowds are already starting to turn away from him. In this context, the parables take on a warning or threatening note: to these people who have already decided against him, the final judgment, a theme of very many of the parables, remains a call to conversion but sounds especially as a threat.

Hence after thirty or forty years of making and of "stock-piling" sequences and series on Jesus in the midst of the community, four authors, Matthew, Mark, Luke, and John, about the years 60 to 80, undertake the mounting. But from the same mass of documents, because each has a different personality, and a different theology, because each addresses himself to a different audience, they produce not **one,** but **four** films: each of them through his mounting will reveal to us—and this is what renders the reading of them so alive—the aspect of the personality of Jesus that struck him the most. The Gospels are not "a verbal presentation of marvelous facts but, rather, the testimony of intimate friends who were in the company of a person and have drawn near to his secret" (Benoit)[2] The witness, says J. Guitton, is a being "pierced through": I have a friend; by entering into close friendship with him, I have discovered a secret which gives new meaning to my life; I cannot help but speak about him and want to bring other people to share in his close friendship. "We cannot speak of what we have seen and heard," said Peter and John to the Jewish leaders.

The Gospels are a **testimony:** here is a new "key" for reading them. We said above: they are a response to the questions of the community. To understand them we must know these questions by becoming familiar with the early Church and have our own questions to put to them (cf. p. 42). Now we add: we cannot understand them unless we become friends with each of the redactors. The more I become a friend of Camus, Bergman, the more their works will "speak" to me. To read the Gospels, we must become friends of Luke, of John. To open their books we must first enter the home of a friend to converse with him about the Person who changed his whole life. Because we do not have the room, we cannot undertake here the continuous reading of each Gospel as we have attempted with the other writings. In these few pages I will attempt only to help you to enter closely into their lives by studying their personality, their centers of interest, their theology. Or better perhaps, for all these studies are still in their beginning stages, I would like to tell you in a few words what my friends, Mark, Matthew, Luke, and John, say to me—and it is too bad if this is not the most important.

The Gospel according to Mark
"Who Is This man? . . . The Son of God."

Who would have dreamed of such an opportunity as to follow the life of Jesus with the eyes of Peter? This is what the Gospel according to Mark offers. There is no doubt about the author: "Mark, the intrepreter of Peter, who wrote accurately, but not in order, all that he recalled of the words or actions of the Lord."[3] Here indeed is the fisherman from the Lake of Galilee: everything is concrete, living, first-hand. Very often we must replace the impersonal plural of the verbs with a "we." We came to Capernaum. . . . then we went home. My mother-in-law was in bed . . ." (1:21f.). The scenes are described in the present with "everyday" words which the lovers of literary style find awkward and which Luke carefully avoids: when Jesus, for example, tells him that he will deny him, Peter replies "even more earnestly" (Mark 14:31). The visual details are added as they are seen, and often without logic. Note the numerous "and's" which intersperse the account or the "because's" which fall almost haphazardly in the text: the daughter of Jairus is revived "because she was twelve years old," or again "the women saw the stone was rolled back from the tomb because it was very large." The masterpiece of this kind is the account of the cure of the blind man in Bethsaida: "Jesus put spittle on his eyes. . . . Do you see any thing? . . . The man, who was beginning to see, replied: I can see people; they look like trees walking about. . . . and afterwards, he could see everything plainly and distinctly" (8:24-25). Mark is a marvelous popular storyteller, stressing the important words, changing the speakers, studding the text with picturesque words and dimunitives.

But beneath this popular and attractive exterior, this Gospel conceals a dramatic character.

The Gospel before Easter:

The Gospel of Mark is a question, a single question: "Who is this man?" And he who learned the answer from Peter attempts to lead us to recognize with him: "This is the Son of God."

Son of God: This title is set before us from the opening line of his book: "The beginning of the Good News about Jesus Christ, the Son of God." For him the word has the full sense which we now give it.[4] While Matthew uses it frequently, Mark uses it on only three occasions in the life of Jesus:[5] at the baptism of Jesus (1:11), and at the transfiguration (9:7), God declares him his Son. Finally at the foot of the Cross, the Roman centurion (a Gentile) cries out: "Truly this man was the Son of God" (15:39). To lead us to the same faith, Mark invites us to walk the same path that Peter trod. And this path has two stages.

After his baptism, Jesus preaches in Galilee, first to the **crowd**; then as they become more and more hesitant and wavering in their acceptance, he turns to his **disciples**, and finally to the **Twelve**. After this long period of teaching and living with them, Jesus risks "the question" with his apostles: "Who do people say I am? . . . Who am I for you?" Peter in his usual impetuosity cries out, "You are the Messiah" (8:27-30). We get the impression that Jesus breathes freely again: finally a first step in complete openness! For his apostles he is not merely a prophet, he is "the" Prophet, the Messiah (or the Christ, the Greek translation of the word Messiah). This confession of Peter in Caesarea thus marks the turning point in the life of Jesus: now he will be able to work to bring their openness to the next stage. He is indeed the Messiah, but not the kind they are expecting: he is not a glorious, but a suffering, Messiah.

The solemn declaration of God at the baptism, "You are my Son" had inaugurated the first stage. A similar testimony, addressed this time to the disciple-witnesses, will give rise to the second stage: "This is my Son," proclaims the voice of the Father at the Transfiguration. And from that moment, Jesus starts for Jerusalem, for his death. At the end of this stage, at the moment he is dying on the Cross, the Roman centurion, in the name of all the Gentiles, recognizes him as "Son of God." This is the point to which Mark wanted to lead us by revealing the Good News to us: that we, the Gentiles, recognize Jesus as Son of God. "To reveal" the Good News to us: the Gospel is an "**Apocalypse**": a second title of Jesus will bring us to understand this.

Son of Man: This is the only title Jesus uses of himself. Jesus seems to have a special liking for it because of its ambiguity: in the current language of the times, this expression meant "man" ("son of" corresponds to "of the class of," of the species of"). Since the time of Daniel and in relation to his visions (cf. OT, pp. 176, 231) it designates someone heavenly, this mysterious person who was to come at the end of time to complete history and make the judgment. By insisting on the human or the heavenly aspect as the event demanded, this title manifested what Christ wanted to reveal and at the same time concealed it: it allowed him to express his proper mystery and yet to be understood by his listeners in a common way. The peak of the Gospel according to Mark is that moment in which Jesus before the Sanhedrin solemnly proclaims himself the Son of Man (14:62).[6] Why did he wait till then? We must say a word here about "the messianic secret."

The Messianic Secret: One fact has always struck the readers of Mark: In Mark, Jesus imposes secrecy on his true personality. He refuses or, only after qualifying the names, accepts the titles they give him (e.g., Son of David); he forbids the demons to say who he is; he forbids Peter and the Twelve to speak of the revelation they have had (as in the Transfiguration). Until the "Son of Man has been raised from among the dead." Novels have been written about this imposing of silence.[7] As a matter of fact, this was a necessity for Jesus: He could not, without running the risk of misunderstanding, allow a statement of his identity before he had shown who he really was by his deeds. To do this from the beginning would have been to confirm his listeners in their notion of a glorious Messiah. (Did they not want to make him king after one miracle?) Thus it is only at the moment of his death that he breaks this silence. There is no longer any danger that they want to make him king; his death is decided. The Sanhedrin poses the question of his identity. Jesus is to die and he must say not exactly who he is in order that his death take on it full significance of sacrifice willed and accepted. "Are you the Christ, the Son of the Blessed One?—This is what you say, replies Jesus.[8] But this is how I present myself: you shall see the Son of man seated at the right side of God and coming with the clouds of heaven. . . . He has blasphemed!" At this solemn moment Jesus breaks the silence by proclaiming explicitly for everyone who is able to hear—and his adversaries are able because they know the Scriptures—what he is conscious of being: **the Son of David,** this glorious Messiah charged with remaking the Kingdom of God, whom the Lord will introduce to his right side (ps. 110) and the **Son of Man** of Daniel who will come from the heavens to pass judgment. At the same time because he designates himself thus at the moment in which he is condemned to death, he manifests himself as the **Suffering Servant** announced by Isaiah and Zechariah. When he is sure of being rightly understood, Jesus breaks the silence he has imposed. Hence the silence is due first to his pedagogy. But it is also inherent in the apocalyptic form. God is God and he is incomprehensible to man. Man cannot "grasp" him or comprehend him. Even when God reveals himself, he remains the unknowable. Mark brings us to share here in the experience of Peter who only very gradually perceived the personality of his Master, and Mark was very aware of this lack of understanding of the man. In the presence of the mystery, he is "closed." In fact, Jesus makes this complaint: "Do you not understand yet? Are your minds so closed?" (Mark 8:17).[9] At the great turning point of his life, after the confession of Peter in Caesarea, Jesus wishes to reveal himself to his disciples as the Suffering Servant and Peter does not understand this! "God forbid that . . ." In the Garden of Gethsemane, after this struggle during which his close friends are asleep, Mark shows us Jesus plunging alone into the night of his Passion: the last to want to follow him has fled, naked: **naked:** Here is the concluding word of the passage and it gives this account an atmosphere of catastrophe. This is also what Mark tells us when we enter his home, this solitude of the condemned Jesus, during his life and to the end of time, not to be able to say clearly who he is because our vision is blurred and our heart hardened (16:14). But to every man of good will he presents himself as a question, as the question: "For you, who am I?"

Because our entire existence depends on our response, Mark urges us to answer with the centurion: "You are the Son of God."[10] And at the end of his Gospel in its present state[11] he shows us the apostles, all Christians, sent into the entire world to proclaim this Good News. **Sent,** but not alone—and this is the last word—"The Lord works with them."

PLAN OF THE GOSPEL ACCORDING TO MARK

Mark's Gospel is not a thesis and the plan is difficult to establish. However, several indications can help us here.

Theological indications: We noted the turning point in the life of Jesus at the moment of the confession in Caesarea and the three proclamations of Jesus as Son of God. We can already determine two major parts, starting each with a declaration by God (baptism and Transfiguration) and ending with a profession of faith on the part of men: "You are the Messiah"; "This was the Son of God": the mystery of the **Messiah** unveiled gradually and recognized in Caesarea; the mystery of the **Son of man** revealed in an obscure way and then clearly by Jesus before the Sanhedrin and recognized on the Cross by the Gentiles.

Geographical indications: Some topographical data intersperse this Gospel: baptism in Judea; ministry in Galilee; trip outside of Galilee; arrival in Jerusalem and the Passion.

By adding a few literary indications (little summaries,

for example, punctuate a story), Father Xavier Léon-Dufour proposes this plan:

Prologue (1:1-13): Preaching of John Baptist. Baptism. Temptation

I. **The Mystery of the Messiah** (1:14-8:30)

Judea
Galilee

Three Sections

Each one **starts** with a summary of the activity of Jesus and an account of the disciples

Each one **ends** with mention of the attitude toward Jesus

A. **Jesus and the People** (1:14-3:6)

1. Introduction: Beginning of the preaching of the Kingdom and call of the first disciples (1:14-20)
2. A typical day's work in the ministry of Capernaum (1:21-45)
3. Five controversies and a few stories (2:1-3:5)
4. Conclusion: the Pharisees decide on the death of Jesus

B. **Jesus and His Own** (3:7-6:6)

1. Introduction: Cures, exorcisms, and choosing the Twelve (3:7-19)
2. Stories: for or against Jesus (3:20-35)
3. Parables (4:1-34)
4. Three miracles (4:35-5:43)
5. Conclusion: Jesus misunderstood by his own (6:1-6)

C. **Jesus and His Disciples** (6:6-8:30)

Outside Galilee

1. Introduction: Mission of the Twelve (6:6-30)

2. Two multiplications of bread each followed by miracles and instruction (6:31-8:26)
3. Conclusion: Confession of Peter in Caesarea and secrecy demanded (8:27-30)

II. **The Mystery of the Son of Man** (8:31-16:8)

Toward Jerusalem

A. Going up to Jerusalem: (8:31-10:52)

This going up is interspersed by three announcements of the lot of the Son of Man, each followed by an instruction on the lot of the disciples.

1. First announcement (8:31-33): instruction; transfiguration; cure (8:34-9:29)
2. Second announcement (9:30-32)
   a. Instruction en route (9:33-50)
   b. Deeper instruction (10:1-31)
3. Third announcement (10:32-34)

In Transjordania

   a. Instruction which is given while going up to Jerusalem (10:35-45)
   b. The Son of David proclaimed by the blind man of Jericho (10:46-53)

Jerusalem

B. The Judgment of Jerusalem (chs. 11-13)

1. Judgment in deeds: Messianic entrance with palms. Salesmen in temple (11:1-26)
2. Judgment in words: Controversies and parable of murderous vine-dressers (11:27-12:12)
3. Instruction (12:13-44): Announcement of destruction of temple and end of the world (ch. 13)

C. **The Passion and the Resurrection** (chs. 14-16)

1. From conspiracy to arrest: The interior aspect of the Passion (14:1-42)

a. Preludes: Foreknowledge of Jesus "handed over" by the Father (14:1-16)

b. Sacramental fulfillment: the Eucharist (14:17-31)

c. The interior offering of Jesus (14:32-42)

2. From the arrest to the death: the external unfolding of the Passion (14:43-15:47)

a. The arrest (14:43-52)

b. The trial with the Jews: Jesus condemned as Messiah by Jewish leaders (14:53-72)

c. The Roman trial: Jesus condemned as king by the Gentiles (15:1-20)

d. Crucifixion and death (15:21-47)

Epilogue: The Empty Tomb: "Jesus is living, he goes before you . . ." (16:1-8)

Appendix: The appearances of Jesus Risen establishing the Eleven as his witnesses (16:9-20). (**Translator's Note:** The original account would have stopped with verse 8 because this Gospel was primarily intended as a kerygma in the beginning. It is primarily for people who are coming to accept Jesus for the first time. Whereas the Appearances of the Risen Christ are primarily to deepen the faith of people who already believe.)

The Gospel according to Matthew

"We Have Found the Messiah"

On opening the Gospel according to Matthew we enter a completely different universe. With Mark, we get the impression of walking side by side with a friend on the paths of Palestine. This is wonderful: each village, each hill recalls to his mind an anecdote, a word of Jesus, each detour in the path stops him as he tells us what happened there: children who came running up, a blind man who is begging, or the Pharisees who attack, the eager, open face of Peter rises—or John—or James—or the disciples in a hot dispute. Luke will recall more the warm friendship of the host welcoming us into the room where, throughout the vigil, in a brotherly, heartfelt conversation, he will tell us of him whom he loves, of his disturbing friendship with the Lord Jesus. Matthew brings us into a church. The Christ whom we shall meet is less the prophet wandering on the shores of Lake Tiberias, the friend at whose feet we sit as Mary sat, than the Messiah careful to fulfill, by his words and deeds, the mission entrusted to him by the Father. He is the Christ whom we meet at each Mass continuing to the end of time his presence and his mission through the preaching of his Church and through the sacraments which perpetuate his saving acts. Christ is less living than in Mark, more priestly, but also more fascinating.

All this flows from the personality of the author, a Christian come from Judaism,[12] as well as his audience: Matthew introduces us into a Judeo-Christian church of Palestine. These people are not Christians from yesterday —we could say they are Christians of fifteen centuries— in hope. For ten or fifteen centuries, this people Israel, of whom they are the issue, lived with the Word of God who dwells with them. They meditate on it, diligently dig into it, make it their rule of conduct. What does this Word say to Israel? Rather than confidences about God, it is a recalling of the work he has done, an announcement especially of what he will accomplish when the Messiah comes. But the Messiah has come! He has fulfilled this work! To know Jesus, for these Christians, is first of all situating him in the plan of God at the end of this long waiting and their hope; it is to see how he brings into reality these prophecies of Scripture, prophecies that are mysterious and at times seemingly contradictory. In fact, this is so true that Israel did not recognize him and crucified him! But now that he is here, now that the Church is alive, is organized, lives by the sacraments, all this becomes clear. Matthew will multiply the quotations from the Old Testament to show their fulfillment in Jesus.

Whatever you may think of the result, in choosing to carry this Gospel to the movie screen, Pasolini has grasped well that the Christ of Matthew is, before all else, one who has a work to accomplish, a mission to fulfill: and hence this very swift-moving film in which Jesus runs all the time, tiring us out, where the scenes follow one another in an ever faster rhythm. This work is the Kingdom of God (or "of the heavens" as Matthew says more often, but it comes to the same thing). But while they were expecting a Messiah to establish this Kingdom in a single act, Jesus does it in "sacrament": He is this Kingdom fully in his own person and he has inaugurated it through this Church whose foundations he has laid. Thus the Church will be the center of the considerations of this Gospel. Jesus lays the foundation by gathering together disciples and by choosing from among them the Twelve, the future leaders of the true Israel of twelve tribes.[13] He structures this "apostolic body" by giving it Simon as their leader, whom he has made the "Bedrock" (Kepha) of the foundation of his Church.[14] Jesus, Word of God, turns all his attention to the instruction of this Church. He does this by his words—and Matthew gives us the fullest picture of this—and by his acts: his miracles as well as the events of his life are also Word of God. On two occasions, and this sums up well the thought of the author, he tells us: "Jesus went through all the towns and villages **teaching** in their synagogues, **proclaiming** the Good News of the Kingdom, and **curing**" (4:23; 9:25). This interest for the

Church appears clearly in the five great discourses which span the Gospel.

1. **The Sermon on the Mount** (chs. 5-7) is the sermon-program of Jesus in Matthew. We shall take a little time out on this section to get a better acquaintance with Matthew.

If Matthew had been a florist he would not have known how to make a bouquet: to keep only one rose, for example, and a dead branch, while letting the rest of the blossoms fall, would have been impossible for him! He is interested in the whole armful of flowers. His gift is, first, that of compilation. And we understand this. Matthew is a pastor, a shepherd, concerned about teaching his faithful. To let words of Jesus fall would seem impossible. His sermon on the Mount is a good example of this. At first glance it seems like a disconcerting conglomeration of different thoughts put end to end. Actually there was an original outline that was simpler. He attached other sayings of Jesus which were related to the same subjects so as to lose nothing. But did they lose a little in clarity? This is possible. But what riches in this ensemble with its profound unity around this fact: the gospel is the new law by which Jesus "completes"[15] the old law by making it internal and identifying it with himself. Look at this more closely.

Specialists have sought for the basic outline from which Matthew starts: J. Dupont reconstructs it thus:[16]

The Beatitudes (5:3-12) for the introduction to a discourse made up of three parts

(a) **Perfect Justice:**[17]

A general statement (5:17, 20) relates this to the justice given by the old law: "I did not come to destroy the law but to complete it."

Jesus gives **five illustrations** of this:

5:21-24: Not only "do not kill," **but first respect your brother.**

5:27-28: "Do not commit adultery," but **first cleanse your heart,** the source of all sin.

5:33-37: "Do not perjure yourself": **Be a man of your word!**

5:38-42: No law based on revenge: **grant real pardon.**

5:43-48: Love all men, even your enemies.

(b) **Good Works:**

A general directive: "When you do anything good, do it for the Father; and don't play the gallery" (6:1)

Three examples to illustrate:

6:2-4: "When you give an alms or help a friend, don't blow a trumpet."

6:5-6: "Don't pray out in public so as to show off and win the admiration of others—but pray from the heart, from conviction."[18]

6:16-18: "When you mortify yourself, don't put on a long face: wash your face and comb your hair."[19]

(c) **Three Warnings:** Illustrated by history bring this sermon to an end:

7:1-5: "Do not judge others—like the man who tried to remove the splinter from the neighbor's eye while he had a timber in his own."

7:16-20: "Do not trust those who come to you with beautiful words as they set out on shady deals: Look at their acts: a good tree is known by its fruit."

7:21, 24-27: "A little action is a lot better than many good words: It is good to say, Lord, Lord! to go to Mass, to take part in a movement but first we must roll up our sleeves."

By rereading the present text of Matthew, you will have no difficulty in finding the additions that were made, and in recognizing also that this does not alter the general structure. It is perhaps more important to seek the central idea that unifies this discourse. By proclaiming the **gospel,** Jesus gives us a **new law** in relation to the old, because he has "interiorized it and personified it in himself."[20] Jesus has rendered the law **interior:** the deeds do not count as much as the disposition which motivates them. And this disposition has a name: **love**. If love thus becomes the foundation, this interior law becomes an **absolute**: This does not mean there are some Christians who have it and some who do not! This law is absolute for everyone, and yet for everyone **impracticable**! Or it would be totally impracticable if Jesus had not **personalized** the law in his own person. The law is not a regulation which falls on us from above or from the outside. It is the very person of Jesus that we are treating of imitating, or better, in whom we must let ourselves be identified so that he acts in us.[21] This shows the value of the Beatitudes which are placed at the beginning of this discourse and thus reveal its meaning (a proclamation of the Good News) and point out the beneficiaries: the "poor," the little ones, the persecuted, in a word, those who can only receive.[22] To these God can only give. The gratuity of this all-powerful love allows us to understand the Beatitudes as a program of perfection, without being crushed by it: "Come to me, Jesus says, and if you welcome me, I will do in you what you could not do: Love the Father, and love others."

We took a little extra time with this discourse, so we shall have to pass quickly over the other four. But you will recognize the same spirit.

2. **The "Mission Discourse":** Jesus sends his apostles to proclaim the Good News (ch. 10) which is exactly what

they will have to do and what we have to do to the end of the world. And this mission is terribly demanding of those who accept it.

3. **The "Discourse in Parables"** (ch. 13:1-52): The crowd, toward the end of his ministry in Galilee, begins to abandon Jesus—but some remain faithful: this Discourse in Parables presents the Kingdom in its humble and disconcerting aspect. It is a final appeal of Jesus to choose for or against him, a true dichotomy. We have to choose the kind of land we are to be: the stony ground or the good soil. And these parables have their value always for us who are already in the Church: this is the field where the good and the bad grain grow. Let us choose to be good grain before the time of harvest when the Church, cleansed of all that is bad, will be changed into the Kingdom of God.

4. **The "Christian Community Discourse":** After the failure of his preaching in Galilee, Jesus turns full force to the formation of his disciples. He sketches with them a first outline of the Kingdom and gives them the "**rule for the Christian Community**" (ch. 18): the dispositions of children, pardon (seeking the lost sheep, mutual correction, pardon without limit, and the gift of this power to pardon to his Church), presence of Jesus: "Where two or three are gathered together into my name, there I am in the midst of them."[23]

5. **Apocalyptic Discourse:** Finally, in Jerusalem, after he had clearly announced his death by the parable of the murderous vine-dressers or sharecroppers in which he presents himself as the Son of God and has wept over the rejection of his people (the mother bird and the little ones), Jesus announces how the Kingdom will be brought to reality: there will be a great final crisis (of which the

destruction of Jerusalem is an image) and then the "coming" of the Son of man.[24]

Besides this regrouping of the words of Jesus, we note other collections: the ten miracles of chapters 8-9 and the series of controversies with the Pharisees (chs. 22-23).

Another specialty in relation to Mark: Matthew, like Luke but from another point of view, gives us **an account of the infancy of Jesus.** This is new. In studying the kerygma, the proclamation of the essentials of the message, in the early Church (cf. ch. II above), we noted that the life of Jesus seemed to begin with the preaching of John the Baptist and the baptism of Jesus (reread for example, the discourse of Peter). The fact that they are now composing accounts of the infancy is a sign of a deepening. Only gradually did the first Christians become conscious of the mystery of Jesus.[25] With Father Benoit, we can distinguish five stages in this becoming conscious: (1) Jesus is for his disciples a man, a prophet; (2) then from the confession of Peter in Caesarea Philippi they recognize him as the Messiah (always a man); (3) the resurrection and Pentecost lift the veil of his humanity for them and mark the decisive step; they preach Jesus as the Messiah who is God; (4) but in what sense is he God? (You cannot **become** God. If he is God now, he was before his death. By rereading his life in the light of Easter, they have no trouble in discovering that Jesus, discretely but clearly, declared that he was Son of God.[26] This is the depth that had been reached at the time of the discourse of Peter. But the faith of the community had to continue this quest of the real personality of Jesus.) (5) **Son of God:** he is not only from his baptism by John but he is since his birth (infancy accounts of Matthew and Luke); he is from all eternity (Prologue of John). About this life previous to his earthly birth, two men of genius, Paul and John, attempt the first theological reflection: John presents him as the eternal "Word" of the Father, Paul as the "Image" of God, the reflection of his substance.

These two chapters of the infancy narrative are a marvelous summary of the mystery of Jesus. The first chapter presents us with his paradoxical **personality:** man-God; chapter 2 presents his **mission.** Who could doubt that he is man after his genealogy[27] in which the music is more important than the words: this numerical acrostic of three times fourteen names gradually creates in us the certainty that he who is born at the end of the list is surely of our race, son of David, son of Abraham. But he is God also as the "annunciation to Joseph" shows. Because Joseph is "just," knowing that he has no part in this conception, Joseph does not wish to take Mary as wife and thus impose his name on this miraculous child. And God asks him to accept the role of bringing this child into our human family by giving the child his name.[28] Matthew then sums up the mission of Christ for us with the help of five Old Testament questions. Jesus takes up the essential points of the history of the people in order to bring it to fulfillment. The exodus, a symbol of deliverance from sin, is finally completed, since God has "called his Son out of Egypt." The announced Savior, son of David, is born in Bethlehem, as Micah announced it. The neo-Babylonian captivity was the great cleansing of the people. Jesus will fulfill this cleansing definitively by bearing this suffering in himself: Matthew presents Rachel, the tribal "queen-mother" of the people, weeping over this suffering as formerly over the pillars of the condemned that were set in Rama (north of Jerusalem). The prophets had said that from the sinful people there would be a "remnant" of the poor who would accept salvation: the true "Remnant," the starting point of a new people, is what is called "the Remnant" (in

Hebrew: **Nazoreen,** which is close to "Nazarene"—this seemed close enough for Matthew, who is not concerned primarily with the philology!). Of olden times, when his people came back from the exile to the Holy Land, God gave them a glimpse of an extraordinary future: all peoples would come up to Jerusalem to adore God (Isa. 60). This "epiphany," this "manifestation" of God to all the peoples, Matthew sees realized in sign in the visit of the wise men. A wonderful and tragic digest of the mission of Jesus. In his birth, his destiny is prefigured: man-God true Moses,[29] saving mankind, he fulfills all the marvelous deeds that God had announced for Messianic times. And though the Jews (Herod) reject him, already the Gentiles are running to him. Two great chapters. It would be wrong to allow the questions brought up about historicity to keep us from noting the wealth of theology.[30]

PLAN FOR THE GOSPEL ACCORDING TO MATTHEW

Five great discourses all ending with the same conclusion set off for us five collections of stories (7:28; 11:1; 13:53; 19:1; 26:1). Hence this Gospel is frequently presented as being composed of five "booklets," each made up of a story-section and a discourse, the whole of it preceded by an introduction (the infancy narrative) and ending with a conclusion: the Passion-resurrection (cf. the Introduction in the Jerusalem Bible). This is a very practical way to locate yourself easily in this book but "this seems to indicate a more profound study" (Léon-Dufour). For the moment I will gladly use again the plan proposed by Father Léon-Dufour who brings out the drama of the revelation: "Jesus demanded of his people an unreserved adherence to his Person, he proclaimed the admission of Gentiles into the Kingdom of the heavens. This meeting was to have been the fulfillment of the people of God. But because of the refusal of Israel, it becomes a separation, a tearing away. According to the plan of God, the Church is not the true people of God, Israel."

Prologue: 1. **The being of Jesus:** man-Son of God
2. **His mission:** to fulfill the Scripture. Rejected by the Jews but accepted by the Gentiles.

I. **The Jewish People refuse to believe in Jesus** (chs. 3-13)
Introduction: John the Baptist. Baptism. Temptation (3:1-4:11)
A. Jesus all-powerful in words and in works (4:12-9:34)
1. **Introduction:** Journey to Galilee. Nazareth. Capernaum (4:12-25)
2. **Powerful in words:** Sermon on the Mount (chs. 5-7)
3. **Powerful in works:** A triumphal trip. Miracles (chs. 8-9)
B. **Jesus sends his disciples to extend his announcement of the Kingdom** (9:35-10:42)
C. Jesus demands that they choose for or against him (chs. 11-13)
1. The works of Jesus oblige several kinds of listeners to choose:
a. John the Baptist does not understand the manner of acting that Jesus adopts. Jesus answers him by his works (11:2-15)
b. The crowds who do not really change in outlook (11:16-24)
c. The Pharisees who attribute his miracles to Beelzebub and decide on his death (ch. 12)
d. The disciples to whom the Father reveals his secrets because they are committed (11:25-30)

Because they do the will of the Father, they are in the true family of Jesus (12:46-50)

2. The parables also oblige them to choose for or against Jesus (ch. 13)
   Jesus speaks the parables to the crowd and explains them to the disciples. The parable of the farmer sowing grain sums up this first part and lets each of his listeners see what kind of soil he is, how he welcomes the Word of God.

II. **The Passion and the Glory** (chs. 14-28)

A. **Toward Jerusalem** (chs. 14-20): **This account is centered in the disciples**

1. Jesus withdraws and sets about founding his Church (14:1-16:20)
   a. The withdrawal in three stages (14; 15; 16:1-12)
   b. Jesus prepares the foundation of his Church on "Peter" (16:13-20)

2. Jesus goes up to Jerusalem and instructs his Church (16:21-20:18)
   The withdrawal divided by three announcements of the Passion (16:21; 17:22; 20:17)

TRANSITION: In Jerichō, Jesus is recognized as Son of David by two blind men who see in spite of their blindness and follow him (20:19-34)

B. **In Jerusalem** (chs. 21-28): This account is centered **in his enemies:**

Introduction: The Son of David enters Jerusalem and takes possession of the temple (21:1-22)

1. Jesus confronts his enemies: 21:23-23:39
2. **The Great Judgment:** 24:1-27:66
   a. **The world judged by Jesus:** eschatological judgment (chs. 24-25)

b. **Jesus judged by the world:** the Passion (chs. 26-27)
   1. From conspiracy to arrest: the interior aspect of the passion (26:1-46)
      a. The preludes: Jesus himself puts the different actors in place (26:1-35)
      b. The sacramental fulfillment: the Eucharist (26:20-29)
      c. The interior offering of Jesus (26:36-46)
   2. From the arrest to the death. The external unfolding of the Passion (26:47-27:66)
      a. The arrest (26:47-56)
      b. The Jewish trial (26:57-27:10)
      c. The Roman trial (72:11-31)
      d. The crucifixion and death (27:32-66)

Epilogue: The Judgment of God: the Resurrection (28:1-20) Jesus appears in Galilee and gives his disciples the mission to the entire world.

The Gospel according to Luke
The Joy of God

Nativité by Georges de la Tour. We are introduced into a marvelous universe, warm as the light which makes the dense texture sing, mysterious because of the complete penumbra (half-light) which fills the scene; peace springing from interior depth; the abandon of God within the arms of man. A universe in which it is good to lose onself as in a confidence, but as unspeakable as a confidence. **This is the Gospel of Luke.** Already we have extensive acquaintance with him. But what are we to say of his work? A confidence is not summed up: we listen to it and we communicate it. This section is going to seem confused to you. But I have worked it over ten times and I am convinced that I will not be able to arrange his principal themes in a logical synthesis. It will be better to read as a unit some of the texts in which we shall find all of them. But to explain our choice of these four texts we must begin with a little technical detail.

The Synoptic Problem

A mere glance at the synopsis[31] of the Gospels will show us this:

- Some **texts** are common to Matthew, Mark, and Luke (thus we speak of a "triple tradition") but then their **order** is generally different: Matthew on one side and Mark and Luke on the other.
- Some texts are found only in Matthew and Luke (we speak of a "double tradition") but here again the order is different in the two.
- Some texts are proper to each one: **Matthew** (between 500 and 600 verses out of 1,068); **Luke** (from 500 to 600 verses out of 1,150); **Mark** (about 50 verses out of 661).

The general framework of the life of Jesus is the same for all three. But in Luke two collections have interrupted this common outline: they are composed of texts proper to Luke or common to Matthew and Luke (double tradition).

The following is an outline from the three steps in the formation of the Gospels:[32]

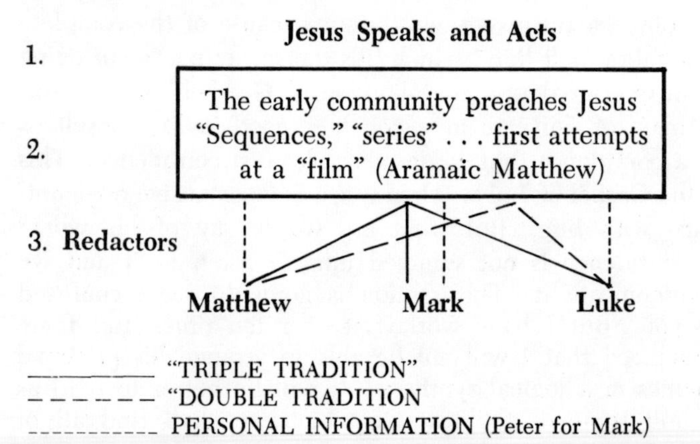

Now let us return to Luke. He follows Mark as to the texts and their order, or better, he follows a common sources previous to Mark which he reproduces quite faithfully. In relation to Mark, Matthew and Luke have a supplement of information (common to the two, or proper to each), but they use it differently: Matthew intersperses these texts throughout the outline common to the three. Luke prefers to "insert" them on two occasions, as two large parentheses.[33] Thus from the point of view of material in Luke, there is a very simple plan.

Plan of the Gospel of Luke

I. Prologue (1-2): Narratives of the infancy of Jesus

II. In Galilee (3:1-9:50): In relation to Mark, these chapters are divided in this way:

3:1-6:19: A collection in common with Mark (chs. 1-3)

6:20-8:3: First parenthesis proper to Luke: the "little insertion"

8:4-9:50: A collection in common with Mark (chs. 4-9) (except for Mark (6:45-8:26, which Luke has omitted without our knowing why)

III. **Toward Jerusalem** (9:51-19:27)

9:51-18:14: Second parenthesis: The "Great Insertion," or the "Ascent to Jerusalem"

18:15-19:27: A collection in common with Mark (10:13-52)

IV. **In Jerusalem** (19:28-24:53): A collection in common with Mark (chs. 11-16) (The same plan as Mark and Matthew: cf. above)

We shall go through four of these texts: the infancy narratives, because in them Luke touches on all the themes dear to him; the discourse in Nazareth, which is Luke's presentation of the "discourse program" of Jesus (4:16-44); the cure of the ten lepers, which teaches us the real key to the "Great Insertion" (17:11-19); and finally the account of the travelers on the road to Emmaus (24:13-35).

The Infancy of Jesus (chs. 1-2)

Luke composed his Gospel after the manner of a Hollywood film known as a "flashback." For example, take the movie **Death, Where Is Your Victory?** The wife of a prominent politician leads a completely dissolute life. When her husband dies, she enters Carmel. The first shot of the movie shows this woman praying, dressed in a Carmelite habit. Thus from the beginning the author presents us the conclusion to warn us that it is in the light of this conclusion that this entire life is to be seen. Mark had chosen to make us relive the life of Jesus as it progressively unfolded in the eyes of Peter. Luke prefers from the beginning to point out to us all that he has learned about the being and the mission of the "Lord" Jesus. He does it in these two chapters where most often people are talking about "folktales," and yet in reality they are nothing less than the "overture" of a vast symphony.

– – – – – –

Translator's Insert on the Meaning and Function of an Overture

In an opera, the story is the essential framework for the music and no appreciation of an opera is complete if the story is unclear to the listener. The overture to the opera, since the time of Glück (18th century) has prepared the audience for the action to follow by including some of the themes or at least by setting the tone and putting the audience into the proper mood.

The overture to **William Tell,** with its Alpine repose, geographical setting, its great storm picture, the injustices mounting, the stirring dance of the Swiss cowherds, the call of the countrymen to arms, and the trumpet call to freedom, Tell's acceptance of the people's desire to have him lead them with a hint of future victory, is one of the most perfect and beautiful ever written.

The overture is completely understood only after all the events of the story have revealed themselves. And at the same time the overture prepares the way for understanding the whole story. However, the overture cannot be understood at all if one knows nothing of what is to follow or is totally disinterested.

– – – – – –

All which years of meditation, alone, with Paul, especially with the Virgin Mary, have uncovered for Luke of the mystery of the Lord, he puts before us in these pages in which, very freely, not dependent on documents, he can expose his theology in his own way.[34]

The fundamental note of these chapters, as well as of the whole Gospel, is **joy**. You find it everywhere in Luke. Everybody sings: Zachary because he will have a child, and Mary because God has done great things in her; John the Baptist and Elizabeth because the Virgin has visited them; the messengers in the heavens and the sinners on earth; the apostles because they are persecuted and the poor because they are filled; Zaccheus who in his joy distributes his goods, and the pagans who hear the call to salvation and Jesus who rejoices at the joy of his disciples; above all, God whose joy as Father, the Father of the prodigal son, radiates through the whole Gospel. For this joy is first of all the joy of God. Reread the Benedictus: this Christian hymn on the paschal victory of Jesus which Luke puts on the lips of Zachary:[35] three parallel strophes (vss. 68-71; 72-75; 78-79) which praise God because he has "visited" his people (I), and has shown them mercy (II), according to the promises made to the ancestors. This is the work "of the merciful tenderness" of our God who has sent us from on high the "visit" of Jesus, the "Rising Sun" (cf. Mal. 3:20) (III). The "marvelous humanity" of God, "his love of mankind," the "philanthropy" (Tit. 3:4) of this "God-Mother." The joy of God is man because he can give him salvation, is the sinner himself because he can forgive him! Reread the three parables of mercy (ch. 15). Jesus recounts them in answer to an attack of the Pharisees, "he welcomes sinners." Elsewhere Jesus had responded to a similar attack by putting himself on the side of sinners. When he goes toward them it is because they need God as the sick man needs a doctor (5:31-32). Here he places himself on the side of God: when God permits sinners to come to him, God has need of them because they are his joy! "My son was dead and behold, he has come back to life." If the joy of God is to **give,** to for-**give,** the joy of man is to **receive salvation**, not to give something, even to God, but to receive, as a child in the arms of its mother. To the woman who cries out: "Blessed is the womb that bore you," i.e., "Blessed is she who **gave** you life," Jesus answers: "Blessed rather is the one who receives and accepts the Word of God": the joy of Mary receiving in herself her Lord, "Rejoice, totally favored one"; the joy of the shepherds on Christmas, "there is born to you a Savior." But God at times grants man his own joy of giving: the joy of the apostle sharing in the labor of Christ, Paul sharing in the sufferings of Jesus (Philippians), Peter and John "judged worthy to undergo outrages for the Name of Jesus" (Acts 5:41); the joy of the disciples of Antioch when Paul and Barnabas were under persecution (Acts 13:52); the joy of Stephen whose death is in the image of the death of Jesus (Acts 6-7); joy of the apostles and the early Church (Acts 4:24-31) and that of the apostles of all times.[36]

Luke 1-2 is made up of a double account, closely

parallel, of the infancy of John Baptist and the infancy of Jesus. They meet at the visitation. The "Annunciation to Mary" is the mother-cell which is the beginning of their relation to each other. Constructed according to the literary form, "Annunciation,"[37] this beautiful text is not surpassed perhaps for its theological depth, except by the Prologue of John. Luke sees fulfilled in it the espousals (the promise of marriage) between God and mankind. Mary, this very real young girl of Nazareth, is for him the symbol of the entire people of God, of all mankind: she is the "Daughter of Zion."[38] As a husband anxious for a response of love from her whom he loves, God (in what manner is of little importance) comes to ask Mary to accept him. Mary the wife of Christ before becoming his mother! God entrusts Mary with her mission at two times. He asks her first to be the mother of the **Messiah-King,** Son of David (cf. 2 Sam. 7:12-16), then to be the mother of the **Son of God** (1:35). This verse 35 is the result of forty years of meditation of the Church. The rare verb, "to-cover-with-his-shadow," designates in the Old Testament the "real presence" of God in his temple (Exod. 40:34-35; Num. 9:18, 22). From the resurrection of Jesus, they knew that God really resided in this "man." They quickly perceived that from his transfiguration God "covered-him-with-his-shadow" (Luke 9:34) and already from his baptism (3:22). Luke can complete the conquest of faith: from the conception of the child, "the Power of the Most High covers Mary with His Shadow," thus making her the true temple in which God-made-man dwells. To this "power" through which God realizes his marvels, Luke can now give his Name: **The Holy Spirit**. Mary thus receives the Word of God which takes a body in her womb: "I am the Servant of the Lord"[39] It is impossible to point out all the themes Luke touches in this account. We will point out the principal ones.

First, he tells us **who** this child is: **the Lord**. Luke is the only one to call Jesus by this title prior to his resurrection. It was enormous as a statement! The "Lord" in the Bible is Yahweh, the Totally-Other, a consuming fire (cf. OT, p. 69). And here the Totally-Other becomes the Totally-Near, a baby in the arms of a young girl! This, and all the other phrases of Luke, had to ring out as blasphemy to the Jewish ears, as an enormous marvel to the ears of the Christian: "The apostles draw near to the Lord"; "Mary sits at the feet of the Lord"; "Zaccheus, standing up, says to the Lord"; in Nain, when he saw a mother bringing a young son to the cemetery, the Lord felt sorry (The Greek reads: "The bowels of the Lord were in turmoil"); and Easter morning, the women "no longer found the body of the Lord"! Jesus, from the time of his earthly life, is the Lord of Glory whom his Church adores! Because he is the Lord, Jesus is **king**, but in a sense completely different from what they expected. Luke loves to show Jesus as king, but king by his suffering and death! See, for example, his entrance into Jerusalem with the palms (19:38), his testimony before the Sanhedrin (22:67-70), his promise to the thief on the cross (23:40-43).

The **mission** of Jesus is pointed out to us by his name, which, for a Semite, expresses the personality: "Yo-Shuah," i.e., "Yahweh saves." Jesus by definition is **Savior**. It is impossible to develop this humanity of God: this would oblige us to reread the entire work of him whom Dante called "The Evangelist of the meekness of Christ."

"The **Holy Spirit** will come upon you." No one has spoken to us like Luke about the Spirit, or better, has shown us the Spirit at work. The Acts of the Apostles is entitled by many "The Gospel of the Spirit." The Spirit is upon Jesus to make him fulfill his mission: to proclaim the Good News to the poor (4:14-18); in the Spirit, Jesus has access to the Father (10:21). Especially, the Spirit is the presence of Jesus continued in our world (cf. the accounts of the appearances of the Risen Jesus in Mark, Matthew, and Luke. According to Matthew, Jesus says: "I am with you to the end of the world," but without telling us how; so also in the finale of Mark, "the Lord works with them." According to Luke, Jesus is content to say—and this corresponds exactly with the preceding statements —"I am sending on you the Promise of my Father," i.e., the promised Holy Spirit). Jesus remains with us, works with us, **through his Spirit.**

Finally, Luke speaks of **Mary.** He "carefully goes over the whole story from the beginning" (1:3). Did he have to pass hours listening to her in the home of John, perhaps in Ephesus?[40] Mary is **in** the Church the model of the believer in whom God can do great things. She is also the figure **of** the Church, since she is from that moment, in image and reality, the Immaculate Virgin whom the Christ can present to himself, the wife whose wedding feast with the Lamb at the end of time is described in Revelation (Rev. 19), the mother in whom each believer can and must say to the Lord in his turn: "Be it done to me according to your word" (cf. OT, pp. 224-225).

We have taken our time over the Annunciation text. Let us quickly run through the other infancy accounts. Christian piety too often keeps only **Christmas** and the **Crib,** precisely the two points that Luke passes over quickly![41] For in this simplicity God wishes to be recognized: "This will be a sign: a baby in a stable." The meaning of the mystery is given to us by the word of the messengers where we find all the themes already mentioned: **joy,** for **all** the people, **David, Savior, Christ, Lord.**

"When the days were fulfilled in which . . . ." Five times this expression comes up in these accounts (The Jerusalem Bible does a poor job of translating: 1:23, 57; 2:6, 21, 22): this time, announced by Daniel and Malachi, in which the Messiah would enter into his temple, has thus arrived. On this occasion, the priest Simeon (nothing is said about his being an old man!) animated by the Spirit, clearly defines "the nature and the manner of the mission of salvation of Jesus. His prophecy is the peak of the manifestation" of the Lord Jesus in these chapters (Benoit). "My eyes have seen your **salvation** . . . for **all the peoples,** a light for the revelation of the Gentiles and the glory of Israel." Salvation is for **all peoples**. The universalism of salvation: this idea almost haunts Luke and he has undoubtedly understood it better in the presence of Paul. We spoke about it in Acts and we shall come back to it again. The glory of Israel is to be the Firstborn, he who benefits first from the Good News but to transmit it to the entire world. But this Firstborn will be for the most part the picture in the parable where he is indignant because the Father sets up a feast to welcome the younger brother who is a sinner (Luke 15:11-32). Thus Jesus will be, again Simeon is proclaiming, in the midst of the people of Israel as this sword of which Ezekiel spoke (14:17) dividing in two the "Daughter of Zion," the People, obliging each to choose for or against him. This option will thus reveal the inner choice that each has made.[42]

The last episode is the best example of a "flashback": **the coming of Jesus to the temple,** at twelve years of age, for the Passover, is a prefiguring of events which are accomplished at the time of his last Passover. We are in **Jerusalem,** in the **temple.** the entire life of Jesus, according to Luke, is centered in Jerusalem. The Gospel begins in the temple (vision of Zachary) and ends there: the apostles, after the ascension, are in the temple to praise God. Luke has simplified the itinerary of Jesus by omitting the trip outside Palestine, by presenting Christ Risen in Jerusalem, not in Galilee (but he knew this tradition, cf. 24:6). The life of Jesus is nothing more than a dramatic **ascent to Jerusalem,** the only place that a prophet can die (13:31). And from Jerusalem, according to Acts, the Gospel will take off for the conquest of the world. "Did you know that I must be in the house of my Father?" This is the first "**I must**" of a long series that runs through this Gospel, the "I must" of the plan of God (Luke 2:49; 4:43; 9:22; 15:32; 18:1; 24:26). Matthew frequently quotes the Old Testament. Luke does this less often, but with more depth. Instead of attaching himself to details, at times minimal, he attempts to bring us to perceive the **History of Salvation** which was announced formerly and is continued and realized now. As a good historian who reflects on the meaning of history, Luke sees the entire life of Jesus as the continuity of the prophecies, especially the Suffering Servant: "Was it not necessary that the Christ suffer to enter into his glory?" he asks the disciples on the way to Emmaus. And he will reread the whole of Scripture with them. "I must proclaim the Good News," "The Son of man must suffer very much," "He must be handed over[43] As a prophet, the great history that unfolds is before all else **the struggle between God and Satan.** All this suffering which reaches Jesus and all men comes in the final analysis from evil. After he was tested, the devil leaves Jesus "to come back at the set time" (Kairos): the devil lost, he can no longer tempt Jesus,[44] but he will get his revenge, he thinks, on the Cross (for "Satan enters into Judas," 22:3). Do not think, however, that this is the "I must" of Stoicism. Jesus knows that he must "suffer"—for Luke this verb means the entire Passion and death—but in his heart as man he experiences all the anguish of it. Reread the Passion account: to recount it to us, Luke situates himself in the heart of the Lord. There the Passion is played in full, in his internal offering terribly resisted by his freedom as man. When the blood of Jesus flows, it is not because of an external cause (the delicacy of Luke could not have shown us his Lord naked, scourged) but only because of this interior commitment of himself: the bloody sweat in Gethsemane. "Why did you look for me? Did you know . . . ." (i.e., have you not read the Scriptures?) Yes! Mary had read them but she did not understand them. Even now she does not understand the words of Jesus, but—and she shows us the interior we should have—"she keeps them in her heart": Jesus points out the words of Scripture she should have, that we must have present in mind in order to understand the events of our life when they arrive. Finally, Jesus in his response, situates himself in relation to God: "Your father and I were seeking you," says Mary. ". . . in the temple of my Father," answers Jesus. The first word of Jesus, like his last on the Cross, is to call upon God, his Father."[45]

His "overture" ends. Luke introduces his account with a solemn Prologue, valuable for the synchronization it offers with profane history. Then after his baptism and the triple test, Jesus sets out for Nazareth.

The discourse program of Jesus in the synagogue of Nazareth (4:14-44)

Luke has succeeded in giving us a "mounting" here in which even the technique is seen! Four sequences: **4:14-15:** a panorama on the activity of Jesus in Galilee: "He teaches in the synagogues"; **4:16-30:** the discourse in Nazareth: "The Spirit has sent me to bring the Good News to the poor"; **4:31-41:** two miracles and an over-all picture of many cures; **4:42-43:** a conclusion that unifies the whole:

"In other towns also, I must proclaim the Good News of the Kingdom of God. And he preached in the synagogues." This skillful mounting gives us the inauguration of the ministry of Jesus in words and deeds as well as the double reaction he stirs up: acceptance and refusal.

The discourse in the synagogue holds in Luke the place that the Sermon on the Mount (put in a secondary place) holds in Matthew. The reactions of the listeners lead us to notice two phrases: first, all is praise, and then suddenly, without apparent reason, all are opposed. The change of tone takes place when Jesus speaks of the miracles he performs in Capernaum—where he does not go until later! This literary handling of details is clear (for Luke is honest): he has drawn together here **two visits** of Jesus to his hometown. In the first one he is accepted. Later, in another visit, he is rejected. By this ellipsis the whole result of the mission of Jesus is prefigured.

Jesus reads chapter 61 of Isaiah, the peak of the work of Third Isaiah (cf. OT, pp. 118-119). The prophet calls to mind the salvation of the end of time: grace and judgment, redemption and vengeance; he awakens the hope of the reign of God through the description of the new covenant, the marriage of God and his people before all the Gentile nations who have gathered together. They are waiting for the commentary that Jesus will give. The thunderbolt strikes in one sentence: "This is T O D A Y !" Suppose some people were living in constant dread of an atomic explosion which would wipe out their city. One day, a messenger is presented to them and he says simply: "It is done!" Imagine their amazement and incredulity. The short "today" of Jesus had to have the same lightning effect. All their messianic hope was to be carried out in this man, their fellow citizen; "T O D A Y": a key word in Luke! "Today, a Savior has been born to you," sing the messengers, and God at the baptism of Jesus declares: "Today, I have begotten you" (3:22); "Today, this house has received salvation," says Jesus upon entering the house of Zaccheus (19:5, 9) and to the thief on the cross: "Today, you shall be with me" (23:43; cf. 5:26; 13:32-33). This word introduces us to a conception of the history of salvation very personal to Luke. For Matthew and Mark, the history of salvation is made up of two times: **Before Christ:** the time of preparation; **With Christ,** the time of realization, of the Church. The life of Jesus is a sort of hingepoint between the two times. In Luke the hingepoint is stretched out to take on an original value: between the time of preparation and the time of the Church, there is the "**Heart of time**": the time of Jesus.[46] Luke defines this time as the year of the favor of the Lord, the opportunity offered to the people. "God sent me, said the text of Isaiah, to proclaim the year of the favor of the Lord (Jubilee Year), a day of vengeance for our God." Jesus interrupts the quotation: he omits "the day of vengeance." Luke will insist on this perspective of judgment, but for the moment he considers only the "time of Jesus"; and this is entirely the offering of favor—offered to the "poor" to whom he comes to proclaim the Good News of their liberation. We have noted already Luke's attention to the "poor," i.e., the unfortunate, but also those who have the soul of a poor man, and of whom Mary is the model. **Their liberation.** He points out to us at once what the only captivity is—that of the devil: Jesus performs two miracles and a series of cures, all of which, in the eyes of Luke, are "exorcisms," expulsions of demons.[47] A year of favor offered to the blind and, first, to the true blind: those who do not believe (cf. Isa. 29:18-19; 35:5-6).

We can understand that in the presence of this extraordinary announcement, his fellow countrymen were "amazed." The word is ambiguous and points out both admiration and scandal. Skillfully he makes a transition here to the second part of the discourse. Jesus reproaches his hearers for not believing in him. This demand for faith in his person was really a shock. Historically Jesus demands it after the miracles in Capernaum. In Luke, these have not yet taken place. In Luke, Jesus demands adherence to his person because of himself. He will do it again later: "no other sign will be given to this generation than the sign of Jonah" (11:29-32), and the only sign that Jonah gave to the inhabitants of Nineveh was to listen to him preach.[48] We do not believe in Jesus because of his miracles, Luke will tell us, but because of his teaching. Jesus continues his discourse: to illustrate the saying: "No prophet is accepted in his own home country," he recalls two signs of the Old Testament. This allows Luke to introduce one of his dearest themes: **the universality of salvation.** During his lifetime, Jesus apparently kept himself to the Jews: "Do not go to the homes of the Gentiles, he hold his disciples, go rather to the lost sheep of the house of Israel" (Matt. 10:5, a text which Luke does not cite). A disciple of the Hellenists and Paul, Luke knows well that Jesus brought salvation to **all** men, Gentiles as well as Jews. Jesus had to preach first to the Jews, since they were the people of God prepared to receive him. But even at that time he was thinking of the others, and Luke is especially attentive to the least details of Jesus' life and preaching which, in advance, legitimate and encourage preaching to the Gentiles. In this discourse program, the two signs that Jesus uses as an example are both carried out in favor of non-Jews and, in the case of Naaman, for the good of an enemy of the Jewish people! Israel rebels in the face of this perspective! They take Jesus outside to stone him. Luke already glimpses this last scene where the people of Israel, through their leaders, will take the

Christ out of the gates of the city to put him to death. Jesus is conscious of this and he voluntarily faces his destiny: "and passing through their midst, he went on his way." "Went on his way"—the actual word is "he went up." Where? Luke will develop this in his "Great Insertion."

The ascent toward Jerusalem: Luke's great insertion (9:51-18:14)

Luke alone recounts for us the cure of the ten lepers (17:11-19). Going through this text will allow us to discover the points of interest in this central part of the Gospel which is proper to him. "Jesus went up to Jerusalem," a refrain which comes up seven times in this section. It is not a geographical notation (he is no more advanced in ch. 18 than he was in ch. 9). It is **theological**: the first refrain introducing this Great Insertion says: "As the time he was **to be lifted** out of this world approached, he set his face resolutely to go up to Jerusalem" (9:51). Jerusalem is the place where he will be "lifted up," a word with a double meaning: his death and his exaltation, and Jesus is going up to it resolutely just as the Suffering Servant set his face like flint before those who struck him down (Isa. 50:6-8). Hence Jesus has only one purpose: Jerusalem where he will offer himself as victim to save us. "As he was going up toward Jerusalem he passed through the borders of Samaria and Galilee": again a geographic note which discourages the topographers—this route is impossible to place. This also is primarily a theological note. Luke is particularly interested in the Samaritans.[49] These dissident Jews, rejected by the true Jews, appeared to him as the symbol of the non-Jews, to whom salvation is offered. Rather than the "cure of the ten lepers," we should entitle it, "the foreigner called to salvation," or "salvation through faith granted to all men." But let us not anticipate: for the moment we do not yet know who these lepers are, but only that they ask.[50] "Jesus, Master, have pity on us!" "Jesus." This "I to You" call is very rare. We find it again only on the lips of the thief on the cross. "Master," a title proper to Luke for the Master of the elements, for him whose Name commands the infernal powers (5:5; 8:24; 9:33; 9:49). "Have pity," our "Kyrie, Eleison"—the Greek equivalent for the Hebrew "favor" and "tenderness" (OT, p. 32). The faith of these lepers is admirable and obtains for them a miracle which they believe on the word of Jesus before they see it. "Go, show yourselves to the priests, . . . and on the way they were made clean." But this is not yet the faith that obtains salvation. For this, one must believe in the person of Jesus. One of the lepers realizes this and comes back to make the "Eucharist," "thanksgiving," by falling prostrate at the feet of Jesus to adore him. Then only when we are filled with admiration for the man, Luke reveals the identity of this leper—he is a Samaritan—and how Jesus draws full attention to this: "Is there no one to come back and give glory to God except this foreigner?" Hence for Jesus he is the symbol of all the Gentiles. And to this "foreigner" he declares: "Rise up, and go, your faith has saved you." The definitive words of salvation through faith granted to every man. We have stressed this enough so as to be able to pause on another idea. "Rise up." To this man who believes in him, Jesus states, as to the disciples sleeping in Gethsemane: "Stand up, the life of a Christian is a struggle and to struggle against temptation we must be standing." "Go": to be consistent with the translation adopted elsewhere, we should read, "go up," or "ascend." "Ascend with me toward Jerusalem, toward my cross, and my exaltation." Here also is one of the characteristics of this Gospel: we cannot open it without sensing immediately that we are called, invited, urged to put ourselves in the following of Christ. The Gospel that "involves" us the most and leads us to self-denial. The evangelist of joy is also the evangelist of the most absolute self-denial. He multiplies the little notices: take up your cross "today," "every day," give up "everything." There is then a hidden connection between renunciation and joy. Only by acting as Simon of Cyrene, by carrying the Cross with Jesus, can we arrive at glory. Jesus explains this to the disciples of Emmaus in the most beautiful page of the book.

> **"Was it not necessary that the Christ endure these suffering in order to enter his glory?"** (Luke 24:26)

All the evangelists have recounted this official appearance on Easter morning in which Jesus shows himself living to his apostles in order to establish them as witnesses of his resurrection.[51] Here Luke is not trying to prove anything, but only to bring us to share in the joy of the disciples finding their Lord again, renewing with him the bonds of friendship broken by death. We already read this page as an introduction to the book (cf. OT, pp. 2-5), so here it will be enough just to take a few of the traits. First of all, the infinite respect of Jesus for every man. He does not impose himself upon a person's faith with soul-shattering "proofs": he tries to win the person's heart by setting it on fire with his Word. He is obliged to do this, because the disciples did not recognize him. We sense here as on very many pages of this Gospel, the astonishment and the sadness of Luke: the disciples did not recognize their Lord! The apostles did not believe as soon as they again saw him living.[52] Yet Jesus did not change—but we: our heart does not love him enough to recognize him.[53] And Luke tells us: Jesus continues to walk with you; but because you do not love him enough, you do not know how to recognize him in the other person who is on the path with you. "Minds without understanding! Was it not neecssary for Jesus to suffer in order to enter his glory?" "**Was it not necessary?**" To recognize him on our humble human paths—the means is Scripture. "He acted as if he was going farther . . . they urged him . . . he entered to stay with them." The delicacy of Christ who never imposes himself. But when he is invited, he will seat himself at our table as he sat at the table of sinners, of tax collectors, welcoming the poor and the sinful women.[54] "He took the bread, broke it. They recognized him, but he disappeared from their sight . . . . **They recognized him in the breaking of the bread.**" This is the "point" of the story. This is what Luke wants to bring out. Jesus has renewed with his disciples some bonds of human friendship, but as soon as they recognize him he disappears, leaving in their hands his eucharistic body.[55] "Christians of the twentieth century," says Luke to us, "like the apostles you can know a life with Jesus of truly human friendship. Jesus is always present with you, walking on your roads, sitting at your tables. We are not dreaming of the past, seeking in distant memories a sense-contact with the humanity of Jesus: it is there entirely in his eucharistic presence."

"Immediately they set out" to proclaim the Good News in Jerusalem. The meeting with Christ is never for ourselves alone. It snatches us up by the bootstraps and puts us on the roads of the world to announce him to our brothers. The Eucharist which gathers us together among Christians to meet with the Lord ends with the mission: "Go to all your brothers in college, in the office, factory, neighborhood, and family: there is only one Savior."

The Gospel according to John

"Jesus, the Way, the Truth, and the Life"
Visit to the Parthenon

I went up the first time on a night of full moon. I

came from the marvelous country of my childhood to the shadow of "the irreproachable arrow," sung by Peguy. Bramante, Michelangelo, and so many others, during a year in Rome and Florence, had made me enthusiastic. But when suddenly, at the opening of the propylaeum, there appeared to me the Parthenon in the bluish shadow, I had the closest experience possible to the revelation of perfect beauty. Immobile, fascinated, I passed the night there, trying to understand: why such a fullness born of such a simplicity. I have gone back since to the Acropolis, I have "visited" the Parthenon, but if you were to ask me to guide you there, what could I do but lead you, in silence, to this unique place where the ensemble leaps out in its unity, where knowledge moves into contemplation.

For me, John is Parthenon. How do you wish me to guide you through him? When we leave the Synoptics, and their richness flowing over into stories, episodes, miracles, words of Jesus, bits of advice, as if going out on innumerable walks, we finally discover the unity toward which they are all leading. In John, everything is simple, unified: a few miracles, but well explained (7, only 2 of the 29 recounted by the Synoptics), ample discourses constructed on a single theme, a few central ideas that unify the chapters. The many precepts for Christian life are reduced to one: **faith flowering forth into love.** And this expressed in everyday words. Like standing before the Parthenon: we have an impression of fullness which heaps us up to overflowing and makes us despair because we do not know how to talk about it. Where do we find this unique point which would allow us to grasp the ensemble in its unity? Father Mollat likes to say: "The best commentary on St. John is the hundredth reading of St. John!" We shall attempt to contemplate the Johannine

Christ, then study the **faith,** the attitude which his revelation must stir up in man. But first—here is a rare idea—I would like to detour into depth psychology: it will help us to answer the question: "Why is such a fullness born of such great simplicity?"

A visit with C. G. Jung and Mircea Eliade

A leader of a crowd knows instinctively how to find the themes that sway the crowd: he will speak of **bread** and **freedom,** he will cry out for the **truth** which is also a liberation and the **right to work** by which a man expresses himself, he will stigmatize **hatred** and call them to **love.** If he is sincere, he will always touch us because he reaches something deep, something "visceral," something that forms part of the consciousness of every man. On their side, psychologists, like Jung, or historians of religions, like Eliade, ponder these great universal symbols that form a sort of subconscious of mankind and resound strangely in every man: masculine symbols like **father,** associated with everything that is strong, instilling life, giving life; the **light,** again, a symbol of life, victory over death, and **darkness** which calls to mind slavery; feminine symbols like **water,** a distant remembrance of this liquid universe where we lived before our birth, maternal water which calls to mind the conception of life, new birth, youth.

We open the Fourth Gospel: Is it not extraordinary that we, involuntarily, start making inventory of the themes he develops? John speaks to us of only one thing: the basic aspirations of man. It is no surprise that he interests us. But in reading him, where do we get this impression of fullness? **The person of Jesus!** John knows well that Christianity is not a religion of divinized values: freedom, human love, however beautiful they are, cannot fill the heart of man. All our human values are a call, an inspiration. And God, in Jesus Christ, fills all of them. Christianity, we can never repeat it too often, is the acceptance of a Person, of a Person who not only does not destroy our humanity but because of his respect for it gives it that to which it aspires and which it is incapable of giving itself. John, the most "philosophical" of the Christian writers, starts with man and his needs, but does this by speaking only of Christ who fills them. He could do it because his Gospel is the testimony of a man who has for a long time lived that which he is speaking.

A testimony

John was already quite old when he set out to write.[56] Since the distant past, the years 28-30, when he left his first master, John the Baptist, to follow Jesus on the roads of Palestine, fifty or sixty years have passed. A half-century of intense life: he has preached Christ in Jerusalem and the areas roundabout (Acts 4; 8:14-25), in Antioch, in Asia Minor. He has suffered for Christ, was exiled to the isle of Patmos during the persecution of Domitian (81-96). From Ephesus where he has returned (and where he will die at an advanced age), he can contemplate the mystery of Christ at work before his very eyes: the Church spread out to the whole known world continually makes the message of Jesus relevant by meditating on it and by deepening it in order to adapt it to the new needs, and already it must defend itself against the first heresies. The deeds of Christ continue their marvelous action in the sacraments. The Church sings the praises of her Lord in worship.[57] From a distance of fifty years, the two years lived with Jesus take on their fullness of meaning, not that John thinks of adding anything whatsoever, but he understands the richness better. The Yes that married people pronounce on their Golden Wedding anniversary is not different from the Yes of their marriage; but what the former contained in hope, a half-century of joy and sorrows shared, of failures and successes together, gives it the complete density of life. The testimony of John about Jesus is rich with a half-century of intimacy with him in his Church.

A "**testimony**": in contrast to the Synoptics, John does not use the word "gospel," but constantly he "bears witness." And his testimony bears on what he has "seen." "**To see**": a frequent word under his pen, frequently associated with the word "believe." **We must believe in order to see.** "The essential is invisible to the eyes," and it is of this essential that he testifies, not so much of the facts which he has seen as of the invisible reality which he believes beyond the vision. This is already true of all human knowledge: in the ordinary deed of a friend, I "see" a sign of his delicacy, because in advance I "know" his delicacy. My "vision" is here guided by my previous experience. The vision of the witness in John is guided by his faith. Thus his work is called the "spiritual" Gospel: only the Spirit could have allowed him this rereading in faith, in the light of Easter, of the deeds and words of this man with whom he lived, in order to discover there the words of this Word of God.[58] It is spoken of also as the "symbolic" Gospel: the ordinary deed of my friend is for me a sign, a "symbol" of his delicacy; John is a Jew and everything speaks to him of God;[59] especially he was the friend of the man-God, and from now on all the deeds and words of the man-Jesus reveal God to him. He attempts frequently to make us feel this by using words which have a double depth of meaning: "To follow" Jesus is to walk with him, but more yet, to "believe in him" by becoming his disciple. The temple designates a monument in Jerusalem, but above all, the Body of Christ.[60] Does this mean that it is not historic because it is symbolic? This would mean that you understood nothing of the nature of a symbol. **It is a sign only if it really exists!** The more symbolic a fact is for John, the more sure you are of its historic reality.[61] The Gospel according to John is testimony. But of whom?

"The Only-begotten Son has made God known to us"

Of whom does he give testimony? He states this in his conclusion: Among many others, "these signs have been related that you may believe that Jesus (this man like us, "son of Joseph") is **the Christ, the Son of God**" (20:30). His testimony bears on a unique subject: the **very person of Jesus.**[61A] Another "theologian," Paul, had attempted this same work earlier. It is enlightening to compare them.[62]

With **Paul**, we are thrown into the dynamism of history, of a history "oriented to," remade by Christ because sin had falsified it, the dynamism of two "worlds" that are opposed but, by following each other on the same line, **the new creation** takes on the lifting up of **creation**. In Paul everything is organized into a "before" and "after" (which he himself experienced on the road to Damascus): between the two is the Cross, the radical cleavage, the drawing out from one to the other.

"BEFORE" "AFTER"

THE CHRIST
IMAGE OF GOD
NEW ADAM

NEW CREATION
TOTAL CHRIST

CREATION
ADAM
(created in the image of God)

"Before" is the world of Adam created in the image of God, but become sinful, the world of mankind enslaved by sin, enclosed in the law, marching inexorably toward death.

"After," because the "image of God," the Son, the new Adam, has assumed our condition as man even to death, and has made his death a sacrifice, because the Father has raised him up, giving him the power to pour out the Spirit upon the world; we are from now on in the "new creation," of the Spirit, of freedom, on the march toward the center and peak of mankind and the cosmos, who is the Christ of the end of time. The entire message of Paul is centered in the paschal mystery, this ordeal of the Cross, where God in Jesus Christ, to save us, has refounded the world, re-created it.

John did not experience the same divisional point in his life. It is in a human friendship, by entering ever more deeply into the intimacy of Jesus, that he understood that his life and the sinful world in which he lived were transfigured by the presence of **the Word of God:** the Word come down, a light in this darkness, yet everything remained as it was, but everything was changed by the incarnation of the Word. In John we find this opposition between the two "worlds," but this time they are superimposed. In John everything is organized into an "on high" and a "here below."

The World "ON HIGH" — Father

God — Son
Breath, Love — Spirit
Freedom, Light . . .

The World "HERE BELOW" — ✝

Man
Flesh, Hatred
Slavery, Darkness . . .

In Paul we are in a universe of re-creation, but in John we are treating, rather, of an atmosphere of **Revelation.** There is the world "on high," the world of God, of the Breath, where everything is love, light, and freedom. And there is the world "here below," where we live with all our aspirations, which is the world of hatred, slavery, enslaved to Satan, "prince of this world." And this is the marvel that John never tires of contemplating: to save ourselves we must know this invisible God, we must be aware that he is the only goal of our desires, we must be able to involve our existence totally in his presence, in an existential decision. Hence he who is the Thought of the Father, his Word, his only Son, becomes one of us to reveal God to us. For John, Jesus is first the **Ambassador** of the Father (the Sent One) charged with revealing him to us. All that John teaches us about the Word Incarnate and the way in which he saves us could be summed up in this "parable" (in the mathematical sense): the Word comes from God and goes back to God, leading men in this movement, in this "Pasch," which means "passage" or "exodus": "Before the feast of the Pasch, Jesus, knowing that the Father had put all things into his hands, and that he had come from God and was returning to God . . ."[63] The earthly life of Jesus unfolded entirely between these two hymns, which express the whole mystery: the hymn to the Word coming into the world (Prologue, 1:1-18) and the paschal prayer of Jesus giving back to the Father (the "priestly" prayer, John 17). Let us read both passages quickly.

The Prologue is well known. Like the overture of a symphony, it touches on the principal themes of the revelation, and the reactions that it will provoke. In three successive waves (cut off by two couplets on John the Baptist) in a very Semitic rhythm, marked by the balancing of phrases, words that are welded together, parallelisms, John deepens his thought. The **first strophe** (1:1-5) carries us boldly into the very bosom of the life of God:[64] The Word, a personal being at the side of God, and God himself, pre-exists creation and creation exists only through him. From eternity the life and the light that men need are in him; they are contained in him to be manifested and given in the Word Incarnate. But already we know that this manifestation will be a struggle, for this light has to shine in evil surroundings, the surroundings of Satan, into which men are cast by their birth. The **second strophe** (1:9-14) leads us to contemplate the historic coming of the Word in the flesh, the way in which the light has come to shine in the world. This incarnation of the Word is only the term of a long series of "comings" of the Word into the world: The Word came into the world through creation (1:10), then through the revelation "to his own," i.e., to his people (1:11). The Word habituated himself to live with men and he wanted to prepare them to receive him, but neither the world nor "his own" received him! A small "remnant" of his own, the poor, accepted him: the Word Incarnate, because he is begotten of God,[65] will give them the power also to be begotten of God, to become children of God. And this is the definitive coming, the incarnation: the Word, like the Wisdom that prefigured it (Sir. 24:7-22), "pitched his tent" among us; he became man. We have seen shine in him the "glory," i.e., God himself insofar as he is manifested, insofar as he is "grace" and "truth" (these two names which God inscribed on his "visiting card" of old, (cf. OT, pp. 31-33). The **third strophe** (1:16-18) after the testimony of John the Baptist can show us from the inside this work of redemption: through this incarnation we have entered into the new covenant far superior to the one made by Moses because through it we receive the grace of divine filiation in fullness. This is what the Word has come to reveal to us: in him we are called, through grace, to become a son and thus, in him, we "see" the Father. Against him the darkness can do nothing, it cannot overcome him.[66] It will attempt this, however, and this will make the incarnation of the Word painful.

The **paschal prayer** of Jesus as he makes his pain-filled return to the Father through the Cross. In this chapter, 17, John reveals to us the prayer of Jesus at the "H-Hour" of his life, the dispositions of his heart at the moment of the Supper as well as during his Passion and resurrection.[67] Jesus talks first of the hour of his **definitive** glorification (17:1-8): he asks the Father to glorify him through the exaltation-ascension, but he himself has already glorified the Father by completing the word of redemption that was entrusted to him. "Now"[68] his disciples—all those who believe in him—**know** that the Son is sent by the Father, because they have the Word of Jesus in them. Then he **prays** for them (17:9-19), and not for the "World."[69] He asks the Father, first of all, to keep them in his Name (17:11-16): God gives us the gift to believe and keeps us in the faith. This is our joy! Then he begs the Father to consecrate them, to sanctify them as he consecrates himself to the Father. Then Jesus extends his prayer to all those who will come after (17:20-23); they will believe because of the preaching of the Church. Let them be **one** so that the world may believe that the Father has sent his Son. Jesus gives them, gives us, his glory in order that they may be **one** and that men may know that the Father loves us as he loves his own Son.[70] Jesus completes his prayer (17:24-26) by summing up the purpose of his life: "That the love with which you have loved me, Father, may be in them and I also in them."

Jesus, the One sent by the Father to reveal him to us

Jesus reveals the Father to us first by his **Word**: In John as in Matthew, Jesus speaks very much. But what a difference between these discourses! The Sermon on the Mount, for example, unifies a great number of statements on different subjects. But the discourses like the one on the Bread of Life, the Work of the Father, the Good Shepherd, or the conversations of Jesus with Nicodemus or after the Last Supper, a little abstract at times, but always constructed around a single theme and carefully composed.[71] Jesus reveals himself as a marvelous pedagogue. In the **first stage,** he starts from the concrete needs of the man and his aspirations: the water that the Samaritan woman came to draw, the bread multiplied, freedom ("If you remain in my word you will be my disciples, then you will know the truth and the truth will make you free"). He starts from these human aspirations because they are true, but he sees them especially as a call to a higher revelation, an expectation of his person which will fulfill them. Then frequently an interruption from the listeners shows that they have remained on a narrow-minded plane. "Give me this water always so that I no longer have to come to draw"; "We are sons of Abraham and we have never been slaves to anyone"; "Am I to return to the womb of my mother to be born again?" Now Jesus can pass to the **second stage,** reveal the spiritual meaning of these aspirations": The water that I give leaps up to eternal life. . . . I am the Messiah." "The real bread is my flesh." "He must be born from on high." Intense discourses: We see here in his search for man, God wanting in Jesus Christ to meet man. The dialogue with the Samaritan woman is from this point of view a model for the meeting of two people. This dialogue is, first of all, a confrontation because it is necessary to begin with, in order to be true, that the masks be removed. Jesus wishes to meet this woman—and each of us—as she is with her concrete hopes and her sin. In removing her mask he is not out to crush her but to free her. Revealed in her intimate life, without humiliation, knowing that she is understood and loved as she is, this woman is open to the revelation which is grace and pardon. "He is the Savior of the world."

Jesus reveals the Father by his Word, but just as truly by his works, his miracles, or rather, keeping the Johannine term, his **Signs**. These are not prodigies to astound the people but works which have only one purpose: to manifest **the** work which Jesus came to accomplish, the salvation of men realized in the painful passage from the Cross to glory. This "passage," this "pasch," is made once for all, but Christ wishes in the course of ages to lead all men to it. And the liturgy with its sacraments will render this only Pasch present until the end of time. Thus, the miracles become "signs" both of the Pasch and of the sacraments. John is writing in a period in which these sacraments are lived in the Church and "he wishes to show in each account the identity that exists between the Jesus of history and the Christ present in the Church. There is no alternative. The events are like a prefiguring of what is taking place in the life of the Church, especially, in worship and the sacraments" (I. de la Potterie). The cure of the man born blind, for instance, is a real miracle performed by Jesus, but it is even more for John a sign of what takes place in baptism: through our sinful nature, we are blind, we do not know how to recognize God. Baptism is an illumination, a new look which allows us, with the eyes of faith, to recognize the Son of man and to say with the cured man, "I believe, Lord!"

"I believe": this is John's goal for each of us. For he knows that this is our whole life.

"To be or not to be"—The stake of faith

The Gospel of John is dramatic. There is only one purpose: to put us in the presence of the person who reveals the Father to us. And the consequence of this is great: put in the presence of the living God, man is concerned with the very heart of his existence, he must decide, must choose for or against him, with his entire being. For faith is something total: "the fundamental step of man giving himself in Jesus Christ to God who reveals himself and comes to him to save him" (Mollat; reread OT, pp. 28, 66, 70-71). Since the testimony of John has only one object, the person of Jesus, there is also only one purpose: to stir up in us an attitude of faith. He tells us this in his conclusion: "These signs have been written in order that you may **believe** that Jesus is the Messiah, the Son of God, and that **by believing,** you may have **life** in his name" (20:30-31). This theme shines out everywhere, and the vocabulary for it is very rich: pay attention not only to the words "**to believe**" (97 times) but also to the numerous equivalents, "to receive" Jesus, his testimony, his words; "to come to him," "to listen to him," or to listen to his voice; "to follow him," "to dwell in him," or in his Word, or in his love. The existentialists have recalled to us that man exists only in the free choice that he makes of his existence, that he passes in this decision from **Vorhandensein** to **Dasein**, as Heidegger puts it, i.e. from "any existence," from "a simple fact of being cast there," to "existence" of him who is capable of understanding himself and of disposing truly of himself.[72] A long time ago, the Bible had seen in this decision the grandeur of man: "before you: life or death: choose," states God in Deuteronomy (30:19). But the Bible confers on him a character more tragic by far than very many of the modern existentialists: this decision is not concerned merely with our earthly life, it involves eternity! Man is defined by the Bible as a creature, i.e., as a being only in his "relation" to God. To accept this relation freely is to live forever. To refuse it is sin, death, the "nonidentifying," or, what is worse, establishing oneself in the separated existence of him who separates himself from that which is his life. From this comes the particularly dramatic character of the faith as John presents it. To believe is not only to decide on a change of existence, to consent to pass from the "existence-here-below" to the existence-on-high. But it is also, and in a sense no philosopher has yet glimpsed, to opt for or against the Existence, for or against the Life. The "stake" of faith is "to be or not to be," but an existence so much more intense than that which disturbed Hamlet. This is a question of Life or Death, the only important question. "He who believes in life . . . . he has passed from death to life" (5:24). "You do not want to come to me in order that you may have life" (5:40). "If you do not believe 'I am,' you shall die" (8:24). "You shall see me, and shall live" (14:19). Through the act of faith, man accepts being snatched by God from the "world" of darkness. He approaches the light of true existence, the existence of the children of God. And therefore John can call faith a "victory."[73]

This faith blossoms forth into **love** or, rather, in a sense it is love. Jesus explains it to us in his Testament.[74] He wants to console his disciples for the sadness of the separation: "I am leaving you and yet in fact I am not leaving you, or, rather, I am leaving you in order to allow you better to find me. This carnal presence with you had a character of warm intimacy which hurts me also to break. But the presence was still only partial, limited by this same carnal aspect. Beyond death, I will be present with you even more intimately, with a spiritual presence. This will be for the end of the world: where I am going you cannot come, but the end of the world is already there for him who believes and loves." In this conversation of chapter 14,[75] Jesus attempts to make his disciples pass from the intimacy which they have known with the Christ of flesh ("with you") to the intimacy with the mystical Christ ("in you"). This conversation is deeply stirring because Christ is experiencing in his heart of flesh the pain of separation and passing from one to the other.

We find these themes in the second conversation (chs. 15-16). It is more composite and regroups perhaps some elements which serve as the outline for the first conversation and the priestly prayer. We find two texts about love: the allegory of the vine-stock (15:1-8: the Johannine development of the body of Christ in Paul and the Kingdom of the Heavens in the Synoptics) and the commandment of love (15:9-15). A transitional verse sums up these two texts (15:16-17). Because this love must be lived by men in concrete circumstances, living in the world, two other texts describes for us **the hatred of the world** for believers (15:8-16:4) and the manner in which God defends them: the Paraclete, **the Holy Spirit**, will come into the heart of the believer and will himself defend him by showing that he is right in believing, that Jesus is indeed the "Sent One" of God, and that the world is wrong in rejecting him (16:4-11). But here the disciples are not following him anymore! Jesus then stops short and reveals to them another role of the Spirit: He will bring us to understand the teaching of Jesus and guide us "to the entire truth" (16:12-15). Finally, Christ forewarns his apostles against the scandal that his Passion will be to them—and this is true always for us—this suffering and his death in which we share are only the painful labor in the begetting of a new world (16:16-33).

The believer, a passive being?

Faith is the supreme activity of man, since it is an existential decision. In fact it is the only "work" that God expects of us (6:29). To speak of faith, John uses a certain number of expressions to indicate the effort involved: we must "follow" Jesus, "listen" to him, "serve" him, "keep his commandments." Hence we must live a life that conforms to the life of Jesus. This activity is, however, quite a source of curiosity, since it consists in accepting, in welcoming, the coming of God in Jesus Christ. But the real paradox of the faith is even more profound: the faith is a favor, i.e., it is given to us by God. For us to believe, to accept the Word of God who comes before us, this Word must already be at work in us (5:38). You see the calm with which John states this apparent contradiction: "You do not believe because you are not of my sheep," i.e., "You are not of my sheep because you are not" (10:26; cf. the note in the Jerusalem Bible). To us this appears contradictory, perhaps, only because we have forgotten the **Holy Spirit**. The Spirit in the Trinity is the movement toward the Father by the Son. And this Spirit, God has poured out on the world through Jesus Christ.[76] Since Pentecost, there is at the heart of the world a "dynamism," a divine Person who is extended toward the Father. In every man, no matter who he is, the Spirit who is extended toward the Father is present. This presence can remain unknown for a long time. The non-believer or the atheist in good faith can live basically under the dynamism of the Spirit without being conscious of him.[77] In order that this presence be revealed to men, something external has to be presented to him: **The Event, Jesus Christ**. At that moment, the man must choose: accept or refuse him. To choose for him, "to believe," is to accept consciously this movement of the Spirit which tends in me toward the Son and the Father, to let myself get into this movement. Man is thus at the "Crossroads of God." God in him, through his Spirit, tends toward Jesus Christ, to adhere to him.[78] The conversion—we must now complete what we said earlier—is to accept consciously and freely to be led into the dynamism of the Spirit.

We must add: this act of faith is made **in Church**. John tells us this: faith is born of testimony. Without exception, to make this leap of faith from one world into another, we are held by the hand. See, as examples, the call of the first disciples (1:19-51): Andrew and his companion "follow" Jesus because John the Baptist leads them to him. Then Andrew goes to look for Peter, and Philip for Nathanael. And in his first letter, John "bears witness in order that you also may be in communion with us," i.e., John and the community. Once this communion is established, the other is established also by the very fact: "As to our communion, it is with the Father and with his Son, Jesus Christ" (1 John 1:3; cf. the Introduction to **De verbum,** the **Constitution on Revelation**).

After all these detours in the thought of John, it is perhaps time to come back to the starting point to attempt to get an over-all view of his work.

The Parthenon in the light of the moon, or the plan of the Fourth Gospel

A drama in very slow rhythm, which leads us inexorably from the struggle between Light and Darkness to the glorification of Jesus on the Cross. A very slow rhythm: a movie about Christ according to this Gospel would be the exact opposite from the movie of Pasolini. There would have to be wide sequences with very long series frequently using the panoramic technique to show us the different reactions aroused in the listeners by the Word of Jesus. We go forward in this drama by episodes and each forms a unit in which we receive, each time, the ensemble of the revelation brought by Christ and the reactions that he arouses, **faith** or **the refusal.** It is progression in a spiral: in each episode we cover the whole question, but each time we have progressed in his mystery.[79]

A very simple statement points out to us two great parts in this Gospel. Jesus speaks frequently of his "Hour" to designate the moment of his return to the Father (death, resurrection, exaltation), but for twelve chapters he tells us it has not arrived (e.g., 2:4; 7:30; 8:20). In 12:23, we see the hour has come. Then the whole change of outlook is seen from chapter 13: "Since Jesus knew that **his hour** had come to pass from this world to the Father . . ." (13:1). The life of Jesus is divided into two great periods: the **second** is the period of his hour. He realizes it is the true "exodus," his own return and the return of all mankind to the Father. But this mystery is so rich and will be realized so quickly (a few hours) that the disciples, like ourselves, run the risk of not understanding it. So in the **first** part of his public life, Jesus explains in advance and anticipates by "signs" what he will accomplish in this hour. To warn us, for example, that this hour will be the hour of our entrance into true life, Jesus raises Lazarus; that it will be the moment in which the light will finally be victorious over darkness and Satan, he restores the sight of a man blind from birth; he explains in advance to Nicodemus that it will be a new birth for us. In a word, all the works that Jesus performs during his "public life" are sign and anticipation of the unique work of our salvation realized in his hour.

"Overture": 1:1-18: The Word Incarnate revealing the Father to men, arouses two reactions: **Faith** and the **Refusal to believe** (un-faith)

I. **"The Book of Signs"**: 1:19-12:50: During his public life, the Son of man manifests what he will be and do in his hour

A single question is put to Jesus: "Who are you?" But it is asked on two different levels:

A. **Section of Signs** (1:19-4:54)

"Who are you?" The question here is especially the question of the Jewish expectation: "Are you the Messiah?" And Jesus manifests who he is. He is the "Temple"; he is the one through whom we obtain the new birth proclaimed by the Old Testament (3:10); he is the "Bridegroom"; and finally he will say clearly, "It is I, the Messiah, who is speaking to you."

In the face of this progressive revelation, John shows us different types of believers (among whom we have no difficulty recognizing ourselves): the disciples **see** the sign of Cana and they **begin to believe** (2:11); the Jews believe, but it is not solid (2:23); to Nicodemus, who says, "We have **seen** your signs and we **know**," Jesus answers: It is not necessary to see in order to know, but to be "reborn," i.e., **believe** in order to **see.** The Samaritan woman believes without seeing signs; the royal official, to whom Jesus has recalled that faith founded on signs is weak (4:45), **believes** in the word of Jesus and **therefore sees** the miracle.

Hence Jesus responds here to the Jewish expectation: he is, indeed, the Messiah; but they must go forward; they must believe in order to see the more marvelous still.

B. **Section of Works** (chs. 5-10)

Far beyond the Jewish expectation, by his works, Jesus manifests himself as **one** with the Father. He shows his divine origin and the consciousness that he has of it. These works are summed up finally in **the** great work of our salvation, which is conjointly the work of the **Father** and the **Son:** the gift of **Life** to men.

- Jesus declares himself **source of Life** with the Father (ch. 5).

  Reaction: Unbelief of the Jews.[80]

- Jesus declares himself **Bread of Life** (ch. 6). He announces the Last Supper, and John who will not recount it tells us here all that he understood of it.

  Reaction: Unbelief of the disciples and faith of a small "Remnant": (the Twelve).[81]

- Jesus proclaims himself more and more solemnly **Light** and **Life** of the World (chs. 7-10; decisive explanations with the "Jews"). Promise of the Living Water, the Holy Spirit, a promise which John sees fulfilled on the Cross (7:37-39; 19:34).

- Cure of the man born blind. Good shepherd.

  Reaction: Incredulity of the "Jews," who pass from hesitation to decision with regard to putting Jesus to death.

C. The "Sacramental Aspect" of the Death-Exaltation (chs. 11-12)

The liturgy renders present for us the paschal mystery, the sacrements re-present it **after** it has taken place. It is just as extraordinary—but no more so—that Jesus wished to "celebrate" this mystery **before** it is realized: a series of acts of Jesus "play" his death and his glorification in advance. He announces his own resurrection through that of Lazarus (and when he weeps over the death of his friend, he is also weeping over his own). The "anointing at Bethany" is his burial. The entrance with the palms announces and anticipates his entrance into heaven by his exaltation at the time of his resurrection and his definitive return into the heavenly Jerusalem at the end of time.[82]

Reaction: The "Jews," symbol of the sinners of all times, condemn him to death (11:25, 33; in the course of this Passion, there will be no Jewish court trial in John, before the Sanhedrin, since Jesus is already condemned).

II. **The "Hour" of Jesus** (chs. 13-20): He brings into reality all that he has prefigured

A. Discourse after the Supper (chs. 13-17).
Intimate revelation made to the disciples.
Strengthening of the disciples in the faith.

B. Apparent victory of unbelief: but in fact, the Passion is the "Epiphany of Christ-King" (Jesus ascends the Cross as his throne of glory), the "manifestation" of the mystery of the Word Incarnate, who founds his Church. It leaps from his opened side, symbolized by the two sacraments: Baptism (water) and Eucharist (blood). Thus his action of life can continue in the world (chs. 18-19).

C. **Resurrection:** Exaltation, Gift of the Holy Spirit (ch. 20).
The Christian faith is definitively founded.

Epilogue: (ch. 21—added by disciples): **The Church in action.** Under the leadership of Peter it sets out to fish for men.

Is John a heretic who does not know any better? Whence comes his originality?

The originality of John in relation to the other writings of the New Testament is a fact. Recall his dualism: "light-darkness," "life-death," "truth-lie"—his way of contrasting the world from above with the world from below, instead of the world-present with the world-to-come; the images which depict Christ: "Bread, Light, Life, Vinestock" and especially the term "Logos," Word. Hence this question arises: "What is the origin of his thinking? And this is all the more true since these themes are met frequently in the religious currents of that time, currents of the non-Christians or of the heretical Christians: the Hellenist mystery religions, "Gnosticism,[83] and the writing of Philo. At one time there was a penchant for explaining John through all these currents. But a healthy reaction began to make itself felt with the appearance of the Qumran texts. At present we can say that the teaching of John certainly comes from Jesus,[84] but he has deepened it by his own personal meditation, by his Christian experience in an organized Church. He remains profoundly Semitic and his thought is rooted in the Old Testament, especially in the sapiential and apocalyptic currents. Here he is a "cousin" (undoubtedly through his master, John the Baptist) and not a "son" of the thought of the Essenes of Qumran. And yet his language and expressions are no longer exactly those of Judaism: they take on a new coloring in this environment of Asia Minor in which he lived and thus he finds himself adapting to the thought patterns of the Christians of this region.

John is in no way a "heretic" (in fact he is always struggling against heretics), but he teaches us to rethink unceasingly our Christianity, the Person and the message of the Christ, in order to present it to our contemporaries in a manner which is true for them. An effort at pedagogical, pastoral adaptation which is rooted in the personal experience that we have of Christ through the sacramental life and diligent meditation. This "experience" of Christ is the precise object of the First Letter of John.

The First Letter of John

"I thank you, Lord, because I love you . . ."

"I thank you, Lord, because I love you . . . As the hand glides over the

> zither and the strings speak, so the Spirit of the Lord speaks in my members; and I speak through his love . . . .
>
> "From my lips bursts forth a hymn for the Lord because I belong to Him . . . ."
>
> **Odes of Solomon,** ca. A.D. 100-120

"My brother, Christian, you who believe in Jesus Christ, do you not know that Jesus Christ is your entire life, that the Holy Spirit animates you, that you live at every instant in communion with the Father? Awake! Stir up this life which is yours: you live in communion with the Father and the Son." It is to this Christian "experience" that John invites us. The "mystical" life—when this does not evoke for us something that is nebulous or unreal—we think to be reserved for the "saints-who-have-ecstasies." The **mystical life** is nothing else than the **Christian life.** John is undoubtedly writing this letter to the church of Asia Minor. He urges the faithful to live their Christian life to the full, without toying with doctrines, more or less heretical, which are in vogue at that time.[85] In the Gospel, his purpose was to lead men to "**believe** that Jesus is the Son of God," to possess, through faith, "Life in his Name." Here he is writing for believers "in order, he says, that you may **know** that you have **eternal life,** you who **believe** in the Name of the Son of God" (5:13).

Communion with God: a unique theme with numerous nuances: to be born of God, born of God, Son of God, to dwell in him, to possess the Son, to dwell in the Light, in the truth, and especially "to know God," an expression which means "to experience profound union with God" (de la Potterie). But some pseudo-intellectuals destroy the true meaning of this experience, and so John is concerned with giving **criteria** to recognize that you live with

God: they are summed up in **faith** and **love**. Let us run through this text in which a complete commentary would destroy the freshness.

Introduction: 1:1-4: To communicate with God, we must pass through the humanity of Jesus Christ. In him, God and man meet. He is the only path to this same meeting.

First Part: 1:5-2:29: **Communion with God: Walk in the Light**

For all those who fear that Christian life puts them to sleep, John, with the entire Bible, repeats: Mystical life is not "contemplating God" but "walking with him"! How does a person know whether he is walking well? There are four conditions or criteria which John will take up again in the second part:

1:5-2:2: Break with sin.

2:3-11: Keep the commandments and first of all, love your brothers. "By this we know that we are in Him."

2:12-17: Do not love the "world," i.e., Satan and all that through which he entices us.

2:18-29: Proclaim your **faith**, and a faith that is clear of all compromise.

Second Part:

3:1-4:6: **Communion with God: Live as children of God.**

For we are sons. And right now (3:1-2)! Here are the same criteria to see whether we are truly sons:

3:3-9: Break with sin.

3:10-24: Keep the commandments, which are reduced to love of each other. "We know that we have passed from death to life because we love our brothers."

4:1-6: Proclaim your faith in the face of the world and all compromises.

Third Part:

At the source of **love** (4:7-21) and **faith** (5:1-12), there is this reality: **God is love: God loved us.** We know that we love our brothers when we love God.[86]

Conclusion and Epilogue: 5:13-21.[87]

[1]The principal works appeared after 1950. But scholars like Dodd were working in this sense since 1930.

[2]"There is no question that the Gospel is presented as the history of a secret which is gradually discovered, of an intimacy which is proposed more and more, of a shadow which shelters you and makes you productive, of a friendship in which it is good to lose oneself, even when it is urging strong demands. Beyond the words and acts of Jesus there is his person. It is with this person that his witnesses form community. And it is on this person that the weight and stress of their testimony bears" (J. Guitton).

[3]The testimony of Papias who writes about 110 and quotes his master "John, the Elder." Mark undoubtedly writes from Rome about 65, for the pagans.

[4]Does this restriction surprise you? For us "Son of God" means "Son of God"! For a Jew it also meant this, but not in the same sense. Every Jew is a son of God, since he belongs to his people. Some have the title in a special way, and first of all, the *king*. In the entire ancient East, the ceremony of the enthroning of the king consisted in the reading of an oracle of God declaring him his son. When Israel established the kingship, they used the same ritual and God took on this situation (cf. 2 Sam. 7; and Ps. 2). In the time of Jesus, to claim to be "son of God" was understood as a claim to be the Messiah: "I am this son of David whom God promised to send his people." We know that Jesus was very quiet in the presence of this title: he had to accept it, since he truly was, but he refused the content which generations had deposited in it, the *glorious* aspect of the Messiah. Hence in this sense, to declare oneself "son of God" was a weaker statement than to call onself "son of man" in the technical sense of Daniel.

[5]It appeared twice in the mouth of demons: 3:11 and 5:7.

[6]While Matthew presents the coming of the Lord to us "under the aspect of the Kingdom of God, Mark centers it on the person of Jesus, who is the Kingdom in person. In Mark everything converges on the mystery of the Son of Man" (Léon-Dufour).

[7]Wrede, in a thesis that is still famous, concluded: Jesus actually never declared that he was Son of God or Son of Man . . . because he was not. After Easter, his disciples in their faith (and their good faith) believed that he was. Troubled, when reproducing his words, to note that he had not declared himself Son of God, they said: he *did not wish* to declare himself such!

[8]Actually, Mark has Jesus answering more affirmatively: "You said it."

[9]Cf. the note in the Jerusalem Bible on Mark 4:13.

[10]It is very difficult to see the centurion making such a profession of faith at this moment. According to Luke the centurion said: "This man is innocent," and this is more probable. In this recognition of the justice of this condemned man, Mark sees the starting point of the true faith and makes it explicit.

[11]The finale of Mark (16:9-20) raises some questions. Cf. the note in the Jerusalem Bible.

[12]Who is "Matthew"? The answer is not simple. All the lists of apostles mention him. They recount also the calling of a tax collector whom Mark and Luke call Levi and the First Gospel calls Matthew. Are these men the same person? Was Levi surnamed "Gift of God" or "Matthew"? About 110, Papias and Origen, followed by tradition, tell us that Matthew wrote in Hebrew (which means Aramaic) a collection of the sayings of Jesus or, according to another interpretation, a Gospel. Must we then admit a Gospel of Matthew written in Aramaic (partial or complete), written by this apostle about 50 to 60? In any case, we do not know the author of our present Greek Gospel. Though it is impossible to prove its dependence on the Aramaic Matthew (however it exists) or on the apostle Matthew, we do not have reasons for rejecting the tradition. But you see what is meant by this name "Matthew," and how we must be prudent when we call him an "eyewitness."

[13]From the schism of Jeroboam to the death of Solomon, Israel never again counted twelve tribes. But the number remained the

symbol of that time when the Kingdom would be remade in its entirety.

[14]The text "You are Peter . . ." is found only in Matt. 16:17-19, at the time of the confession of Peter. It is very probable that Jesus did not pronounce these words *at this time.* But that he pronounced them is beyond doubt: from the very archaic make-up, retranslated into Aramaic, they form a sort of couplet, in full rhythm, full of alliteration, capable of being engraved on Semitic ears at the first saying. Moreover they are only a part of the triptych formed by this text: cf. Luke 22:31-32 and John 21:15-17.

[15]In the two senses of the word: it leads to *perfection* and hence *puts an end* to the old law.

[16]The book of J. Dupont, *Les Beatitude* (Bruges, 1958), is at present the "summit" in the matter.

[17]"Justice": something like "the true attitude before God." We would perhaps translate it in our period as "holiness."

[18]Matthew attaches here the prayer that Jesus taught us: the "Our Father."

[19]A good occasion to recall here the thoughts about the true treasure, or abandonment to Providence.

[20]X. Léon-Dofour, *The Gospels and the Jesus of History*; cf. pp. 236-238.

[21]"It is I attempting rather than you experiencing the thought as to whether to do well this or that absent thing: I will do it in you if it happens. Let yourself be led by my rules, as I have led the Virgin and the saints who have let me act in them" (Pascal, *Le Mystère de Jesus).*

[22]Here again, Matthew has added. Like Luke, he depends on a previous document very much more concise, which no doubt had only four Beatitudes. When he takes them up, Luke insists more on the real conditions which they imply (material poverty), whereas Matthew is more concerned with the interior attitudes which they presuppose (spiritual poverty). The thought of Jesus takes in both aspects: to understand his thought, we must not choose Matthew *or* Luke. Rather, the two interpretations complete each other.

[23]Note the force of the expression for a Jew who knew the adage: "Where several have gathered to study the Law, the *Shekkinah* (i.e., the Holy Presence of God) is in their midst."

[24]But Jesus says nothing about the "when." He is announcing the destruction of Jerusalem, and this is one of the texts used as a basis for dating the Gospels. But the proof is a delicate matter. The text of Matthew and Luke, some say, prove by the precise details that the authors were present at the destruction in 70 and they have given precision to the very vague announcement of Jesus. In actual fact, these texts do no more than make, in Old Testament style, a stereotyped announcement of catastrophe. What are we to conclude from this?

[25]Note the expression: "become conscious of," and not "invent."

[26]For example, Mark 14:36, in which Jesus calls God "Abba, Father"; the parable of the murderous vine-dressers in Matt. 21:33-46; Luke 20:9-19.

[27]Undoubtedly constructed on the numeric value of the name "David" in Hebrew, which comes to 14.

[28]The role of Joseph is important in the incarnation of the Son of God. Mary gives him his being, Joseph by giving him his name inserts him into the human condition, in history. This virgin birth, moreover, will help Christians to understand the text of Isa. 7, which in this period they understood in a symbolic fashion and never in a real fashion. (**Translator's Note**: "In dogmatic theology today, Christology, supported on the data of modern anthropology, is more attentive than formerly, not only to the fact of the incarnation, but to the consequences that flow from it for the understanding of the economy of salvation. It insists upon the fullness and the realism of the incarnation. The Son of God is personally man and this man is personally God: they refuse to depersonalize the humanity of Christ more or less. A human act of Jesus is a personal act of God in a human form. God is love, but it is in man that he shows it: his human love is the human form of his redemptive love of God. The words of Christ are the human words of God; the acts of Christ are the acts of God in human visibility. In Jesus Christ, the Son of God, through a human word, addresses himself to man, person to person." This note is taken from *Theologie, Science du Saint*, by René Latourelle, p. 256.)

[29]To describe him for us, Matthew describes for us the events of this birth by taking up the historic and legendary traits of the life of Moses. A dream warns Joseph, like Aram, father of Moses. Herod, like Pharaoh, is afraid for his throne; and both

consult the divines or priests. Both order the massacre of children, but, in each case, Moses and Jesus escape from death. The inconsistency of Matt. 2:20, "they are dead" (in the plural) is explained as a quote from Exod. 4:19.

[30]How are we to treat this question honestly in a few words? Let us be content with a few generalities. First evidence: Matthew quotes the Old Testament abundantly. He wishes to show us how Jesus fulfills the Scriptures. Hence his intention is first of all theological. He does this with his complete knowledge of the Bible and of Jewish legends. But this does not prejudice the historicity of the facts. A poet who is present at a volcanic eruption could see a manifestation of the wrath of the infernal gods, but this does not say that the eruption did not really take place! Second evidence: our faith is not attached to the historicity of these facts as it is to the resurrection of Christ. For example, we could come to admit that this detail or this story is a "parable" without bringing about the destruction of Christianity. For a very long time we took the story of Jonah as "statistical history"; now we recognize it as a parable in satire (cf. OT, pp. 125-128). We have merely come to do justice to the intent of the author. We must recall that we have to approach the texts without preconceived ideas, we can no more say "this could not have happened" than "this happened exactly as it is described, word for word." The problem is in the final analysis a problem of the literary order: What is the "literary form" of these chapters (cf. OT, pp. 23-24)? This is difficult to answer at the present moment. May I give you my own actual attitude? It does not seem to me that it is proved that the episode of the wise men is impossible, and so I will retain the basis of it (but some Catholic exegetes are more radical). The massacre of the children, even in the morals of Herod, has surely been intensified. The flight into Egypt seems to me especially literary. The star is very real: it is the Messiah who has been born and thus fulfills the announcement of Num. 24:17. In our remarks on Luke we shall come back to the basic agreement between the two accounts.

[31]Or better: pick up the surprising *Concordance of the Synoptic Gospels* (Desclee, 1956) in which Father Léon-Dufour by a clever use of colors makes pleasant and easy the comparison between the texts and their interrelation.

[32]An outline gladly simplified. The compositions vary almost infinitely according to the imagination of the specialists.

[33]Exegetes, who are not lacking in imagination, have called them the "little insertion" and the "great insertion."

[34]Some think that Luke translated a Hebrew or Aramaic text into Greek here. This does not seem too improbable to me.

[35]By adding vss. 76-77 to adapt it to the circumstances; cf. above, note 12, p. 55.

[36]In No. 139 (July, 1965), in the magazine *Jesus Caritas,* you will find a development of this theme.

[37]Cf. as an example Judg. 6:11-24. This form contains: the coming of God, the salvation which he is directing by giving a "new name" (a name which does not describe the person as he is, but announces what he is to become), the mission entrusted, a reflection of the person involved; "how," an answer to the objection, and finally a sign given by God confirming the mission. Hence this literary form is an "announcement of a mission": the interest of the writer is found more in this mission than in the person himself.

[38]The two texts are parallel in OT, pp. 77-78. Cf. also Joel 2:21-27; Zach. 2:14-17.

[39]Mary, just like all of us, had to grow in her faith. She learned from her Son and from his resurrection what he was. To discover this a little more at length, cf. *Promesses,* 12 March, 1966.

[40]On this point, as in very many other circumstances, especially in the accounts of the Passion, Luke is very close to John. This is bound to cause surprise in a disciple of Paul. Paul's influence also is seen (for example, the theme of salvation through faith), but the influence of John is more evident. This is not extraordinary: Luke is transmitting to us especially the preaching of the Hellenistic churches (Antioch, Asia Minor?) where John had preached (cf. also note 56, p. 274).

[41]Do not embellish this too much. Mary was from Nazareth. It is not impossible that Joseph was from Bethlehem, or at least that he had a house there, in which Mary lived with him until she was obliged to withdraw to give birth to the child in the only place that peasants could find calm and warmth: the cave which served as a stable, for there were too many people in the "living room." The word which is translated "inn" in Mark and Luke designates the "cenacle," the "upper room" (to say "inn," Luke uses another word: cf. Luke 10:34).

[42]This sword divides *the people.* This sword does not, it seems, announce the "sorrows of Mary" as an individual person, but of Mary insofar as she is the "figure" of this people whose tragedy she carries in her heart. "This is the sorrow of the Woman who carries in her heart the destiny of an entire people, in fact of the human race" (P. Benoit).

[43]Cf. in the book already cited by J. Guillet, *Jesus Christ hier et aujourd'hui,* the chapter on the obedience of Jesus to his Father in the events of his life.

[44]Jesus vanquished once and for all "every form of temptation." In this Gospel he will no longer be tempted. Temptation will reach his disciples, ourselves.

[45]These infancy accounts of Luke do not pose the same problems of historicity as those of Matthew. Certainly, Luke has reread in depth the events and knew how to draw a theology from them. But we are walking on solid ground. Matthew and Luke do not depend on each other, nor on a common source. Their agreements are all the more significant. In short: "A Virgin, named Mary, engaged to Joseph, son of David, has conceived by the Holy Spirit a child whose name will be Jesus. After they had lived together and undoubtedly in the time of Herod, in Bethlehem, Mary brings Jesus into the world. Finally, they take up their dwelling in Nazareth" (Léon-Dufour).

[46]Luke establishes a parallel between these two times: the time of the Church, for example, like that of Jesus, begins with the outpouring of the Spirit, in Pentecost and in the baptism.

[47]Yes, even the cure of Peter's mother-in-law. She is "possessed," since she is sick, Luke tells us, and he points this out with a word: Jesus does not "cure" her but he "exorcises" the fever. Look up note 30, p. 57.

[48]Matthew will transform the sign of Jonah to make it a prefiguring of the resurrection of Christ (Matt. 12:38-42).

[49]And very particularly in this "Great Insertion": the "ascent" begins with a Samaritan village (9:52). Jesus sends the "seventy" on a mission into Samaria it seems (10:1). He recounts the parable of the "Good Samaritan" (10:29-37), and here the only leper who comes back to give thanks is a Samaritan. Would Luke thus be pointing out to us the source of his special information: the traditions of the churches evangelized by the Hellenists? Cf. above, p. 46.

[50]Luke frequently insists on prayer and gives us numerous examples of it. In the Gospel of Luke, Jesus lives all the great events of his life in prayer (cf. the Jerusalem Bible, Luke 3:21). With true discretion he is pointing out to us a line of conduct.

[51]A stylized scene, an apparition among very many others, in which each sums up what the "forty days" of living with Jesus has brought them to discover (Acts 1:3).

[52]Luke is surprised. But because he is delicacy itself, he always makes an effort to excuse the apostles. At times he succeeds even to the point of making us feel sorry for them: the disciples are asleep in the Garden: but it is because "of sadness," and though they did not recognize the Risen Christ, it is because they experienced such a great joy!

[53]Jesus has not changed (contrary to the note in the Jerusalem Bible). Just as in John, Mary Magdalene takes him for the gardener, not because Jesus is disguised but because the eyes of Mary are filled with the tears of despair. Her faith will permit her to recognize him.

[54]We must pass up, with regret, reading together some texts, such as Luke 7:36-50, the sinful woman who loves Jesus very much because she has been forgiven very much.

[55]Did Jesus prepare the Eucharist that evening? The Eucharist consecrated by Jesus can only be unique. But Luke wishes to show us that the meals with Jesus Risen are recallings of this event and the sign that, when the Church breaks bread, she is celebrating the Eucharist of the Risen Lord.

[56]Some have doubted at times that the Fourth Gospel is indeed the work of John the apostle, but the reasons they advanced are not convincing enough to abandon tradition. It is probable, however, that a disciple put the final touches to his work (which is surely true for chapter 21). Father Boismard would see St. Luke as this disciple.

[57]This liturgy will be found in the Apocalypse.

[58]Read 1 John 1:1 "Something . . . that we have heard, and we have seen with our own eyes, that we have watched and touched with our hands: the Word, who is life—this is our subject." What we have seen, touched—he is treating of concrete events. It is not of these that John bears witness, but of the facts-which-reveal-the-Word. He does not say, "We have seen the Word," but "What we have seen of the Word," what we have seen from

the outside which permitted us to recognize the Word. In his Gospel, note these reflections: "Recalling . . . they began to believe" (1:22; 12:16; 13:7; 20:9). Cf. the note in the Jerusalem Bible on John 14:26.

[59]Reread OT, p. 33 or pp. 227-228.

[60]The note in the Jerusalem Bible points out for us some of these words.

[61]Scientists, pay attention: We are not dealing here with a mathematical "symbol." We are speaking of knowledge through a symbol to contrast it to knowledge through a concept: the concept is a handy label placed upon reality, which defines it, but does not enrich my knowledge: I say that a man is "courageous" (the mathematical symbol is the most refined of concepts). The "symbol" is a reality which I know well and which I use to suggest a reality: I say that this man "is a lion"; I project on him all that I know of the lion, on the condition that, for me, a lion is something other than a marble statue spitting water in a square.

[61a]Cf. Translator's note above, in fn. 28.

[62]Pardon the simplicity of this comparison, which I borrow essentially from the works of Father Benoit.

[63]Note these numerous expressions: "descended from heaven," "come into the world," "go back to the Father," "to be lifted up," "to be exalted," "he who has sent me."

[64]The Synoptics started from a definite point in human history: Mark with Isaiah (1:2-3); Matthew from Abraham (1:12); Luke from Adam, son of God (3:38).

[65]In vs. 13 it will undoubtedly be better to read the singular "he who is born not of the flesh," i.e., of human marriage—which would be witness to the Virginal Birth—rather than the plural, which is however attested to by all the manuscripts.

[66]In vs. 5, instead of "The darkness did not receive him," we should translate, "could not overcome him."

[67]Some traits of this prayer can be explained only if Jesus has already been raised and exalted: He is "no longer of this world," he has "received glory." The Synoptics "report several prayers of Jesus in the course of the Passion. John has kept only one, but he gathers all the prayers of Jesus into this chapter 17, which expresses the entire sense. Before describing in detail, from the outside, the successive episodes of this Pasch,

he gives us first the meaning in the thought and the prayer of Jesus. He used a similar procedure in his Prologue, which, before his account, gives us in a single summary the entire Gospel from the incarnation to the paschal glory. Thus this chapter 17 is not a prayer before the Passion, but it is the paschal prayer of Jesus in the indivisible unity of the mystery of the suffering and the glory" (A. George, *Jesus, Nôtre Vie* [Equipes Ensiegnantes, 1958].

[68]A word which runs through this prayer. Jesus makes a balance-sheet of his work before "passing" to the Father.

[69]Note this double-meaning word in John (cf. the note in the Jerusalem Bible on 1:10).

[70]The only proof that Jesus leaves us of his mission and his divinity: that all Christians are one. "Lord, what have we done with your unity?"

[71]This discourse has evidently not been given by Jesus as it is. John has gathered together, developed, and made explicit the different parts. Is this a betrayal? Suppose that a friend, a priest, said something to me some time ago and I thought it was really important but I did not completely understand it. After a few years I discover the meaning and the depth. If I report it then, what will be the **truest** report: to reproduce it in its original material tenor? Or to bring out all the meaning that it contains?

[72]To recall this is not mere pedantry. It is in these categories that Bultmann, the great German Protestant exegete, tries to translate the message of the New Testament.

[73]A. Decourtray, "La Conception johannique de la foi," a thrilling article that appeared in the June, 1959, issue of *Nouvelle Revue Theologique*.

[74]Chapters 14-17 form the "discourse after the Supper." There arise questions of a literary order which we must set aside, especially the fact that we seem to have two discourses: 13:31-14:31 (cf. 14:31) and chs. 15-16.

[75]14:1-4: by *faith,* you are already in heaven with me and the Father.

14:15-26: by *love,* heaven is already in you because the Father and I are in you. The Spirit will come upon you in order to lead you to understand from within.

14:27: I bequeath you my *peace.* Goodbye.

14:28-31: summary of the conversation.

[76]Pentecost day: what John sees prefigured by the water leaping from the side of Christ on the Cross. In the bosom of the Trinity, the Spirit and thus a gift of the Father through the Son, a gift of the Father to the Son, communion of one with the other.

[77]To recognize the "signs of the times" as the Council invites us, to discern the Christian values lived by the unbeliever is nothing else than being attentive to this invisible action of the Spirit in the world and in man.

[78]To say, as is done too often, "In this unbeliever, Christ is at work," is a half-truth harmful to pastoral work. If Christ is at work in him, I have no need to announce Christ to him, merely to make him conscious of this. In fact, *however, the Spirit is at work and is waiting that Jesus Christ be announced to this man in order that he be able consciously to let himself be led in this dynamism.*

[79]A difficulty in commenting on John: to explain a single episode, we have to say everything.

[80]Note the meaning of the word "Jew" in John. It is no longer an ethnic term, denoting a people, but a theological term: the "Jew" for John (whatever may be his origin by reason of ancestry: Jew, Greek, Roman, or American) is he who refuses Jesus. It is very sad that anti-Semitism could have found its foundation in a false reading of this.

[81]Here John sums up the essential of the "confession of Peter in Caesarea," the importance of which we have pointed out in the Synoptics (cf. above).

[82]Note the extraordinary synthesis John makes in this text (as in many others). A good synopsis will permit you to see that in this account of the entrance with the palms are gathered together the following Synoptic episodes: the palm branches, and also the transfiguration and the Garden of Olives.

[83]*Gnosis* means "knowledge": Gnosticism is a "system of religious philosophy whose followers claimed to have a complete and transcendant knowledge of everything" (Larousse).

[84]The scholars are being more and more impressed by the basic comparisons with the Synoptics and the primitive character of some of the geographic and historic data, which are frequently preferred to those of the Synoptics. Apostolic preaching is the basis of his Gospel.

[85]These heretics, followers of Cerinthus, did not believe in the divinity of Jesus, claimed to know and live in communion with God while their conduct gave this the lie. John is thinking of them, but his letter is not polemical: it is addressed to his Christians. A good example of apologetics: not to cut error in half in his adversaries, but to give back to the Church and to Christians a face that is true and attractive.

[86]Never has this truth that the love of God and the love of our brothers is *one* been so forcefully expressed. This is consoling when we truly love others, when we see an unbeliever love others. But it is a demanding truth: on this love we must gauge the quality of love of God and our prayer!

[87]*The Second and Third Letters of John:* Two notes written, one to a church which John calls "The Lady, the Chosen One," and the other to a certain Gaius. Perhaps the advice which is found here to conduct oneself in a Christian manner in these times in which heresy threatens, and which are the same as those of the first letter, were the outline for this last letter.

VI.

JESUS OF NAZARETH

"Behold! The Bridegroom is coming, let us go to meet him'"

Matt. 25:6

One volume of this series (**Je sais, Je crois**) is dedicated to Jesus Christ. Hence we have to resist the temptation to sketch here, according to the Gospel, a portrait of our "loved Brother and Lord Jesus." We shall attempt in more modest fashion to point out that this is possible, to see also that it is the task of exegetes to work at it, and that each of us, in opening the Gospel, can find there his own countenance.

Recall the path that we must follow: there are three stages in the formation of our present texts: (1) Jesus speaks and acts. (2) The apostles, in the community, in different "milieus of life" and to respond to the needs of the Christians, recall to the memory of the Christians their own remembrances. They understand them better now because of the resurrection, which has made him "Lord" and because of the Spirit who animates them. (3) Four "theologians" gather these memories and make a "mounting" of them, thus tracing for us four portraits of Jesus. But does not the intense effort at reflection which these last stages presuppose hide the first stage from us? Can we actually get back to the Jesus of Nazareth? What do we know about him?

Bultmann's answer: "We can no longer know practically anything of the Jesus of History." Jesus is only a man. But God spoke to us on the occasion of his word and his life.

God calls to us and urges us to respond to him by a decision which determines our entire existence: faith. This conviction, that on the occasion of Jesus, God has spoken to us and that he saves us through our faith, led the community to project on this man, Jesus, their certitude of being saved, to make him the Messiah, the Son of God.[1]

All that we have said up till now, has convinced you, I hope, that the portrait of Jesus handed on by the apostles and the evangelists was not a betrayal but a comprehension in depth. Yet it is perhaps worthwhile to give a brief summary of the data of the problem.[2] It can be presented in these terms: A Jew, named Jesus, lived at the beginning of our era in Palestine. Toward the middle of the first century, a Jewish sect, detached at that time from Judaism, believed and proclaimed that this Jesus was the Son of God: These two points are admitted by every historian, even the unbeliever. Granted that we know the thought and life of this Jesus almost solely through the texts of this sect,[3] what can a historian claim to know about him? As a historian, can he go back beyond Easter?

The generalized skepticism, common for a while, has for the last ten years been seriously attacked, even by the disciples of Bultmann. There is a continuity between the community after the Pasch and before the Pasch, a continuity which we recognize from different ways.

Jesus was a Jew and he delivered his message in a Jewish milieu which was in the habit of using the oral memory. Recent studies have shown how, in contemporary Jewish milieus, the instruction was presented by the rabbis: the student memorized, by the little sections which he repeated, the phrases of the master, which were very much stressed. He arranged these sections in a way that recalled them by "catch-words."[4] Jesus had to use the method current in his time and by translating some of the texts into Aramaic, the Beatitudes for example, the formula "You are Peter and on this Rock . . ." and many others, we get phrases so well-balanced that they had to be impressed with the first saying in the memory of people accustomed to this method. It is found in the instruction in parables followed by the explanations for the disciples. But we admit that this is of value only for some of the words of Jesus.

Another way consists in testing the stability of the tradition on some particularly important points. This is the minute work of the exegetes, studying each text, to discern what comes from the redactors or the community and what goes back actually to Jesus himself.[5] The results obtained from these detailed studies are sufficient to give us confidence in the ensemble of the Gospels.

Finally, and especially, Bultman's method itself, pushed to its foundation, allows us to establish our confidence. This method gives great importance to the "milieu of life" in which a tradition is born. But its first followers were interested only in the milieu of life of the community **after** Easter. Today, we realize that it is helpful to find out also about the milieu of life **before** Easter: this group of disciples established around a master, Jesus. This team of twelve was structured, with a certain primacy recognized in Peter. Jesus associates his apostles in his ministry by sending them on mission. Thus they would be led to repeat the parables and explain them, to recount the miracles, to take up the principal teachings of Jesus. Jesus sent them again to baptize (John 4:1-2). Hence from that moment, they began to memorize certain words and acts of Jesus. The starting point of the tradition found in the Gospels is not to be sought in the primitive community but in this community before Easter. One last important remark: We must not exaggerate the difference between the faith of the apostles after and before Easter. The resurrection is certainly an important point, and, in a sense, changed everything, but it is not the only important point of history. There is still the Parousia, the definitive coming of Jesus. This central point takes its place in the **plan of God.** And from this point of view, the faith of the apostles after Easter is not essentially different from that of before. Before the resurrection, they believed in Jesus as the Messiah, i.e., in their minds, a man who fulfills the plan of God announced by the Scriptures. After Easter, their faith will remain the same: they believe in Jesus who has fulfilled this plan. What is new and what they could evidently not have suspected, is that the Messiah is the Son of God made man. Before Easter, they were already on the way toward the paschal faith, and the resurrection was a threshhold which brought them explicitly to this faith.[6]

Can a "life of Jesus" be written?

"The Gospels," concluded Father Lagrange at the end of a lifetime of work on them, "are the only life of Jesus we can write. We have only to understand them in the best way possible." The different "lives" that have been written, in spite of their interest, no longer satisfy us. And what exegete would dare to run the risk of writing one at the present moment?[7] To give a "chronology" of the life of Christ is impossible, just as to want to follow him on all his journeys. Are we then reduced to knowing nothing about him at all? Of course not! We can establish with certainty the general framework of the life of Jesus and point out the great moments in it. Let us try.

IN JUDEA: The public life of Jesus begins here with his baptism, his testing in the desert, and "a period of ministry on the banks of the Jordan in the shadow of John the Baptist" (John 3:25-26) (Léon-Dufour).

IN GALILEE: Jesus addresses himself **to the crowds.** He preaches the Kingdom of God and calls to penitence. He does this:

- by his Word: To show this to us clearly, Matthew has gathered together very many of the words of Jesus in the Sermon on the Mount, and Luke has some in the homily in Nazareth. (Do the principal parables date from this period? Mark and Luke seem to say this when they regroup them here. Hence they have been looked on principally as an imaginative and picturesque instruction on the Kingdom of God. Should we perhaps prefer Matthew?)

- by his deeds: His miracles (agreement of Matthew, Mark, and Luke).

Then, from his first successes in the presence of the crowds (here we follow Matthew), Jesus sends the twelve on mission. Their first duty is to preach the imminent coming of the Kingdom of God.

Then, Jesus invites the crowds to make their choice: this is the moment of the controversies with the Jews.

Finally (with Matthew again), he speaks in parables. These modify the preceding preaching: the Kingdom is coming, but it will not take place in a single act, it will know a period of growing;[8] he announces that before the Parousia, there is the time of the Church. Coming to the end of this Galilean period, at a moment when the crowds are starting to turn away from him, the parables take on a threatening character: the last chance is offered to the Jews.

Then takes place the **breaking** with the crowds who reject him.

The refusal of his fellow citizens in Nazareth is the

first sign of this (Luke prefers to anticipate this scene at the beginning of the Galilean ministry in order to warn us in advance that he will be a complete failure).

We can easily see several motives for this break:

- the threats of Herod, the tetrarch of Galilee (Matt. 14:1-12 and par.);
- the error of the Jews about his messianism: Jesus refuses to be their king;
- the opposition of the Jewish leaders (Matt. 12:22-24).

In this context the multiplication of the loaves takes on the character of a farewell meal.

(With all probability, it is in this period that Mark and Luke place the sending of the Twelve on mission.)

TO THE ENDS OF GALILEE: Jesus addresses himself **to the disciples**. He "ascends" toward Jerusalem and toward his Passion.

In Caesarea, Peter recognizes Jesus as the Messiah: this marks the turning point of the life of Jesus. The transfiguration anticipates the glory of the resurrection for the apostles, but the announcements of the Passion give them the goal of going up to Jerusalem.

IN JERUSALEM: Jesus speaks **to the inhabitants of Jerusalem.** Solemn proclamations **concerning his person.**

He remains three months in the Holy City, makes a sojourn in Transjordania, then returns to Jerusalem ("The Palms"). He then clearly announces his destiny in the parable of the murderous vine-dressers.

Then we have the **Passion** and the **Resurrection.**

This outline can be upheld as one of the solid results

acquired from the critical study of the Gospels. This result is important; it permits us to place certain words or certain acts in the life of Jesus. A simple example: It is very clear that Jesus did not pronounce the Sermon on the Mount as such. Matthew has made a mounting here. Take only the ninth Beatitude which Matthew adds as a commentary on the last. "This detailed announcement of the persecutions which await the disciples certainly does not belong originally to the inaugural discourse which breathes of the joy of the Good News, but rather to the final period of the life of Jesus when he came face to face with the irresistible opposition of his adversaries" (Jacquemin summing up J. Dupont). In the place in which it is now, it could pose a question for the historian: could Jesus have pronounced such a word at this moment? Replaced in its original context, it takes on all its probability.

But in the presence of all this display of science and criticism, I feel a question is arising in your mind: How then are we to read the Gospel? Is it not a work reserved for the specialists?

"The dried up breasts of exegesis . . . ." (P. Claudel).

Under one aspect, the study of the Gospel is the work of a specialist, of an exegete. I would compare it to a good travel-guide: he has to forbid certain routes where there would be danger of getting lost in good faith. And especially because of his extensive knowledge of the back-country, he knows how to guide us in the right direction, to orient us toward the discovery of untold riches.[9] The exegetes seem to write poorly (frequently because they are always trying to shade their statements). At times they use an esoteric language, but when we do find good ones, use or follow them: the effort which they demand will be big, but they will help you to hear the harmonies of the Word of God ringing out.

There is no question here of giving their method in detail. The scientific study of a Gospel text is a work of art which demands a professional man, who has extensive knowledge in many fields (from ancient languages to archeology, from the history of religions and their institutions to the rules for textual criticism while using modern languages); at times it has the sense of the hunt, and always requires very much humility! It takes only a few lines to see whether you are taking a chance in their writings.

Open the table of contents in the book by X. Léon-Dufour, **The Gospels and the Jesus of History.**[10] He proposes to bring us to the very heart of the texts in four stages. (1) "The four-form Gospel": i.e., the teaching and the person of Jesus in a global fashion as the first Christian generation understood him. (2) "The Four Gospels": He questions each of these separately, presents the theology, the perspectives, the favorite themes of each.[11] Here we are at the level of the redactors. (3) "The Gospel Tradition": This is the gospel before the Gospels: the traditions about Jesus and from Jesus on the level of the original community. (4) Finally "Jesus of Nazareth": The first impression that can be drawn from this glance is that the exegetical method is related to the tasting of artichokes. They set aside the leaves in order to get to the heart or essence of it. When we have eliminated what comes from the redactor, the details and interpretations added by the community, we arrive finally at the essential, at the message and deed of Jesus found in all their purity.[12] No impression can be more misleading as we know now. Thanks be to God, we do not have a "photo" of Jesus in person. Otherwise we would no longer be able to know anything about him. A photo does not speak of itself, but must be explained to us: "Who is this?" "Where was this taken?" "Why does he do this?" We do not have a photo, but a **portrait**, or better, **four portraits**. This means that those who knew Jesus most intimately, who entered, guided by the Spirit, most profoundly into his personality, have attempted to explain him to us by restoring his countenance. We do not study the Gospels in parallel forms, or in "synopsis," in order to set aside details which do not agree or in order to add to them. This would be dismembering four mosaics in order to reconstruct a single scene from this pile of stones. It would probably be monstrous, but in any case it would be mine and no longer that which the artists wanted. We are not treating of adding up a pile of stones or adding to it, but of comparing four collections. The true countenance of Jesus is not veiled or distorted by the interpretations of the apostles or the redactors, but rather, it is explained to me: I can know it only through the interpretation they have given me.

The method of Father Léon-Dufour follows the order in which the exegete studies his text. But frequently, in order to explain his results, he will prefer, in order to be more clear, to follow the order of origin: he will ask us to have confidence in him on the seriousness of his research, and he will render us present at the genesis of our present texts: (1) What Jesus did and said; (2) what the community understood and how it interpreted these words and these actions; (3) How the final redactor understood all this to make a synthesis of it.[13]

"This is all well and good, you say to me! It is magnificent! But what about me? I who am not a specialist. Am I condemned to close the Gospel?"

Like a confidence of a friend

There was in the manner in which our parents and our ancestors read the Gospel in faith, a certain simple freshness which is now lost to us: listening to the very words of Jesus, following him in each of his acts has become impossible for us. We know too well the part which the community and the redactors had in putting it into writing. But we have gained so much more: Instead of a merely objective photo of Jesus, we have four portraits of him made by his intimate friends and they bring us thus into his very heart. With a series of photos we would have been left to our subjectivity, to our personal interpretation. With a portrait we are guided by authentic witnesses and finally by the Spirit himself. What, for example, could I draw from a "snapshot" of Jesus looking at a young man: all I would say is that he is looking at him! Was the picture taken at a moment in which he was turning away his glance in anger? Or was it the ordinary passing glance given to an unknown person who is walking up? "No," Mark tells us, "Jesus looked at him and loved him."

We have to open the Gospels as we would enter into the home of a friend, to listen to him speaking of a person who has upset his life, read them as a **testimony**. The skilled exegete will do this with all his scientific knowledge: this will help him to distinguish, perhaps, what is "historic" and what is interpretation. But the Christian who does not know all of these problems will also be at ease here. He will not always know how to distinguish what is actually taking place and what his friend Mark or Luke is telling him about him. What will this mean to him? He knows that everything is "true," that this detail, perhaps invented, is "true" in this sense that it truly expresses what Jesus wanted to say or do. As before two pictures of one and the same painted by different artists, we compare the details to perceive better what each has grasped from it; so before two or three parallels of one and the same event, the reader can pause on the details, discovering there the moving confidence of a friend. What sentiments did Jesus have in his heart at the moment he was dying on the Cross? A photo would tell me nothing of this. By recounting this scene with the help of traits borrowed from the poems of the Suffering Servant in Isaiah, the evangelists tell us: he was conscious of saving the world, of offering his life in atonement for our sins. But how did he live this death in his freedom as Man-God? He prayed, Mark and Matthew tell us, with Ps. 22: "My God, My God, why have you deserted me?" This psalm: a blasphemy become a prayer; by passing through the prayer of Jesus, all our rebellions themselves become a prayer and are redemptive.[14] Luke puts on the lips of Jesus another psalm. The scholar will discuss whether Jesus actually recited Ps. 31 on the Cross. But he, like the simple Christian, will listen to this confidence of Luke opening to him another aspect of the heart of Jesus: Luke, more than any other, in his account of the Passion has pointed out the interior suffering of Jesus, has shown him as the conqueror by his patience, to the point that he is able to be concerned only for the suffering of the others (Peter, the women, Zion, the good thief, the murderers) and not for his own. He shows us his Lord Jesus after the terrible internal struggle in the garden, and the intensity of the sweat of blood, abandoning himself like all the little ones, the lowly, the "anawim" of the Old Testament, in an unlimited peace, into the hands of the Father.

Concretely

Read the Gospels as a "witness" or "testimony" of friends of Jesus without always posing questions about the historicity. This testimony is "true"; it leads us, without falsifying it, into the heart of the historic Christ.

Read the Gospel **in "synopsis,"** not to add details or suppress them when they do not agree, but to let yourself be guided by them, confident of your witnesses, toward the different aspects of the unique person of Christ.

Read the references from the Old Testament given in the notes or the margins of your Bible.

And above all, put the Gospel **into practice.**[15] To the degree that we bear witness to him in the world, we know Jesus. By striving each day to live the Gospel, you will be surprised to note how much more it gradually "speaks" to you. **The Gospels were not written to occupy the time of the scholars but to form witnesses.**

[1]Cf. note 8, p. 54. In thus summing up a difficult thought, I hope that I am not making a caricature of Bultmann, who is a great scholar and a sincere believer. When he speaks of Christian faith or Christian existence his intensity is very moving.

[2]It is clearly impossible here to treat this at its very roots. These few lines are only an outline and intend to guide you in the readings of more scholarly works: e.g., the *Gospels and the Jesus of History,* by Father Léon-Dufour. I took my inspiration from some of these pages.

[3]A small book of the collection "Idées" (N.R.F., Gallimard), *Le Christ,* by R. Dunkerley, helpfully gathers together the indications about Jesus furnished by texts other than the Gospels. (Eng. edition: *Beyond the Gospels,* published by Penguin Books.)

[4]Consider the children's word games.

[5]J. Jeremias for example has dedicated his life to this work. Among his works see *Central Message of the New Testament* (New York: Scribner, 1965) and *Parables of Jesus,* trans. Hook (New York: Scribner, 1963).

[6]This is important for pastoral understanding. When someone is on the way toward the true faith, we must not feel urged to introduce him to the totality of this faith. He will not understand it and this could block his actual progress.

[7]The last dated one from a Catholic (1960) is that of the history professor, A. Nisin, *Histoire de Jesus* (Seuil). Although he is in the current of present-day research, the book is not without defect (which comes frequently from the preference which he gives to

Mark). If you read it, it could be the occasion for a fruitful dialogue with your chaplain.

[8]Cf. the numerous parables which, in one form or another, put a delay between the sowing and the harvest.

[9]Claudel was born too soon to have the benefits of the works of exegesis.

[10]We are treating here of a global study of the Gospels. The same method is applied to some precise texts in his *Etudes d'evangile* (Seuil).

[11]All this presupposes as a preamble a minute study of the texts. A synthesis can be drawn up only at the end of a patient analysis.

[12]This is the one complaint we have against the book. It is excellent if we look at only one stage of the work of J. Jeremias, *Parables of Jesus.* But when he comes to the fourth stage, he claims a synthesis of the thought of Jesus which is actually only the synthesis of Jeremias.

[13]At present, there is not in French a satisfactory commentary on the Gospels except *L'Évangile selon Saint Matthieu,* by the Protestant, P. Bonnard (Delachaux, 1963) which deliberately remains on the third level: to understand what Matthew said of Jesus. Several series of Catholic commentaries have been announced. On the other hand, numerous magazines or the collection "Assemblees du Seigneur" (each volume is dedicated to the liturgy of one Sunday) publish excellent articles on particular texts.

[14]Cf. the commentary in OT, pp. 202-204.

[15]The wisdom of this advice of Kierkegaard: "Yes, there are some obscure passages in the Bible, and some books are almost entirely puzzles. But what obliges you in the Word of God, are the clear passages which you can immediately put into practice. Scripture will be intelligible only in an event; you must obey it immediately, without being obstinate over the pages which seem puzzles to you. The Word of God was given to complete you and not in order to exhaust you with exegesis or the discussion of its obscurities. If you read it without considering that every smallest detail that you understand obliges you, you are not reading it."

VII.

"AS A YOUNG BRIDE PREPARED FOR HER HUSBAND"

The Apocalypse (Revelation)

"Periods of saturation and mean minds have never found the Apocalypse to their liking."

J. Könn

Close your eyes for an instant: in your mind call up the word "apocalypse." Undoubtedly "catastrophic," "incomprehensible," or, with Larousse, "obscure and too allegorical." "If I were a god, said the Chinese wise man, I would begin by giving a meaning back to word!" Etymologically, Apocalypse means **Revelation**, a light which enlightens the way, a message of hope because it gives back a meaning to life: we know where we are going.[1]

At the end of our reading of the Old and the New Testaments[2] and with this vivid book, the third part of Scripture is opened. It is very short. Because it is still to take place! The Old Testament recounted for us the history of the people, a "witness," a "priestly" people, whom God has chosen to take on all the anguish of mankind, its hopes and its expectations, to whom also he gave a presentiment of the manner in which one day he would fill them. With Jesus this day has come. And before this fullness, everyone puts himself, the apostles, Paul, John, Mark, and Matthew and Luke, the entire world, in order to reveal to us this fullness lived in the heart of daily life.

And this was the New Testament. There remained two things to say, not the easiest: How will all this end? What will be the condition of Christians in the meantime? Hence God, before he closes his family album, has gone forward into the future. He has taken a prophet, John,[3] and for him has **drawn back the veil** (in Greek: **apokalypto**) which closes the end of time. John saw this end of time—and it was a history of love—and God invited him to read in this light the destinies of his people with one another. John "saw." But how can he speak the unspeakable? When we cannot recount, there remains only the suggesting. The only solution being offered was to do as those who, before him, benefited from the use of visions and imagery. The reading of the book of Daniel has already familiarized you with this dazzling literary form, with its amazing symbols, difficult to interpret. Its purpose is twofold: to give courage to the faithful who are being persecuted, and to do this by teaching them the fundamental truths upon which their hope is based. And there is need of this. John is writing in dramatic circumstances. "The Apocalypse is published on the verge of the persecution of Domitian who is demanding that they worship him. The Apocalypse traces out one's duty: to remain inviolably faithful to Christ and to refuse to worship Caesar. The handful of Christians will be shown to be right over the totalitarian state. The Church will be victorious through the blood of the martyrs just as Christ was victorious through the blood of Calvary. And history will show that the author of the Apocalypse is right" (Feuillet). We note an essential difference between the Jewish apocalypses, for example, Daniel, and the Apocalypse of John: the victory of God is no longer announced as a distant hope (which leads some Jews to a defeatist attitude: since God will do everything, they need only sit back and wait with folded arms), but as a fact established in its principle: Christ **is** already the victor.

This must remove every desire to evade the struggles of the Christian people: victory is a reality already active in the heart of every believer and it mobilizes all his energies to carry it to its term.

The broad divisions of this book are clear, even though the development of the thought within is not quite so clear!

1-3: "The address" of the message: the CHURCH INCARNATE, very real and concrete, a holy Church of sinners, represented by seven churches.

4-20: The CHURCH IN ACTION: In the world between the resurrection of Christ and his second coming, the Church comes to the relief of Israel, whose "judgment" in the year 70 is the end (4:4-11). It is confronted by the pagan world, the persecuting Roman empire and all those who in the course of the ages will imitate it (4:12-20). But it is constantly sustained by Jesus Christ, the victor.

21-22: The CHURCH TRANSFIGURED: into the Kingdom of God where, in joy, she is united forever to her Husband, the conqueror of death.[4]

1. **The Church Incarnate** (chs. 1-3): The Letters to the Seven Churches

John's message is rooted in the heart of the Trinity. Note the name given to the Father. "He is, and he was" places us outside of time, and then we would expect "and he will be," but John writes "he is coming" and this reassures us: the purpose of God is the meeting with men in their history. Then in a few words the entire work of Jesus Christ is recalled to us: incarnate and crucified (a "faithful witness"), raised as "firstborn," seated at the right side of God, "prince of the kings of the earth." He loves us and redeems us and now he is coming. A joyous security which the Apocalypse gives: from the outset one fact is posited: our salvation in Jesus Christ and his coming constantly into the life of each of us and the life of his Church until his definitive coming at the end of time.

In Patmos, where he is deported (under Domitian in 96, according to St. Irenaeus), John has a "vision": The Messiah appeared to him as Judge at the end of time and entrusted to him the care to write to the seven churches of Asia Minor.[5] Each of these letters is built on the same plan: an address from the glorious Christ to the local church; the body of the letter consists in a community examination of conscience (Laodicea receives only blame, Smyrna and Philadelphia only eulogies); the finale is an exhortation to fidelity or a threat of punishment, then a promise to the victors in the form of images which will be found in the last part: the final glory of the Church is already anticipated in her earthly life.

These letters are quite earnest because they are a visit to very concrete churches face to face, like ours, with holiness and sin, and because also, they give us a model for "an examination of conscience" established by Jesus himself.[6] To these very real churches and through them to the whole Church of which they are the symbol (as the number seven indicates), to our Church of our times, John now addresses his message.

2. **The Church in Action** (chs. 4-20)

We enter now into the truly prophetic part of the work. Before we launch out into it, let us give you a few "keys."

Apocalyptic language freely uses the movie procedure called "mounting by synchronism."[7] Before describing for us a scene which is to take place on earth, they show it to us played out in heaven. An example: in chapter 13,

John describes the persecuting Roman empire, represented by the beasts, struggling against the Church and finally conquered by Christ. Immediately before, he has us assist at the heavenly version of the event: a battle between Michael (Mi-cha-el=Who is like God?) and the dragon. The battle in heaven and the struggle on earth are thus not two events which we set one after the other chronologically, but they are a single event: the struggle on earth whose deep meaning is revealed to us by the battle in heaven. This is a picturesque or imaginative way of giving us the religious significance of the events of our history.

We find these continual goings and comings between heaven and earth in the **liturgy**. The Apocalypse is a liturgical book in which you constantly find: "alleluia," "amen," "holy, holy, holy," "Glory to God," "Glory to Christ." By this liturgy, are we being introduced into a Christian church of the first century or into the courts of heaven? It is impossible to say. But is this not also true for our own present liturgy? The liturgy, especially the eucharistic worship, is the place and the action in which is effective the osmosis between heaven and earth, or better, the liturgy renders present, actually, in his Church, Christ the conqueror glorified. With this precision however, that it renders him really present, but especially as a pledge of his definitive presence! "We proclaim the death of the Lord until he comes" (1 Cor. 11:26).[8] An actual meeting of the Church and its Lord, even more, a proclamation and anticipated realization—which only increases the expectation—of the eternal wedding of the Bride and the Groom.

Science-fiction or history? Real history, but studied with such a depth that it becomes symbolic of all history. It is undeniable that the back-drop for the Apocalypse is contemporary events: the Jewish war and the destruction of Jerusalem in 70 (chs. 9 and 11), the Roman emperors and the persecutions of Nero and Domitian (17:10-14). But John's first interest is their religious significance: in them the struggle or battle between God and Evil is being carried out. Thus they take on universal significance.

A good test for your **knowledge and recognition of the Old Testament!** Try to count the explicit quotations from the Old Testament and the marginal references! This book could be defined as the "rereading of the Old Testament in the light of the Christian event" or "the Christian flowering forth of the Old Testament" (Feuillet). Its richness is disconcerting: a word, an image, suggest an entire scriptural theme, sum up the expectation of Israel and through it of mankind to show us how it completely filled up in Christ.

Must we really comprehend it? We shall try without always succeeding! But this is perhaps not so important. We must draw out the essence of the message and then let ourselves be carried along by the flow of images, by the brilliance of the colors. Frequently it is less a matter of reading than of "seeing." In front of "Guernica," the fresco by Picasso painted in fury a few hours after the attack of the Nazi planes on the Spanish village, we feel ourselves carried away by the power of the indignation, we communicate in the suffering of a world disintegrated by the diabolic will of man in exactly the same way as the bursting forth of the blood-red or the plague-green horses of John. And Lurçat in his tapestry of Assy, by the warmth of tones causes us to dwell more in the universe of the Apocalypse than many commentaries.

But since we must here introduce a person to the reading not with color but with text, let us proceed.

The prophetic books of the Old Testament (from which

is born the apocalyptic genre) are comprised of two parts: oracles against Israel and oracles against the Gentiles. We seem to find this division here. We have in fact not one, but **two** apocalypses, since chapter 12 is a second start. Chapters 4-11 are interested in the relation between the Church and Judaism; chapters 12-20 in the relation between the Church and the pagan nations. Chapters 21-22 concern only the end of time and the conclusion of these two parts.[9] Take a look first at the outline on the following pages: we shall attempt to give you a summary view of these parallel passages.

Chapters 4-11: The Church and Israel

Because they have rejected Jesus, their Messiah, Israel will be rejected by God. But not totally. The prophets announced that a "Remnant" would be saved. This "Remnant" is the Church.

ch. 4: Vision of **God** who is controlling history.

ch. 5: The Book of the Seven Seals=the Old Testament, which announces the destinies of Israel. They announce the "lion of Judah," the offshoot of David" (=the glorious Messiah of the Jews), and there arrives the LAMB AS SLAUGHTERED=the summary of the paschal mystery.

chs. 6-11: Definitive passage of Israel to Christianity: it is described in two forms:

6:1-8:5: SEVEN SEALS=	**8:6-11:19:**
the heavenly vision=the seven woes:	**SEVEN TRUMPETS:** =earthly realization
First 4 are vague	First 4 are vague
Last 3 are detailed	Last 3 are an allusion to some historic events in the Jewish war:
	9:1-12: Troubles under Festus

	9:13-21: Expedition of Cestius
	ch. 10: Intermediary: before the destruction of Jerusalem we pass over to the evangelization of the Gentiles
Heavenly Liturgy (7:4-8:5) —the 144,000="Remnant" of Israel	ch. 11: Destruction of Jerusalem in 70 11:1-13: religious significance 11:14: realization
—The large crowd that is joined to them=the Gentile nations who will be converted and joined to the "Remnant"	11:15-19: Announcement of the Reign of God (15:5: takes up this vision and prolongs it) (11:17: "God will reign . . .") (11:18: Announcement of the final great revolt of the Gentiles and their passing victory)

Chapters 12-20: The Church and the Gentile World

Rome, the symbol of all the persecutors, pursues the Church with is hatred. But Christ is the victor and sustains his Church. The Gentiles are called to be converted.

ch. 10: The Little Book (=the Gospel) announces this universalism

12:1-14:5: The Great Fresco of the PASCHAL MYSTERY and its fruits

12:1-6: The two antagonists: The Woman (=the People of God giving birth to the Messiah in the suffering of the Cross and the triumph of the Pasch) and the Dragon representing Satan

12:7-17: The struggle in heaven between Michael and the Dragon symbolizing

13:1-14:5: the struggle on earth between the faithful of the Lamb and the followers of the Dragon represented

by the beast coming up out of the sea (=Rome) and the beast coming out of the earth (=the religious doctrines coming from Asia Minor, which the Roman empire uses)

The Faithful of the Lamb: the 144,000=a first small percentage of the multitude of converted Gentiles

14:6-15:4: "The Small Apocalypse": summary announcement of the end

14:6-13: Announcement of the end

14:14-20: Execution

15:1-4: Completion of the end=the new exodus comes to its fullness

15:5: The events are no longer seen as starting with the temple of Jerusalem which has been destroyed (thus starting with the relation between the Church and Judaism) but starting with the true Temple which is in heaven (=the body of Christ passed through death and raised). These events are presented here in two forms:

15:6-16:22:
Heavenly Vision:
The SEVEN CUPS: punishments inspired by the plagues of Egypt, to con-

17:1-19:10: Earthly realization
17:1-18:8: Fall of Babylon (=Rome)
(18:10-14: The seven

vert the persecutors, but in vain

emperors: John can "announce" them because he is writing about 96 and with literary license places his visions about 70)

18:9-24: Weeping on the earth (extraordinary lyricism. Inspired by Ezekiel)

19:1-4: Joy in heaven

19:5-10: God has taken possession of his Kingdom

19:11-20:10: The Battle of the End

20:11-15: The Judgment of the End

Now that you have an over-all view, we can take time to consider more in detail a few of the more important passages.

A. Chs. 4-11: What is the lot of Israel and what is the relation between the Church and Israel?

With a richness of imagery borrowed from the Old Testament, here John simply develops the teaching of Jesus in his "apocalyptic discourse" (cf. Mark 13; Matt. 24-25; Luke 21). He can do it for two reasons: the Holy Spirit has led him "to the entire truth" (John 16:13); and what Jesus was announcing is already in part fulfilled. We have a similar teaching on the final conversion of Israel in Paul (Rom. 11:25-32).

Ch. 4. God: The entire apocalypse is dominated by

this vision (inspired by Ezekiel, Daniel, and Isaiah); God is seated in heaven, adored by the "twenty-four elders" (undoubtedly the saints of the Old Testament, a prefiguration of the Church and in her of sanctified mankind) and the "Four Living Creatures" (a probable symbol of the cosmos). If we accept that the "Seven Spirits" designate not angels, but the "seven-form Spirit," the fullness of the Spirit, we have here a beautiful description of the Trinity: God the Father, invisible, perceived only in the glory which radiates from him, adored by mankind and the cosmos, ruling and directing history, with the seven-form Spirit and the Risen Christ.

Ch. 5. The **"Lamb as Slaughtered":** Two words suffice to call up the entire paschal mystery in John. Christ is the "lamb" who offers himself as sacrifice for our salvation (Isa. 53), he who seals the true covenant with God in his blood (the Pasch of the exodus and of Holy Thursday). The elder announces the "lion of Judah"—the Messiah awaited by the Jews—a "Lamb slaughtered" arrives! Messiah he is, not glorious, but the Suffering Servant. And yet he is glorious: because of his sacrifice, and because he has raised and exalted him, God puts in his hand the sovereign control of history. But Christ the King dwells in heaven as the "Lamb slaughtered," i.e., keeping our humanity and carrying the scars of his Passion.

Ch. 6: He alone is capable of opening the sealed Book of the Seven Seals,[10] of unveiling for us the meaning of the Old Testament, which, in advance, proclaimed the destiny of Israel.

Ch. 7: Will there be only 144,000 elect? You are too aware by now of the symbolic language of our book to fall into such an error.[11] Israel is represented by its twelve tribes: from each of them 12,000 are the elect. This determined number designates the "little Remnant" of Israel, the fraction of the Chosen People who accept Jesus as their Messiah, in contrast to the great number of the Jews not yet converted. And to these elect are added the innumerable crowd of the Gentiles.[12]

Ch. 10: In this section dedicated to the relation between the Church and Israel, John inserts a vision which announces the second section. As he had seen the destiny of Israel announced in the Book of the Seven Seals (the Old Testament) he sees now the destiny of all the peoples contained in a small book which is undoubtedly the teaching of Jesus. It is not without importance that John anticipates this vision: conversion of the Jews and conversion of the Gentiles are closely intertwined. Recall the evolution of St. Paul: he saw the conversion of the Jews first in order to obtain the conversion of the Gentiles, but he understood that the conversion of the Gentiles would precede and prepare for the conversion of Israel (cf. p. 76).

Ch. 11: The allegory of the "two witnesses" makes the same idea explicit. These two witnesses, whose traits are borrowed from Moses and Elijah, do not designate real persons, for example Peter and Paul, but rather, symbolize the testimony which the Church gives to Christ "in the face of Judaism stubborn in its unbelief" (Feuillet).

The announcement of the end of the world terminates this chapter and this first section. Rather, we should say: the announcement of the end of a world: the world of Judaism of which the catastrophe of 70 marks the end. But through this "coming" of God, John, following the lead of Jesus in his apocalyptic discourse, catches a glimpse of the definitive coming: "now" the Kingship is established for God and for Christ." But this is still in the future: "he will reign for ages upon ages." It is only later that he can write in the past tense: "he has taken possession of his Kingdom" (19:5-10).

B. **Chs. 12-20: The Church at work in the world.**

Ch. 12: The Woman crowned with stars: The Catholic, guided by the liturgy, instinctively recognizes Mary here. This is not wrong. However, there is a danger of forgetting the essence. Just before, John had presented the paschal mystery in these words, "The Lamb as Slaughtered." Now he paints a gigantic fresco of this mystery and its fruits. Never, perhaps, had God been so explicit on the role of man in his religious history. God alone can save us and he does this in his Son. God does everything in our salvation. But this demands that man do everything also. To be saved by God demands of man a total cooperation which, in order to be accepted, demands his entire initiative. "The biblical man sees himself before God as a woman giving birth from her entire love to a fruit which is the common work of God and Man.[13] The New Mankind is born in this great painful childbearing of the Cross on which the Son of God, carrying in himself the entire sinful mankind, has effected once and for all the great passage from death to life, a childbearing of the Cross, which opens out on the Ascension and the triumph of Christ in heaven. God, the Son of God, does everything . . . on the condition that Mankind, represented by the People of God, does everything. The Woman, here, symbolizes the People of God, the Church, giving birth to the Messiah in the drama of Calvary. The Dragon, Satan, is all set to devour him, but the Cross which he thought was surely his victory, turns out to be his defeat: God saves his Son from death. Satan then cuts loose against all the other children of the Woman, all Christians, and wages war throughout the entire time of history. God does not save the Church, the Woman, by withdrawing her from the world, but by protecting her, by "nourishing" her in the world throughout her entire earthly history.[14] To be saved by Jesus Christ does not mean that the Church and each of us, her children, are snatched out of our condition as men, but this salvation throws us right into the midst of the world, into the struggle against evil, protected by Christ, the conqueror of evil. "The time of the Church is first of all and before all else the time of **the presence in history** of the risen Christ" (Feuillet).[15] The seer now presents this struggle in two ways: the victorious struggle in heaven between Michael and the Dragon should help us to read the victory of God in the struggles which the Church attacked by the world sustains. Two beasts are the symbol of this world: one comes up out of the sea and represents the persecuting Roman empire (but in the course of the ages, so man, political or economic powers, will continue this persecution), the other comes from Asia Minor and undoubtedly represents the religious ideologies of the period (and all periods) which the powers use (from racism to religious intolerance). Does evil seem to be gaining in the world? Let us keep right on struggling but with real hope. Through these struggles, the march toward the Promised Land is accomplished: the vision of the 144,000, or the multitude of men already arrived in hope at the goal of the exodus, is a source of encouragement for us.[16]

14:5-15:4: A "small apocalypse" shows us, in summary form, how the end of time will be accomplished.

15:5: To this end of time John will now dedicate the rest of his work.[17] The description of the punishments striking the persecutors is less detailed than in the first section: John "foretold" in that first section some woes that had taken place right before his eyes. Now he passed over to the future. In part only: in 17:10-14, for example, pretending to write about 70, he can describe the "future" with a certain exactness, the Roman emperors following one another up to 96 (the approximate date of the final redacting of the work). The chapters that follow could be put in three columns: the first would contain the "plagues of Egypt," according to the book of Exodus; the second, chs. 15:6-16:22, the "seven cups," a heavenly version of the events described in 17:1-19:10 (third column). The lyricism of the lamentation on Babylon-Rome is not inferior in any way to that of Ezekiel or Jeremiah from which it is inspired.

19:1-10: The nuptial theme now makes its appearance as a hymn to the joy long sought before it bursts forth in the final chorus: "Behold: the wedding feast of the Lamb, and the Bride gets herself ready . . . ." But then this is immediately overshadowed by a tragic war chant.

19:11-20:10. The Great Evening: The Lamb has disappeared. There remains only the Horseman in the mantle red with the blood of the enemies he is trampling under foot. We studied earlier the theme of the "Avenger" (OT, p. 210) inspired by Isaiah, and we know that this blood which flows is the blood of the enemies of Christ, the blood of all those who make a pact with Evil, you, me, but first of all, it is the blood of Christ himself whom "God has made sin for us."[18] The blood that soaks his mantle is first of all his own! The Judge of the end of time thus wished to be the trampled sinner. And the Red Horseman is none other than the Lamb Slaughtered. Now we can enter into the account of the judgment, with fear of course, but also with confidence. What is the meaning of all the images which describe it? It is very difficult to say. They express one thing for sure: Christ is the conqueror, the definitive victor, over Evil and over Satan.[19]

20:11-15: The great day of the judgment and the final

resurrection. The hymn to joy will finally unfold on the world.

3. **The Church Transfigured** (chs. 21-22)

> ". . . This book will make sense only when it ends. It is thus that by the art of the poet an image in the last lines awakens the idea which slumbered in the first, revivifies many figures half-formed which were waiting the call. From all these scattered movements I know for sure there is prepared a harmony, since they are already united in discord."
>
> P. Claudel, **Le soulier de Satin**

And now at the end of Revelation, we see the masterful harmony which ties together all the themes. The Bible opened with a "vision," the first creation in which God, in the paths of Paradise, conversed with man his friend, undertook with him the organization of the world. We close the Apocalypse on a vision even more beautiful. The joy which bursts forth is first of all the joy of God: "Behold: I have made all things new!" The joy of God who can no longer be "God" but "God-with": "Behold: the dwelling of God with men. He will have his dwelling with them; they will be His People and he, God-with-them, will be their God. He will wipe away every tear from their eyes; of death there will be no more; of weeping, crying, and pain, there will be no more for the old world is gone" (21:3-4). "The second creation is like the first, but with the Serpent and sin missing" (Planque). There was in Paradise a fountain giving life. It was lost through sin, but men will not cease to search for it. Ezekiel glimpsed it for the future, and this water had found its name: the Breath of God. Jesus had promised it to the Samaritan woman, and from the right side of the Temple which is his body, it had leaped out on the world. John sees it now gushing forth from the bosom of the Trinity, "from the throne of God and the Lamb," and the lost tree of Paradise, giving the fruit of immortality, plunges its root in it (22:1). A vision of beyond history and yet already realized in history: Gushing forth from the Eucharist, the Holy Spirit, baptismal water, gives life to those whom Jesus, the tree of life, nourishes with his body: "Please, Lord, let me see your face." "When can I go to see the face of God?" A side-tracked expectation, finally fulfilled: "They shall see his face and his Name shall be on their forehead" (22:4).

The peaceful and powerful joy which surrounds this revelation has not yet revealed all its fullness: this hymn to joy is in fact a wedding march.

One image actually dominates this entire vision as it unifies the whole of Revelation: the image is MARRIAGE. "I see the Holy City, a new Jerusalem, coming down from heaven from the presence of God: she is as beautiful as a bride all dressed for her husband" (21:2). John succeeds in uniting in this single image the two fundamental themes of the entire Bible: **Marriage and the Temple.** The Temple expressed the aspiration of Mankind to see God dwelling in his home (cf. OT, pp. 211-213) and God, starting with the material symbol of the temple of Jerusalem, has brought us to understand that his desire is not to dwell in a place but in a people. In the new city, John is not surprised at no longer seeing a temple (21:22). There is no need for the symbol since the reality is here: "the sign vanishes now that God is visibly and permanently present among his own" (Brutsch). And this city is at the same time a woman, a young wife. We men sense this need, a deep need, to be artisans of our own happiness. The theme of marriage recalls to us that this fruit of our flesh cannot be born except by the action of God in us (cf. OT, pp. 218-219). This definitive happiness, the Holy City, Jerusalem, the Church, is constructed by Jesus Christ, to whom it is united as the wife to the husband. This unrealizable dream of married people to remain two in order to love one another, even though they form only one being, we see fulfilled in the marriage of Christ and redeemed Mankind. This unity remains for married people the reality toward which they tend and which they signify in the world. And it is also the fulfillment which Christians who maintain virginity for God have the favor of prefiguring in our history. For this reality is already present in our midst. The "young bride" comes down from heaven, and John thus recalls that the definitive Church is not totally identical with our earthly Church, it is a gift of God. And yet, already it is there, in this People who are related to Jesus Christ and live by his presence, while waiting his full revelation.

This, then, is the grand hope which John plants in the heart of our world: Human history has a meaning, it is entirely extended toward its goal, Jesus Christ coming to consummate the eternal wedding with mankind. Mankind, in its earthly march toward happiness, in the midst of the struggles for man which believers and nonbelievers carry on shoulder to shoulder, Mankind is lifted up by this Ferment, it is led toward its goal through the Church, which has only one assurance: the word of Christ the conqueror: "Yes, I am coming quickly," a single prayer which the Spirit cries out with it: "Oh Yes! Come, Lord Jesus!"

[1]Look up what we said regarding Daniel (OT, pp. 172-177), especially about the symbolism of the images. I presuppose this is known.

[2]This book forms a unity with *The Old Testament—Always Relevant.*

[3]"John": It is impossible to be more precise. From the second century up to our days, the Fathers and exegetes are divided on

the identity of the author. They note considerable differences in thought and style between the Fourth Gospel and the Apocalypse, but also surprising likenesses. If they admit the identity of the one author, they think of a disciple who revised the style of the Fourth Gospel.

[4]This simple presentation presupposes already a certain number of choices among many explanations. I will be obligated to them throughout these pages. What should I advise to prolong the study? M. Planque, in his *"Introduction a l'Apocalypse"* (Alsace) is in favor of this idea: the young people need images and one book of the Bible is full of them; why not read it with them, illustrating it through them? *L'Attente du Seigneur* of J. Peron ("Equipes Enseignantes") is a good guide for reading. Among the commentaries (I do not mention the technical studies), the best is that of the Protestant, Ch. Brutsch, *Clarte de l'Apocalypse* (Labor et Fides); that of L. Cerfaux and J. Cambier, *L'Apocalypse de Saint Jean lu aux chretiens* (Cerf) is precious for clarifying the Apocalypse, with the help of texts from the Old Testament abundantly quoted.

[5]Real "visions"? If you wish to hold this you certainly may. But our book presupposes a work of literary elaboration. John constantly uses images borrowed from the entire Bible, from Daniel especially. Were these images which he had known all his life the source of his visions? Or did he choose the images as an afterthought to express what God had brought him to understand in his heart? It really is not too important.

[6]Two letters from the same period invite the Church to vigilance against heresies, in fidelity to Christ. The Letter of Jude (shortly before 90) is based on the Jewish apocalypses, some of which, like The Assumption of Moses or the book of Enoch, will be separated from the Jewish canon in 90. The Second Letter of Peter uses Jude and thus is later than this letter. The author uses the procedure called "pseudepigraphy," current at that time, which means that he uses someone else's name, in this case the name of Peter, in order to reach a larger audience. From this letter we learn that in this period the teaching about the divine "inspiration" of the Scriptures is well accepted (1:20-21) and the letters of Paul are "already canonized for all practical purposes" (Auzou).

[7]"This is the convergence in the same sequence of a certain

number of events which took place in different times and places but tend to the same purpose" (Agel).

[8]It is a quite noticeable lack that the Latin liturgy, especially in the canon of the Mass, does not express this aspect more clearly.

[9]Here more than elsewhere, I take sides. On the whole, for all that follows, I am indebted to the studies of Father A. Feuillet.

[10]They wrote at that time on scrolls. The image is a book composed of seven parchments rolled up on the same base.

[11]This is the mistake at the basis of the "Jehovah's Witnesses."

[12]John here anticipates the second part. We shall find this immense crowd, symbolized in its turn by 144,000 redeemed of the earth, who are a kind of first-fruits. These Gentiles are redeemed because they are "virgins," i.e., in prophetic language, they love God with a unique love by rejecting "fornication" with the idols, with the sin. There is no question here of "virginity" in the sense in which we now understand it.

[13]Excuse me for referring to OT, pp. 218ff., and inviting you to reread these pages.

[14]Time symbolized by 3 times and ½ time, or 1,260 days.

[15]The Woman is the Church. But John was also certainly thinking of Mary, the figure of the Church, Mary who in her personal life had this grace to live the entire destiny of the Church, the sorrowful mother of Calvary, cooperating in the redemption through her acceptance which includes ours, a woman already raised and brought into Glory with her Son.

[16]You have noted how the vision of the exodus, which the Jewish people formerly carried out toward the Promised Land, underlies this entire book: in Jesus Christ, the definitive exodus is effected. In him we finally have access to this happiness from which are excluded tears and death.

[17]The vision of 15:5 follows that of 11:19.

[18]2 Cor. 5:21. Read this in the earlier part of the book, the section on 1 Corinthians pp. 87-97.

[19]The "1,000 years" during which Satan is enchained and the faithful of Christ, raised up, live in peace, have stirred up the most hare-brained interpretations. John takes his inspiration here from Ezekiel 37, from this symbolic resurrection of the People of God, living, after "death," which was the deportation, in a relative peace. It is not impossible that John meant simply to describe the time between the great persecutions of Nero and Domitian, which failed to destroy Christianity, and the Parousia: a moment of respite, favorable for the conversion of the Gentiles.

INDEX OF THE BOOKS OF THE BIBLE